Evil Empire?

Evil Empire?

*Government Officials as Proponents
of the Gospel in Luke–Acts and Beyond*

Christopher S. Chen

WIPF & STOCK · Eugene, Oregon

EVIL EMPIRE?
Government Officials as Proponents of the Gospel in Luke–Acts and Beyond

Copyright © 2026 Christopher S. Chen. All rights reserved. Except for brief quotations in critical publications or reviews, no part of this book may be reproduced in any manner without prior written permission from the publisher. Write: Permissions, Wipf and Stock Publishers, 199 W. 8th Ave., Suite 3, Eugene, OR 97401.

Wipf & Stock
An Imprint of Wipf and Stock Publishers
199 W. 8th Ave., Suite 3
Eugene, OR 97401

www.wipfandstock.com

PAPERBACK ISBN: 979-8-3852-2199-8
HARDCOVER ISBN: 979-8-3852-2200-1
EBOOK ISBN: 979-8-3852-2201-8

VERSION NUMBER 01/02/26

Unless otherwise noted, all Scripture quotations are from The ESV® Bible (The Holy Bible, English Standard Version®), © 2001 by Crossway, a publishing ministry of Good News Publishers. Used by permission. All rights reserved.

Scripture quotations marked (NIV) taken from The Holy Bible, New International Version®, NIV®. Copyright © 1973, 1978, 1984, 2011 by Biblica, Inc. Used with permission of Zondervan. All rights reserved worldwide. www.zondervan.com.

Scripture quotations marked (RSV) are from Revised Standard Version of the Bible, copyright © 1946, 1952, and 1971 National Council of the Churches of Christ in the United States of America. Used by permission. All rights reserved worldwide.

Scripture quotations marked (LXX) are from *The Septuagint Version of the Old Testament with an English Translation*, translated by Lancelot C. L. Brenton (London: Samuel Bagster and Sons, 1851; repr. Peabody, MA: Hendrickson, 2003).

"Drawing on Scripture, church history, and China's story, Christopher Chen invites readers to see how God's sovereignty reaches into the most unlikely places, offering hope for the church in challenging times."

—**Richard Cook**, Professor of Church History and Missions,
Logos Evangelical Seminary

"Every generation of Christians has had to navigate their relationship to governments and cultures, many of which have been opposed to the faith. In this insightful and nuanced work, Chris Chen provides an original and convincing interpretation of Luke's portrayal of centurions as exemplary proponents of the gospel of Jesus Christ. Chen makes a significant contribution to the ongoing discussion of Christ and culture."

—**Jonathan T. Pennington**, Professor of New Testament Interpretation,
Southern Seminary

"Chen's *Evil Empire?* is a compelling work, demonstrating God's providential hand in spreading the gospel even through individuals whom many disliked or even despised, namely, political leaders. This book deepens my appreciation that God's ways are higher than my own and stirs me to pray more earnestly for the 'good guys' in government for the sake of the gospel. Take up and read! This book will rekindle your heart for God's gospel mandate."

—**Peter L. H. Tie**, Associate Professor in Systematic Theology, Christian Witness
Theological Seminary

"Christopher S. Chen's *Evil Empire?* skillfully tackles the question of whether a committed follower of Christ can hold political power. Using the centurions in Luke–Acts as a springboard, Chen draws from the broader biblical text and historical examples from both Roman and Chinese history to make a compelling and inspiring case that it is indeed possible to be a faithful servant of the Lord even within a hostile political system."

—**Daniel K. Eng**, Associate Professor of New Testament Language and Literature,
Western Seminary

"Excellent work mining and examining the biblical evidence and presenting what certainly is in the mind of the Author/author. Chen's analysis and conclusions are impressive and compelling. Additionally, he has provided a graduate course in Advanced Hermeneutics, skillfully blending macro- and micro-observation and responsible, intelligent interpretation."

—**Gary Tuck**, Professor of Biblical Studies, Retired, Western Seminary

To my brothers and sisters across the world who daily navigate the tensions of Jesus' command to "render to Caesar the things that are Caesar's, and to God the things that are God's"
—Luke 20:25

Contents

List of Tables | viii
Preface | ix
List of Abbreviations | xii

1 Introduction | 1
2 Government Officials as Proponents of God's Purposes in the Old Testament | 10
3 Luke and His Audience | 30
4 Centurions in Luke–Acts | 51
5 Government Officials as the "Most Excellent" Proponents of the Gospel in Luke–Acts | 77
6 Roman Officials as Proponents of the Gospel in Early Church History | 96
7 Government Officials as Proponents of the Gospel in Chinese History | 118
8 Conclusion | 149

Bibliography | 155
General Index | 169
Ancient Document Index | 179

List of Tables

Table 1   Military Commanders of Syria and Israel in 2 Kgs 5 and 7 | 26

Table 2   Links Between Luke's Preface and Paul's Trial Narrative | 43

Table 3   Government Officials Who Convert at Key Points in Luke–Acts | 92

Preface

THIS BOOK IS A major revision and extension of a thesis that was previously written for my ThM degree at Southern Seminary between the years 2020 and 2022. I thoroughly enjoyed being a Southern student, which proved to be a productive use of my free time during a global pandemic. While I expected the degree program to further my theological training, what I did not anticipate was the new relationships that would forge in the process. By his grace, the Lord brought wonderful friends like Timothy Ingrum, Zachary Hess, Luke Waite, and William Brown to journey with me through the program. Along the way, God also graciously gave me a supportive wife who traveled with me to attend class in Louisville just four days after our wedding and delivered our first child about two months after my graduation. As I reflect upon all that God provided over these past several years, I cannot help but echo the words of Jacob's prayer, "I am not worthy of the least of all the deeds of steadfast love and all the faithfulness that you have shown to your servant" (Gen 32:10).

The initial seeds of this book were planted during my experiences with Chinese students whose very lives are a testimony of faithfulness to Christ amid persecution. The main argument of the book came to me while thinking about those Chinese believers as I was preparing to lead a small group Bible study on Jesus and the centurion in Luke 7:1–10 in my local church. Many thanks to my brothers and sisters who journeyed with me through Luke-Acts over the years in both the seminary classroom and the local church. I am honored to have called Pathway Bible Church and South Bay Agape Christian Church my spiritual homes—spending well over a decade in each of these local churches—as the ideas for this book were germinating in my mind. Thanks are also due to several local churches who have invited me to guest speak over the years. Your generous honorariums have funded my academic pursuits. May you enjoy the fruits of your kind support.

Converting my thesis into a book was a significant undertaking that resulted in a work that grew to become two to three times longer than the original. Chapters 1, 2, 3, and 5 have been significantly revised to become chapters 1, 3, 4, and 8 of this book, respectively. Chapter 4 of my thesis has been expanded into chapters 5 and 6 of this book. Chapters 2 and 7 of the book are entirely new material that were not in the thesis. Many thanks to Michael Thompson, Matthew Wimer, Hannah Starr, Calvin Jaffarian, and the rest of the team at Wipf and Stock for believing in this project and helping to bring it to fruition.

I would like to thank my thesis supervisor, Dr. Jonathan Pennington, for guiding my research and modeling the life of a scholar who loves God, family, and the church. Morgan Johnson provided insightful suggestions and pointed me to relevant resources at each stage of my thesis research and writing. Dr. Stephen Presley pointed me to helpful resources on the early church and military service. I would also like to express thanks to brothers and sisters who read my thesis and provided helpful feedback: Aaron and Melinda Yakligian, Anthony Baldwin, Jennifer Stec, and Torey Teer. My brother Kevin read multiple revisions of every chapter and gave thoughtful advice on the overall flow of the book, and especially regarding chapter 2. My wife, Jacqueline, and two-year old daughter, Lois, listened to Daddy's book being read either by me or by the soothing voices embedded in Microsoft Word's "Read Aloud" feature for countless hours in car rides and before bedtime. Though Lois generally fell asleep, Jacqueline picked up the slack and was a wonderful dialogue partner who helped me to hone my arguments. Tina Teng-Henson deserves my thanks for not only helping to introduce me and my wife, but also for her encouragement and prayers in the initial and final stages of this project.

I thank God for giving me a family that has supported my academic pursuits throughout various seasons of my life. Dad, thanks for teaching me to appreciate details and to value continuous learning. Mom, thank you for praying for me and cheering me on in my development as a writer and minister. Kevin, thanks for encouraging me to pursue further

PREFACE

theological training and for being both a role model and conversation partner in all areas of life. Thank you to my dear wife, Jacqueline, and daughter, Lois, for making our home a place of love and laughter that has provided much joy during this season of writing. May God receive all the glory for the great things he has done.

Chris Chen

San Jose, California

July 2025

Abbreviations

Ag. Ap.	Flavius Josephus, *Against Apion*
ANF	*The Ante-Nicene Fathers: Translations of the Writings of the Fathers Down to A.D. 325*. Edited by Alexander Roberts and James Donaldson. 1885–1887. 10 vols. Buffalo, NY: Christian Literature.
Ant.	Flavius Josephus, *The Jewish Antiquities*
BDAG	Bauer, Walter, et al. *Greek-English Lexicon of the New Testament and Other Early Christian Literature*. 3rd ed. Chicago: University of Chicago Press, 2000.
BDB	Francis Brown, S. R. Driver, and Charles A. Briggs. *Hebrew and English Lexicon of the Old Testament*. Oxford: Clarendon, 1907.
FJTC	Flavius Josephus, Translation and Commentary
LCL	Loeb Classical Library
LXX	Septuagint
NPNF[1]	*A Select Library of Nicene and Post-Nicene Fathers of the Christian Church*. Series 1. Edited by Philip Schaff. 1886–1889. 14 vols. Buffalo, NY: Christian Literature.
NPNF[2]	*A Select Library of Nicene and Post-Nicene Fathers of the Christian Church*. Series 2. Edited by Philip Schaff and Henry Wace. 1890–1900. 14 vols. Buffalo, NY: Christian Literature.

1

Introduction

> I urge you to beware [of] . . . the aggressive impulses
> of an evil empire.
> —Ronald Reagan[1]

> Pray for those who abuse you.
> —Luke 6:28

On March 8, 1983, Ronald Reagan ascended the podium in Orlando, Florida, to address the National Association of Evangelicals with what is now known as his "Evil Empire" speech. Drawing upon imagery from the popular *Star Wars* movies, Reagan cast the Soviet Union as an "evil empire," calling upon American Christians to stand strong against the expansion of communism. Reagan's rhetoric was clear. The United States, despite being an imperfect nation, was a country founded upon freedom. The Soviet Union represented totalitarianism, which was the worst form of evil.[2] Along with other factors, some recognize Reagan's speech as a pivotal moment in his fight against communism, which culminated in the collapse of the Soviet

---

1. Reagan, "Remarks at the Annual Convention."

2. To be fair, Reagan also acknowledged the wrongs in America's past and present, calling upon American Evangelicals to oppose ongoing evil in their home country. However, he argued that the existence of evil in America does not make the US morally equivalent to a regime whose founding principles confuse right and wrong. Bateman, "Lord over Raging Nations."

Union. Reagan's speech is also remembered for its unique blending of public policy, pop culture, and the personal religion of a civic official.

Indeed, one of the remarkable aspects of Reagan's "Evil Empire" speech is that it begins by reflecting upon the everyday prayer life of the president.[3] Reagan encourages Christians to continue supporting and praying for their government leaders by saying, "I tell you there are a great many God-fearing, dedicated, noble men and women in public life, present company included . . . [who] need your help." These government officials work behind the scenes motivated by the "realization that freedom prospers only where the blessings of God are avidly sought and humbly accepted."[4] Although the government might appear to be an impersonal system, Reagan's words highlight the important roles of individual believers who labor behind the scenes to shape society for good.

But could there also be God-fearing, dedicated, noble men and women serving within the governments of other countries? And what if some of those God-fearers serve within the ranks of what many Christians might perceive to be an evil empire? In addition to praying for public officials who belong to the good guys, how should Christians pray for officials who hold positions of power in hostile regimes? These questions are immensely practical for believers living in parts of the Middle East, Northern Africa, and Asia, where state-sponsored religious persecution is a part of everyday life.[5]

But these same types of questions are also becoming increasingly relevant to many believers in Western contexts. In some Western countries, Christians have enjoyed centuries of peaceful existence under governments that are generally amenable towards the gospel. However, these are changing times. In the United States, for example, many who once thought they lived in a Christian nation now wonder if their elected officials are increasingly clamping down on religious liberty. Other voices highlight the less pristine aspects of America's religious history and point

---

3. Near the beginning of the speech, the president thanks his evangelical hearers for their continued prayers for him and his wife, Nancy. Speaking on her behalf, he said, "Thank you for your prayers. Nancy and I have felt their presence many times in many ways. And believe me, for us they've made all the difference." Reagan, "Remarks at the Annual Convention."

4. Reagan, "Remarks at the Annual Convention."

5. These three regions account for most of the top fifty countries listed in Open Doors' annual ranking of countries where Christians face extreme persecution. Open Doors UK and Ireland, "World Watch List."

towards deeply entrenched patterns of public policy that are opposed to basic Christian beliefs.

The purpose of this book is to suggest that even within an evil empire, there can be officials who become surprising supporters of the gospel. In other words, Reagan's broad characterization of an "evil empire" opens space to explore the possibility that there could be good guys who remain embedded within evil systems. To borrow from Reagan's *Star Wars* allusion, could there be some individuals who work for good while being affiliated with the dark side? If so, what attitude should Christians have towards representatives of a state system that is hostile towards God's people? Could such government officials perform their civic duties while also honoring God? Believers across the ages from all over the world have grappled with these issues.[6] Thankfully, Scripture has much to say about the complex relationship between Christians and the state. This book explores the relationship between the gospel and the Roman Empire by focusing on Theophilus and the centurions in Luke–Acts. Using Luke–Acts as a lens, I will also trace the theme of supportive government officials from the Old Testament through early church history and into the present day. My historical analysis will show how government officials have become surprising proponents of the gospel from the times of the Roman Empire before turning towards later centuries of Christianity's development throughout Chinese history.

Thesis and Purpose

In this work, I will argue that the Gospel of Luke and the book of Acts portray Roman centurions as supporters of the gospel. These centurions demonstrate that it is possible, and even respectable, for Romans to be faithful citizens in the kingdom of God while also holding high status within the Roman Empire. As a corollary, I suggest that there can be a place for believers to hold positions of power even within hostile government systems. While I would not necessarily insist that believing officials must always choose to remain embedded in hostile regimes, I believe there is plenty of biblical precedent for doing so. The propagation of the

---

6. For example, Daniel in Babylon was confronted with the question of how to remain faithful while serving within a government that antagonized believers. In a different context, Dietrich Bonhoeffer took up employment in the German government in an effort to bring down a tyrannical regime that had allied itself with the church. Watson, "Political Theology of Dietrich Bonhoeffer."

gospel through individual Roman officials would have been a topic of great interest for Luke's reader, Theophilus, a high-ranking Roman official who was drawn to the gospel. The pattern of supportive officials extends from the pages of Luke–Acts through church history, appearing in diverse cultural contexts across the centuries. Valuable insights emerge when this theme is examined through the lens of early church history under the Roman Empire and the development of the church in China from the seventh century to the present.

I write this book for all believers who are navigating the complexities of being in but not of this world. As Christians who long to be salt of the earth, there will inevitably be times when being a believer will create friction with societal values. I write for individuals who feel called to serve both God and country but nevertheless find themselves wondering how much longer they can remain in civil service. You are not alone in your struggle as you strive to remain loyal to God while serving within what sometimes feels like an evil empire.

I write this book for Christians in the West who want to understand, support, and pray for their brothers and sisters in other parts of the world where faith in Jesus comes along with considerable risks. I write for believers who are concerned that their own governments are drifting towards increasing hostility towards Christianity.

I write this book for my sisters and brothers in the majority world who daily navigate the tensions of life under oppressive authorities. I write to provide a biblical framework for understanding and relating to officials who may seem to represent the enemy. I hope this book inspires increased engagement with and prayer for those who persecute you. I recognize that I have much to learn from you who are already living the message of this book, and my aim is to help provide a broader biblical basis for you to understand your lived reality.

Approach of This Book

Before going further, it is worth pausing to explain how I will approach my topic. In my treatment of Scripture, I will use narrative exegesis while drawing upon historical backgrounds to support my exegetical claims and to determine applications for the biblical message. In other words, I will employ a dual-pronged approach: (1) narrative criticism to uncover authorially

INTRODUCTION

intended meaning and (2) historical analysis to develop the implications of the Bible's message for both its original and modern audiences.[7]

In broad terms, narrative criticism "attends to the literary and storied qualities of a biblical narrative."[8] When studying Luke and Acts, priority will be placed on understanding the two-volume work as a literary whole, rather than on historical reconstructions based on parallel Gospel accounts.[9] Moreover, I will treat Luke–Acts as "comprehensive applied narrative theology" respecting both the historical accuracy and theological richness of the text.[10] I will seek to uncover the meaning of the narrative on two levels: the story level (consisting of the elements most readers would easily notice) and the discourse level (seeing the narrative through a wide-angle lens).[11] The most relevant historical background is assumed to be found within the text, thus allowing the reader to focus on Luke–Acts as the locus of divine revelation, while paying careful attention to the historical details mentioned by the author.[12]

---

7. This dual-pronged approach is analogous to E. D. Hirsch's helpful distinction between meaning and significance. Hirsch argues that while the meaning of a text does not change, its significance to a particular reader may change. "*Meaning* is that which is represented by a text; it is what the author meant by his use of a particular sign sequence; it is what the signs represent. *Significance*, on the other hand, names a relationship between that meaning and a person, or conception, or a situation, or indeed anything imaginable." Hirsch, *Validity in Interpretation*, 8; emphasis original.

8. Brown, *Gospels as Stories*, 11. See also Brown, "Narrative Criticism."

9. Jonathan Pennington explains that we must prioritize "vertical" over "horizontal" readings of the Gospels. For Pennington, a "vertical reading focuses on reading the individual Gospel accounts as wholes, following their narrative structure and development, as one reads from top to bottom on the page of a book." In contrast, "to read horizontally is to always have an eye toward parallel passages from the other Gospel accounts." Pennington, *Reading the Gospels Wisely*, 149. Mark Strauss describes a similar approach: "Gospel comparisons (horizontal reading) will be done in the service of a narrative and theological analysis of the text (vertical reading)." Strauss, *Four Portraits, One Jesus*, 84.

10. Pennington, *Reading the Gospels Wisely*, 153.

11. Jeannine Brown credits Seymour Chatman for coming up with these "two levels" of meaning. See Brown, *Gospels as Stories*, 11–14. Drawing upon the work of R. T. France, Pennington describes these two levels of meaning as "surface meaning" and "bonus meaning." See Pennington, *Reading the Gospels Wisely*, 117–19.

12. Throughout this book, I uphold the historical reliability of the biblical text. For example, when Luke describes Cornelius as a centurion of the Italian Cohort who fears God (Acts 10:1–2), I accept the truth of his description even if it goes against stereotypes of centurions based on some extrabiblical historical sources. Though some may question the possibility of a centurion of the Italian Cohort being in Caesarea at the time, there are good reasons to believe Luke's account was historically accurate. Keener, "Troops."

Summary of Argument

Among the four canonical Gospels, Luke's is unique because it addresses an individual reader, Theophilus, and it belongs to the two-volume set of Luke–Acts.[13] It is significant that Luke addresses his reader as "most excellent" (Luke 1:3) since elsewhere in Acts he uses this title exclusively to refer to high-ranking Roman officials (Acts 23:26, 24:3, 26:25).[14] If, as this honorific title suggests, Theophilus was a Roman official, we should expect Luke to have much to say about the Roman Empire.[15]

Many scholars have commented on the complex nature of Luke's portrayal of the Roman Empire.[16] In this book, I will focus on the role of Roman centurions in Luke–Acts. Centurions appear at critical junctures in the narrative, and each centurion plays a positive role in the advance of the gospel. Devout centurions are the first gentiles to be saved in both the Gospel of Luke (7:1–10) and the book of Acts (10:1–48).[17] A centurion is the first person to proclaim Jesus' righteousness at the cross (Luke 23:47).[18] Various centurions protect Paul by escorting him away from the violent Jerusalem mob (Acts 21:32), asserting his citizenship rights before

---

13. This does not necessarily preclude the possibility that Luke's Gospel was also meant to be circulated (Bauckham, *Gospels for All Christians*; du Plessis, "Lukan Audience").

The opening lines of the sequel explicitly frame Acts as a companion volume to "the first book" (Acts 1:1). Some have proposed that Luke and Acts originally belonged together as a single composition, based on the arrangement of Codex Bezae (Read-Heimerdinger and Rius-Camps, *Luke's Demonstration to Theophilus*). For more on the unity of Luke–Acts, see Tannehill, *Narrative Unity of Luke–Acts*, 1:1–12.

14. Unless otherwise noted, all Scripture quotations come from the English Standard Version.

15. The Gospel of Luke traces the geographical movement of the good news starting from Jerusalem (1:9, 2:22), to Galilee (4:14—9:50), and back to Jerusalem (9:51—24:53). The driving force of Acts is the spread of the gospel through Spirit-empowered witnesses from Jerusalem, to Judea, to the end of the earth (Acts 1:8). Figuratively speaking, the gospel reaches the "end of the earth" when Paul arrives in Rome and preaches the gospel unhindered for two years (Acts 28:16–31).

16. Walton, "State They Were In"; Rowe, *World Upside Down*; Kuhn, *Kingdom*; Yamazaki-Ransom, "God, People, and Empire"; Kim, "Collusion and Subversion." Ho Sung Kim argues that Luke has a complex relationship with the Roman Empire, sometimes portraying it positively and other times portraying it negatively.

17. Oleksandr Kyrychenko argues that Luke portrays Roman centurions as "prototypical Gentile believers in anticipation of the Christian mission to the Empire." Kyrychenko, *Roman Army and the Expansion*, 8. See also Yates, "Centurions in Luke/Acts."

18. Easter, "Certainly This Man Was Righteous."

INTRODUCTION

the tribune (22:26), ensuring safe passage to his trial in Caesarea (23:23), granting liberty to see friends under Felix's orders (24:23), and facilitating a safe journey despite shipwreck (27:1, 6, 11, 31, 43). While Luke–Acts features many Roman officials (Luke 2:1–2, 3:1, 13:1, 23:1–25; Acts 12:1–6, 20–23; 18:12–15; 21:31–40; 22:24–27; 23:13—26:32), the role of centurions is significant because they appear frequently as representatives of the empire at the "ground level" of the average citizen.

Writing to Theophilus, Luke shows that the gospel message is for all types of people: lowly and influential, rich and poor, men and women, tax collectors and sinners, Jews and Romans, civilians and soldiers. Far from being the enemy, Roman centurions often function as the "good guys" in Luke's story.[19] Indeed, the conversions of two key centurions show that the gospel could subvert an ostensibly anti-Christian establishment. Centurions who supported the advance of the gospel would have served as positive role models for Theophilus, who himself was in a position of power in the Roman Empire. The centurions also convey a positive message for us today, in a world where authorities may be hostile towards Christians. Luke's portrayal of supportive centurions in Luke–Acts encourages us to pray for favor from and conversion of low-level officials who enforce regulations. Seen in this way, the conversion and cooperation of centurions encourages believers to "pray for those who abuse you" (Luke 6:28; see also 23:34).

Outline of Book

I will unfold my argument in the following way. Before getting into Luke–Acts, chapter 2 will demonstrate that the Old Testament also presents government officials as proponents of God's purposes. Chapters 3, 4, and 5 form the heart of the book by focusing on the theme of government officials in Luke–Acts. Each of those chapters covers one aspect of the theme: Theophilus (chapter 3), centurions (chapter 4), and other government officials (chapter 5). Chapters 6 and 7 trace the theme of government officials through church history. I will first cover Roman officials during the first few centuries of church history (chapter 6). Next, I will discuss examples

---

19. Laurena Brink argues that Luke portrays centurions in ways that break from stereotypical characterizations of soldiers in Greco-Roman literature. Brink, "Unmet Expectations," 270–89. Brink focuses on literary analysis and suggests that the Roman soldiers in the narrative were "not necessarily meant to be historical figures" ("Unmet Expectations," 61).

of supportive government leaders throughout Chinese history (chapter 7). Although the chapters unfold in a logical progression that is roughly chronological, each chapter can also be read as a standalone unit for those wishing to proceed in a different order. A more detailed description of each chapter is below.

Chapter 2: Government Officials as Proponents of God's Purposes in the Old Testament. This chapter provides a broader biblical basis for my argument in Luke–Acts. Indeed, the Old Testament also shows that officials in oppressive governments can sometimes serve as surprising proponents of God's purposes. This chapter discusses examples of Old Testament believers who were embedded within oppressive government structures using two case studies: (1) the story of Daniel in Dan 1–6 and (2) the conversion of Naaman in 2 Kgs 5:1–27.

Chapter 3: Luke and His Audience. This chapter discusses Luke's audience and the identity of his named recipient, Theophilus. While affirming that Luke–Acts was intended for broad distribution among a general Christian audience, I also contend that Luke wrote in the first instance to a historical individual whom he calls Theophilus. After surveying various scholarly views on the identity of Luke's first reader, I will argue that Theophilus was most likely a high-ranking Roman official.

Chapter 4: Centurions in Luke–Acts. This chapter examines every appearance of centurions in Luke–Acts, highlighting their roles as proponents for the gospel. After introducing the major themes of Luke–Acts, I will provide a brief historical overview of centurions and the Roman military during New Testament times. The heart of the chapter divides into five major sections which discuss the centurion at Capernaum (Luke 7:1–10), the centurion at Calvary (Luke 23:47), the conversion of Cornelius (Acts 10:1–11:18), the centurions who escort Paul at Jerusalem and Caesarea (Acts 21:27—23:35, 24:23), and Julius the centurion (Acts 27:1–44).

Chapter 5: Government Officials as the "Most Excellent" Proponents of the Gospel in Luke–Acts. This chapter builds upon the previous one by broadening our perspective on the roles of government authorities in Luke–Acts. By examining several other examples in Luke–Acts, I will demonstrate that the theme of supportive officials extends beyond centurions. To do this, I will survey several key passages in Luke–Acts that demonstrate that the gospel is for political leaders. These varied examples show that Luke uses multiple ways to demonstrate the reasonableness of Christianity for government officials.

Chapter 6: Roman Officials as Proponents of the Gospel in Early Church History. While the prior chapters emphasize close readings of the biblical text, the last two chapters of the book focus on historical analysis in two different cultural contexts. Chapter 6 traces the theme of the gospel and political leaders into the first few centuries of church history under Roman rule. During this period, Christian thinkers wrestled with the issue of how to serve God while remaining faithful citizens of the Roman Empire. Two individuals, Tertullian and Augustine, stand out for their engagement with such topics.

Chapter 7: Government Officials as Proponents of the Gospel in Chinese History. Building upon the discussion of early church history under the Roman Empire in the prior chapter, this chapter will survey additional examples of supportive government officials who worked in a very different historical and cultural context. While the story of Christianity in China is often told from the perspective of government persecution, this chapter aims to provide a broader perspective on Christianity's 1,400 years of history in China. While state-sanctioned suppression is a significant part of the story, Chinese Christianity has also developed in part due to the support of government officials. The role of officials as surprising proponents of the gospel from the Tang dynasty (AD 618–907) to the Communist era (1949 to present) is a fascinating story that needs to be told.

Chapter 8: Conclusion. In this chapter, I will provide an overall summary of my argument before exploring implications for Christians and government leaders today. Drawing upon insights from the previous chapters, I will seek to develop a few points of application for contemporary believers.

2

Government Officials as Proponents of God's Purposes in the Old Testament

> There were many lepers in Israel in the time of the prophet Elisha, and none of them was cleansed, but only Naaman the Syrian.
>
> —Luke 4:27

> Of all the Evangelists, Luke is the most intentional, and the most skillful, in narrating the story of Jesus in a way that joins it seamlessly to Israel's story.
>
> —Richard Hays[1]

The central idea of this book is that Roman centurions function as surprising supporters of the gospel throughout the Gospel of Luke and the book of Acts. In later chapters, I will build my argument directly from Luke–Acts. The goal of this chapter, however, is to demonstrate the theme of sympathetic government officials from a broader biblical perspective. If my overall argument is correct, then we should expect to find supporting evidence in how the rest of the Bible portrays the leaders of various nations.

---

1. Hays, *Echoes of Scripture*, 191.

PROPONENTS OF GOD'S PURPOSES IN THE OLD TESTAMENT

My purpose for this chapter is to show that the Old Testament presents government officials as surprising proponents of God's people and plans. Like the centurions in Luke–Acts, some of these individuals become believers in the God of Israel. Some other officials do not necessarily experience conversion but nevertheless play important roles by helping God's people during critical times. From beginning to end, the Old Testament presents a steady stream of foreign rulers who support God's purposes while also holding leadership roles within antagonistic administrations.[2] Although these individuals are generally associated with the bad guys, they surprisingly become the good guys in the story. To demonstrate how this happens, I will examine two extended case studies: (1) the story of Daniel in Dan 1–6 and (2) the conversion of Naaman in 2 Kgs 5:1–27.

In the stories of Daniel and Naaman, we meet several characters who become unexpected sympathizers for God's people while also serving within purportedly evil empires. These individuals range from major characters (such as kings) to minor characters (such as lower-level officials).[3] In the Daniel story, the main protagonists are faithful young Israelites who are taken captive in foreign lands where they face persecution and morally compromising situations. Surprisingly, the Lord directs these young men to assimilate into a gentile culture while also rising the ranks to hold top governmental positions within the most powerful foreign nations of their times.

Naaman is a military commander for Israel's perennial enemy, Syria. Naaman becomes the recipient of God's saving grace despite his own initial hesitations to submit to the words of the prophet Elisha. After his conversion, Naaman's conscience is bothered by the idolatrous practices that he must support as part of his official duties for the Syrian king. As we examine these case studies, we will see the types of complexities and tensions that arise when individuals seek to honor God while serving within hostile kingdoms (1 Pet 2:17).

---

2. Indeed, the entire Old Testament is rich with relevant examples of foreign officials who serve as proponents of God's people and purposes. Examples can be found from Israel's patriarchy to its exile, encompassing most of the historical period covered by the Old Testament. In Genesis, examples include two Philistine kings named Abimelech. During Israel's exile, King Cyrus of Persia plays a remarkable role in advancing God's purposes. Other examples include Hiram, king of Tyre; the Queen of Sheba; and Artaxerxes.

3. The differences between major and minor characters can sometimes be subtle. As Shimon Bar-Efrat helpfully suggests, we can view secondary characters on a continuum of "secondariness." Bar-Efrat, *Narrative Art in the Bible*, 86.

Navigating Hostility: Foreign Officials in Daniel's Story (Dan 1–6)

Our first case study comes from the book of Daniel, which contains several important examples of government officials who become surprising proponents in God's plans. A close reading of Dan 1–6 shows that, despite living as captives to an evil empire, God's people find unexpected support from officials whose ranks span from the lowest to the highest levels of gentile governments.

The first half of the book of Daniel demonstrates God's faithfulness to preserve his people while living under a hostile Babylonian regime. The narrative traces how Daniel, Shadrach, Meshach, and Abednego submit to God's authority while navigating the realities of living under an antagonistic human government. Throughout the book of Daniel, several visions reveal that even the mightiest human kingdoms are but fleeting moments in the grand narrative of history. God, on the other hand, is eternal, and he reigns even during times of political upheaval. The climax of Daniel's prophecies is that one day, the messianic Son of Man will rule over all people and nations forever (7:13–14).

It is not only the major characters who have a story to tell. Several minor characters in the plot also hold significant positions in the narrative. In Dan 1, Babylonian officials of various ranks play important roles by protecting Daniel and representing his interests during critical junctures in the storyline.[4] As we will see in the rest of this book, these Babylonian officials foreshadow the Roman centurions who become supporters of the gospel in Luke–Acts.

Negotiating Exceptions (Dan 1–2)

Tension mounts immediately in the opening chapter of the book of Daniel. After conquering Jerusalem, Nebuchadnezzar takes the temple vessels along with some of Israel's finest young men to Babylon. The depiction of these handsome and wise young men (Dan 1:4, 17) reminds us of how Joseph was viewed in the eyes of the Egyptian royalty (Gen 39:6; 41:12,

---

4. Chen, *Daniel*, 12–13, 25.

33, 39).⁵ Moreover, since these youth belong to Israel's royal lineage, they quickly become prime candidates for service in the king's court.

King Nebuchadnezzar places these young men into a three-year training program "to teach them the literature and language of the Chaldeans" (Dan 1:4). As it soon becomes clear, the goal of this program is not merely to impart knowledge of "literature and language." In addition to their academic studies, the youth are also required to eat daily portions of the king's food and wine (1:5). Under the king's chief eunuch, Ashpenaz (1:3), these Israelites are given new Babylonian names (1:6–7). As was the case with Joseph (Gen 41:45), their new names demonstrate their integration into a gentile culture (Dan 1:7).⁶ Throughout the rest of the book, we are reminded of Daniel's cultural assimilation each time he is called by his Babylonian name (4:8, 9, 19; 10:1).

Pressures escalate in the story when Daniel resolves not to defile himself with the king's food or wine (1:8). As a conscientious objector, Daniel requests an exception from the chief of the eunuchs, Ashpenaz. The Babylonian official faces a conundrum. Because of God's hand in this situation, Ashpenaz views Daniel favorably and compassionately (1:9). On the other hand, his official duties require Ashpenaz to obey the king or face a potential death sentence (1:10). The eunuch's response shows that while he fears the king, his primary concern is to ensure Daniel appears like the other youths (1:10). Would Ashpenaz grant Daniel's request if it did not endanger the eunuch's life?

Newsom insightfully explains that this passage emphasizes "the interplay between knowledge and power and the differentiation between the space 'before the king' and the space away from the king." She continues, "Even though the king is theoretically the most powerful actor [in the story], his commands can be abrogated—but only so long as the king does not know (cf. the similar dynamics in chs. 3 and 6). The king's lack of knowledge creates a space where individuals can exercise their own power."⁷ After ascertaining the dynamics of the situation and grasping the eunuch's concerns, Daniel strategically circumvents Ashpenaz by approaching a lower-level official.

Daniel makes a special appeal to the steward whom Ashpenaz had assigned over Daniel and his three companions (1:11). Newsom points out

---

5. Goldingay, *Daniel*, 16.
6. Goldingay, *Daniel*, 17–18.
7. Newsom, *Daniel*, 49.

Daniel's care in "protecting the vulnerability" of this lower-level official by requesting a brief test: only ten days out of a three-year period.[8] The steward listens to Daniel, granting his request for a provisional ten-day period where the four Hebrew youths would eat only vegetables and drink water. This temporary exemption enables the steward to accommodate Daniel's request without drawing the attention of the ruling officials. After their testing period, the four Israelites are found healthier and in better appearance than the other youths who ate the royal provisions (1:15). As a result, the steward continues to permit Daniel's special dietary requests. With the tension resolved, these youths excel in their acclimation into Babylonian culture and gain the attention of the king (1:17–20). Daniel is appointed to an official position (1:21) and will remain in this role even during later parts of the book under other kings (8:27).

It does not take long, however, before another wave of persecution arises. The stage is set when Nebuchadnezzar has a disturbing dream and demands its interpretation (2:1–3). Since the king offers no clues about the content of his vision, his wise men attempt to negotiate and buy time for themselves to decipher the dream (2:4, 8). The Chaldeans' antics upset the king, causing Nebuchadnezzar to decree "that all the wise men of Babylon be destroyed" (2:12). The king's command is firm and certain (2:5, 8, 10), and his decreed death sentence encompasses Daniel and his companions (2:12–13).

With Nebuchadnezzar's order in hand, the king's captain, Arioch, is tasked to kill all the wise men of Babylon (2:13). Daniel learns of the royal decree through Arioch and prudently negotiates for an appointment with Nebuchadnezzar so that he might show the interpretation to the king (2:14–16). Like the wise men before him (2:8), Daniel's initial request is for more time (2:15). However, because of Daniel's prudence (2:14) and the mediating role of Arioch, the request for time is granted.

Meanwhile, Daniel and his companions seek the Lord for a divine revelation concerning the king's dream. Daniel receives a miraculous answer to their prayers and returns to Arioch to ask that the captain pause his capital punishment campaign and escort Daniel into the king's presence (2:24). Arioch then brings Daniel to Nebuchadnezzar and sets the stage for Daniel to interpret the king's dream (2:25). In a scene reminiscent of Joseph and

---

8. Newsom, *Daniel*, 49. Newsom also points out that "Daniel explicitly leaves the evaluation of the experiment in the supervisor's hands (translating either 'according to what you observe' or 'as you see fit')."

Pharaoh, Daniel wisely interprets Nebuchadnezzar's dream, causing the king to acknowledge God as the "God of gods" (2:47) and to promote Daniel to become "ruler over the whole province of Babylon and chief prefect over all the wise men of Babylon" (2:48). Daniel's three companions are also appointed to official positions "over the affairs of the province of Babylon," while Daniel remains in the king's court (2:49).

Daniel 1 and 2 demonstrate that lower-level officials can serve as intermediaries who help alleviate the tensions that arise when God's people live under oppressive regimes. In Dan 1, both Ashpenaz (a high-ranking official) and his steward (a lower-level official) become surprising allies of the young Israelite protagonists. Pressed between the king's edict and a desire to support God's people, these Babylonian officials model how to simultaneously hold authority within an evil empire while also becoming instruments for God's purposes. In Dan 2, Arioch plays a critical role in mediating between Daniel and the Babylonian king. In a tense situation, Arioch is caught between the king's impatient fury (2:12) and Daniel's request for more time (2:15). On the surface, Nebuchadnezzar's edicts in Dan 1 and 2 require absolute obedience. However, as is often the case in real-life situations, the implementation of official regulations can leave some room for negotiation. Lower-level officials are uniquely positioned to serve as a helpful buffer between a ruler and his people.

Although rulers may sanction regulations from the top down, lower-level officials often have some freedom in how they choose to implement the rules. Based on their relationships with superiors and individual citizens, these officials may sometimes serve as mediators to help represent the interests of God's people. Ironically, such officials can sometimes even help to implement creative exceptions to state regulations. Such exemptions need not always be disclosed to the highest authorities who have already delegated power to their entrusted officials.

It is important to note that the types of tensions raised in Dan 1 and 2 are not necessarily resolvable from a human level. The narrative repeatedly emphasizes that God worked behind the scenes to bring a resolution to an otherwise irreconcilable conflict. From the start, it was the Lord who gave his people into the hands of the Babylonians (1:2). Moreover, God granted Daniel favor and compassion in the eyes of Ashpenaz, the chief eunuch (1:9). After passing their dietary test, God enabled the four young men to excel in learning Babylonian culture and endowed Daniel with supernatural abilities to understand visions and dreams (1:17). Daniel and his companions prayed earnestly for God's mercy and received a revelation of the king's dream (2:17–23, 27–28).

Ashpenaz and Arioch are the only named gentile officials besides kings in the book of Daniel. Their naming emphasizes their importance in the narrative as government officials who support God's people, despite serving within a hostile regime. In Dan 1–2, various Babylonian officials exemplify how God can advance his purposes through courageous individuals who remain embedded within oppressive systems. Indeed, without such officials to serve as intermediaries, there would be less flexibility in the official sanctions, placing the people of God at greater risk for persecution. But how would God's people fare in situations where the official intermediaries are hostile instead of friendly? We will now look at two such situations found in the book of Daniel.

Enforcing Persecution
(Dan 3, 6)

Government officials are not always as supportive as Ashpenaz and Arioch in Dan 1–2. The fiery furnace (Dan 3) and lions' den (Dan 6) are two examples of scenarios where officials enforce government-sanctioned persecution. Although our focus in this chapter is on government officials as proponents of God's purposes, it will be helpful to briefly explore what happens when officials turn against God's people.

In the compositional structure of Dan 2–7, chapters 3 and 6 form a literary frame featuring two similar stories of persecution.[9] The central issue in both chapters is a royal directive that usurps the worship of Israel's God. Daniel 3 features a command of King Nebuchadnezzar that jeopardizes the lives of Shadrach, Meshach, and Abednego, who are officials serving in the Babylonian government (6:12). Daniel 6 focuses on an ordinance from King Darius that is targeted at Daniel, who is being groomed to become ruler over the entire kingdom (6:3). In both chapters, the king's officials hatch a hostile plan to persecute God's people (3:8–12, 6:4–13). In contrast with the named officials (Ashpenaz and Arioch) who served as protagonists in Dan

---

9. There are various proposals for the structure of the book of Daniel. Although the details of each proposal differ, most scholars agree on the parallels between Dan 2 and 7, Dan 3 and 6, and Dan 4 and 5. Lenglet, "Structure littéraire de Daniel 2–7"; Tanner, "Literary Structure," 272–73; Hamilton, *With the Clouds of Heaven*, 77–83.

1–2, the unnamed officials in Dan 3 and 6 are antagonists who reinforce the rigidity of the royal commands (6:8).

The scheming of the officials is designed to amplify enmity between believers and the king (3:12, 6:13). However, as was the case in Dan 1, God's hand is at work to protect his people amid fierce persecution. After seeing the Lord's supernatural salvation, the persecuted believers are vindicated before the officials who plotted against them (3:27, 6:24). Nebuchadnezzar promotes Shadrach, Meshach, and Abednego into positions of power (3:30), while Daniel is restored to a position of prosperity under King Darius (6:28).

Kings Who Give Glory to God

After these dramatic reversals, the gentile kings pivot from persecuting believers to publicly praising God (3:28, 6:26–27). Both Dan 3 and 6 demonstrate that even the most powerful foreign rulers can become surprising worshipers of the Lord.

In the final episode featuring King Nebuchadnezzar of Babylon, the king has another disturbing dream (4:5). After the Chaldean wise men fail to interpret the dream, once again it is Daniel, "the one in whom is the Spirit of the holy God," (4:8) who successfully interprets the dream.[10] Following the dream's fulfillment and Nebuchadnezzar's humiliation, the king praises God in a way that resembles the climactic prophecy of the messianic Son of Man (Dan 7:13–14). Nebuchadnezzar praises Daniel's God, "for his dominion is an everlasting dominion, and his kingdom endures from generation to generation" (4:34). Despite being the ruler of the hostile Babylonians, Nebuchadnezzar surprisingly aligns himself with the God of Israel.[11] The king's new attitude is reflected in his summary statement, "Now I, Nebuchadnezzar, praise and extol and honor the King of heaven, for all his works are right and his ways are just; and those who

---

10. In Dan 4:8, I follow the ESV's footnoted translation "Spirit of the holy God" rather than rendering it "spirit of the holy gods." See also Gen 41:38.

11. John Collins describes Dan 4:34 as a "concluding doxology" that "elaborates the piety of the converted king" (Collins, *Daniel*, 232). Carol Newsom suggests that "Dan 4 humanizes Nebuchadnezzar and indeed presents him in the positive role of the redeemed sinner, completing the development of his character begun in ch. 1" (Newsom, *Daniel*, 149). Although the exact nature of Nebuchadnezzar's transformation is debated among interpreters, many have argued that Dan 4 describes Nebuchadnezzar's conversion. For a survey of views, see Newsom, *Daniel*, 155–56.

walk in pride he is able to humble" (4:37). Shockingly, the same Nebuchadnezzar who earlier enforced idolatry has now turned to trust in the one true God.[12]

In a similar way, God's miraculous deliverance at the lion's den causes Darius to recognize Israel's God. King Darius declares to all "peoples, nations, and languages that dwell in all the earth" that they ought to "tremble and fear before the God of Daniel" (6:25–26). Darius then beautifully declares a message that echoes the "Son of Man" prophecy (7:13–14). In Darius's words, Daniel's God "is the living God, enduring forever; his kingdom shall never be destroyed, and his dominion shall be to the end. He delivers and rescues; he works signs and wonders in heaven and on earth, he who has saved Daniel from the power of the lions" (6:26–27). In his final recorded words in the book of Daniel, King Darius, like Nebuchadnezzar before him (see 4:34–35), boldly proclaims God's rule over all human authorities.[13] The finality of Darius's declaration emphasizes that the gentile king ultimately came to recognize God's eternal kingdom.

The Book of Daniel and Luke–Acts

The book of Daniel provides important background for many New Testament books, including the Gospel of Luke.[14] Like the other Synoptic Gospel writers, the Gospel of Luke frequently uses the messianic "Son of Man" title from Dan 7:13. Moreover, Luke's Gospel also evokes Daniel in ways that are not present in the rest of the Synoptic tradition.[15] Thus, it

---

12. Daniel's relationship with Babylonian royalty continues beyond the reign of Nebuchadnezzar. The famous handwriting on the wall scene of Dan 5 shows that Daniel has gained a lasting reputation among Babylonian royalty. Although the queen recognizes Daniel as one "in whom is the Spirit of the holy God" (Dan 5:11; see also Dan 4:8, 5:14) and Daniel testifies to King Belshazzar of God's mighty works towards his father, Nebuchadnezzar (5:18–21), Belshazzar refuses to humble himself before God and is thus removed from office. In Belshazzar's pride, we find a contrast with Nebuchadnezzar's humility. Belshazzar's story reminds us that not all gentile kings become supporters of God's purposes and that those who fail to acknowledge the Lord will face his judgment.

13. Newsom, *Daniel*, 201; Collins, *Daniel*, 271–72.

14. The New Testament contains many allusions to the book of Daniel. Although the New Testament authors quote from Daniel only five times (Matt 24:30, 26:64; Mark 13:26, 14:62; Luke 21:27), they allude to Daniel about two hundred times. Daniel ranks alongside Isaiah and Psalms as one of the most frequently alluded to books in the New Testament. Evans, "Daniel in the New Testament," 490.

15. Mitchell Chase points out that, outside of the book of Daniel, Luke is the only

is plausible that as Luke wrote, he also had in mind the government officials of the book of Daniel. Just as some of the highest-ranking officials in the Babylonian and Medo-Persian governments served as surprising proponents of God's people and plans, so too, Luke would suggest that Roman officials could also become supporters of the gospel. In our second case study from the Old Testament, we will look at a foreign official who is explicitly named in Luke's Gospel.

Conversion and Conscience: Naaman, the Syrian Commander (2 Kgs 5:1–27, Luke 4:22–30)

The story of Naaman may seem obscure to many modern readers of the Bible. However, the Naaman account is positioned prominently in both the Elisha narrative and in the composition of Luke–Acts. The dilemma that Naaman faces after becoming a believer also has important implications for our later analysis of Roman centurions.[16]

The healing of Naaman is one of the longest episodes during the ministry of Elisha.[17] From a literary perspective, the account of Naaman's healing involves multiple characters and is rich with narrative artistry.[18] Most

---

biblical author to mention the angel Gabriel (Chase, "Angel Gabriel"). Caleb Friedeman argues that the book of Daniel provides an important interpretive key to understanding Luke 1–2 (Friedeman, "Daniel in Luke 1–2").

16. The Naaman story has drawn significant attention in missiological studies. Such studies point out that Naaman's dilemma represents the types of tensions experienced by Christian converts in contexts where there are very few believers. Their situations would parallel that of a Roman official converting to Christianity. Brueggemann, "2 Kings 5"; Effa, "Prophet, Kings, Servants, and Lepers"; Maier, "Naaman in Missiological Perspective"; Nwaoru, "Story of Naaman"; Sauma, "Ancestor Practices."

17. Cohn points out the uniqueness of the Naaman story in the larger cycle of stories of which it is a part. "Its length and complexity set it apart from the many short, independent episodes in the cycle, in particular from the two which precede it (2 Kings iv 38–41, 42–44) and the one which follows it (vi 1–7)." Cohn then points out that Naaman's healing is unique among the prophetic stories in that it describes "the healing of a leper (but cf. Num xii) and worship of Yahweh by a non-Israelite (but cf. 1 Kings xxiv)." Cohn, "Form and Perspective," 171.

18. Hobbs detects a significant increase in the number of characters and complexity of the Naaman story compared to other stories in Elisha narrative. Hobbs identifies a total of ten characters or groups of characters in the story: Naaman, his wife, her servant girl, the king of Syria, the king of Israel, Elisha, Gehazi, Naaman's servants, Elisha's messenger, and the additional servants who carry Gehazi's loot (Hobbs, *2 Kings*, 58–62). See also Cohn, "Form and Perspective."

importantly, since the bulk of Elisha's ministry is directed towards Israelites, Naaman stands out as a gentile who belongs to an enemy nation.

In this case study, I will begin by reviewing the key aspects of Naaman's story as recounted in 2 Kgs 5:1–27. Through his conversation with Elisha, we will see how Naaman's conversion raises tension with his role as Syrian military commander. Next, I will show how Naaman functions as a prototypical gentile believer within the Elisha narrative cycle. The last part of this case study will demonstrate how Naaman's story functions as a precursor for Jesus and the apostles' ministry to gentiles (including Roman centurions) in Luke–Acts. As we will see later in this book, the tension that Naaman faces after conversion is very similar to the pressure that a Roman official would encounter upon believing in Jesus.[19] To set up that discussion, let's first review the story of Naaman, with a focus upon the two climactic points of the story: (1) Naaman's healing and conversion and (2) Naaman's subsequent conversation with Elisha.[20]

Naaman's Healing and Conversion
(2 Kgs 5:1–27)

Following Elisha's ministry to a prophet's widow (2 Kgs 4:1–7), the Shunammite woman (4:8–37), and the hungry group of prophets at Gilgal (4:38–44), the narrative abruptly turns to introduce "Naaman, commander of the army of the king of Syria" (5:1). Naaman is held in high regard by the king "because by him the Lord had given victory to Syria" (5:1). This description is surprising since Syria is one of Israel's perennial enemies, and the text states that "the Lord" granted Naaman military victory.[21] Moreover, Naaman is introduced as a "mighty man of valor" (גִּבּוֹר חַיִל, 5:1), a familiar phrase that biblical authors typically use to portray Israel's leading men (Judg 6:12, 11:1, Ruth 2:1, 1 Sam 9:1, 1 Kgs 11:28). The problem for Naaman, however, is that he is also suffering as "a leper" (2 Kgs 5:1). The author's intricate

---

19. Maier compares Naaman's dilemma in 2 Kgs 5:18 to the stories of Daniel, Shadrach, Meshach, and Abednego (which we have discussed earlier) and to Christians who suffered martyrdom for refusing to burn incense to the Roman emperor (Maier, "Naaman in Missiological Perspective," 191).

20. Von Rad, "Naaman," 51.

21. Commenting on 2 Kgs 5:1, von Rad writes, "The remark is brief, but in ancient Israel no one would have missed it. Naaman was, then, someone for whose sake God had blessed Israel's enemies." Von Rad, "Naaman," 48.

introduction of Naaman amplifies anticipation for what will become of this diseased military commander.

A key character in the story is an Israelite slave girl who had been taken to serve Naaman's wife during one of Syria's raids upon Israel (5:2). Though taken captive to serve an enemy nation, the anonymous slave girl demonstrates compassion on her master by suggesting that he might be cured by the prophet Elisha (5:3). The slave girl exhibits how God's people can offer hope to officials who serve hostile governments.[22] Eventually, the young girl's message is passed along to the king of Syria, who sends Naaman to the king of Israel along with an enormous gift of "ten talents of silver, six thousand shekels of gold, and ten changes of clothing" (5:5). The Syrian king's generous gift shows how much he values Naaman. The king of Israel's response, "Am I God, to kill and to make alive . . . ?" (5:7) demonstrates the difficulty of the miracle that is about to take place through Elisha. When Elisha hears of the king's response, he invites a visit from the Syrian commander so "that he may know that there is a prophet in Israel" (5:8).

Upon Naaman's arrival, Elisha remains in his home and sends a messenger to instruct the leprous commander to wash seven times in the Jordan (5:10). At first, Naaman is offended by Elisha's instructions. Naaman was expecting the prophet to meet him and pray for him to heal his leprosy (5:11). Moreover, to Naaman, the rivers of Damascus back in his homeland are more desirable compared to the Jordan River (5:12). After being encouraged by his servants, Naaman eventually submits to Elisha's command and goes down to wash in the Jordan "according to the word of the man of God" (5:14). Upon doing so, Naaman is healed of his leprosy.

There are several indications that Naaman received not only physical healing but also an inward change of heart.[23] Prior to his healing, Naaman was upset with Elisha for not coming out to meet him (5:11). However, after being healed, Naaman humbles himself by returning to stand before Elisha (5:15). Moreover, Naaman declares, "Behold, I know that there is no God in all the earth but in Israel" (5:15). Naaman's humble attitude is

---

22. House explains, "Despite her captivity, she is not bitter or unhelpful. Rather, she shares what she knows about the Lord and the prophet out of concern for Naaman and her mistress and desire to see God's glory magnified. In this way she acts like Daniel, Mordecai, Ezra, Nehemiah, and other exiles who care for the spiritual and physical well-being of their conquerors." House, *1, 2 Kings*, 272. See also Brueggemann, "2 Kings 5," 265–66.

23. House lists several evidences of Naaman's change of heart in his commentary on this passage. House, *1, 2 Kings*, 273.

matched by his verbal declaration of loyalty towards the Lord. The Syrian commander's newfound faith is on display in his subsequent conversation with Elisha.

Naaman's Dilemma
(2 Kgs 5:15–19)

Following Naaman's conversion, his conversation with Elisha is a second climax in the story (5:15–19). Naaman begins by wanting to repay the prophet using the gift provided by the king of Syria (5:15). However, Elisha turns down the gift (5:16). Next, Naaman makes a curious request for two loads of dirt to help facilitate his worship of the Lord back in Syria (5:17). Although the exact details of Naaman's motivation are debatable, at least one part of his reasoning is clear.[24] Naaman wishes to set up an outpost for worship of Israel's God after he arrives back home in Syria. Naaman also makes a stunning commitment, saying, "From now on your servant will not offer burnt offering or sacrifice to any god but the Lord" (5:17).

Naaman's vow to worship the Lord comes with significant risk, given his close relationship to the king of Syria. Naaman's complex situation is revealed in the form of a final request towards Elisha. Though the wording of Naaman's request appears at first to be needlessly repetitive, it is upon closer inspection found to have a deliberate chiastic structure that centers upon the phrase "leaning on my arm" (נִשְׁעָן עַל־יָדִי, 5:18), which identifies Naaman as the right-hand man of the Syrian king (see 7:2, 17). The chiasm is seen in the following structural layout of 2 Kgs 5:18 which I have adapted from Cohn:[25]

---

24. Maier explains that although Naaman understands that "'there is no God *in* all the earth but *in* Israel' . . . he does not yet comprehend that Yahweh is God *of* all the earth. . . . Accordingly, Naaman deems it necessary to take Israelite soil back to Syria so that he could properly worship Yahweh. . . . He would have a sanctified place for Yahweh in a land unclean, polluted with idolatry.'" Maier, "Naaman in Missiological Perspective," 187; emphasis original.

25. Cohn, "Form and Perspective," 179.

   A   In this matter

       B   may the Lord pardon your servant:

            C   when my master goes into the house of Rimmon to worship there,

                X   leaning on my arm,

            C' and I bow myself in the house of Rimmon, when I bow myself in the house of Rimmon,

       B' the Lord pardon your servant

   A' in this matter.

Naaman immediately realizes that his recent conversion has the potential to conflict with his responsibilities towards the Syrian king, since Naaman is expected to accompany the king into a house of worship for Rimmon.[26] As part of the king's regular routine, he bows to worship while "leaning on [Naaman's] arm" (5:18). The expression "leaning on my arm" (נִשְׁעָן עַל־יָדִי) explains Naaman's role in the Syrian government. At first glance, the wording might appear to suggest that the king is physically incapable (perhaps from illness or old age) and must lean upon Naaman as support while bowing down in the temple.[27] While such a reading is possible, it is much more likely that the phrase "leaning on my arm" is being used metaphorically to identify Naaman as the right-hand man of the Syrian king. The figurative meaning "right-hand man" is confirmed later in the narrative when Israel's commander is described using the same expression (see 7:2, 17). Although Naaman may have participated in this rite of worship countless times in the past, his encounter with the living God has now given him a new perspective on the rituals of Rimmon.

It is significant that Naaman does not ask to be relieved of his duties as military commander. Instead, he asks for help to navigate the tensions of worshiping the God of Israel while working in an environment that sometimes impinges upon his conscience. Naaman will be expected to bow in the house of Rimmon, but he wants Elisha to know that when he does so,

---

26. Rimmon is likely the Syrian name for the Canaanite god Baal. Maier, "Hadadrimmon"; House, *1, 2 Kings*, 273.

27. While the Hebrew verb שׁען can mean "lean or to support oneself" (Gen 18:4, Num 21:15, Judg 16:26, 2 Sam 1:6), it is usually used figuratively to mean "to depend upon" or "to trust" (2 Chr 13:18; 14:10; 16:7, 8; Job 8:15; 24:23; Prov 3:5; Isa 10:20; 30:12; 31:1; 50:10; Ezek 29:7; Mic 3:11). The phrase "to lean upon the hand" appears only in 2 Kgs 5–7. See BDB 1043.

his actions do not represent the true state of his heart. Inwardly, Naaman is committed to worship the God of Israel, even if outwardly he is required to stand in the house of Rimmon to fulfill his duties to the king.

How would the prophet respond to Naaman's request? Elisha's response, "Go in peace" (לֵךְ לְשָׁלוֹם, 5:19) has drawn various interpretations. On the one hand, some take Elisha's words as an approval for Naaman to participate in the Syrian religious rituals since he was inwardly a worshiper of the Lord.[28] Others have pointed out that Elisha's response does not necessarily express approval. Elsewhere in the Old Testament, the phrase "go in peace" (לֵךְ לְשָׁלוֹם) is used simply as a blessing upon one's journey that does not carry a sense of ethical endorsement (see Exod 4:18, 1 Sam 20:42). As Keil notes, Elisha wishes Naaman "the peace of God upon the road, without thereby either approving or disapproving the religious conviction which he had expressed."[29] Since Naaman had not asked Elisha's permission in the matter, the prophet "could do nothing more, without a special command from God, than commend [Naaman] . . . to the further guidance of the Lord and of His grace."[30] Elisha does not directly confer the Lord's forgiveness but leaves Naaman with the hope that God would accompany him upon his return to Syria.

Elisha's response to Naaman, "Go in peace" (5:19), shows that the prophet understands the difficulty of Naaman's situation as a believer who also holds an official position as Syrian military commander. It is important to note that Naaman is a tender new believer who recognizes that it would not be right for him to worship both Rimmon and Yahweh.[31] Effa explains, "Elisha's enigmatic response might at least suggest that God is patient with those who have just turned to him and gives them time to discover what it means to worship him in ways that do not require an immediate separation from their culture."[32]

---

28. Crenshaw, *Old Testament Story and Faith*, 149–50; Sauma, "Ancestor Practices," 334–35.

29. Keil and Delitzsch, *I and II Kings*, 321.

30. Keil and Delitzsch, *I and II Kings*, 321.

31. As Maier points out, Naaman is a new believer who still has much to learn about the Lord. Elisha recognizes that Naaman's spiritual growth will take place over time. Maier, "Naaman in Missiological Perspective," 191–92.

32. Effa, "Prophet, Kings, Servants, and Lepers," 311.

Naaman as Prototypical Gentile Believer

Naaman is a fascinating example of a gentile who believes in the God of Israel and becomes a partaker of salvation. Moreover, in the immediate context of the Elisha narrative, Naaman also serves as a contrast with two of his Israelite contemporaries: Gehazi (2 Kgs 5:19b–27) and the commander of the army of Israel (7:1–20). I will now briefly compare Naaman to each of these individuals.

Naaman as a Contrast with Gehazi (2 Kgs 5:19b–27)

The Naaman episode ends with a dramatic account where Gehazi's greed is exposed (5:20–27). This final interaction provides a stunning contrast between Naaman and Gehazi. As Naaman ponders how to remain faithful to the Lord while serving the king of Syria (5:18), Gehazi is plotting to maximize personal gain while outwardly serving Elisha (5:20). After Naaman leaves, Gehazi chases down the Syrian commander so that he might get a portion of the lavish gifts that Elisha had refused (5:16). Although Gehazi thinks that he has secretly secured a portion of Naaman's presents, Elisha is fully aware of his servant's deceitfulness (5:26). As a result, the leprosy from which Naaman was healed is transferred to Gehazi and his descendants forever (5:27). Ironically, Gehazi serves Elisha but lacks integrity, whereas Naaman serves the Syrian king while remaining devoted to the Lord. Gehazi's proximity to Elisha does not guarantee that his heart is pure. Naaman's leadership role in the army of Israel's enemy does not mean that he is an enemy of God. Even though he will return to Syria, "Naaman can serve YHWH in spite of all idolatrous conditions to which his duty and environment may expose him."[33]

Naaman as a Contrast with the Commander of Israel (2 Kgs 7:1–20)

As mentioned earlier, the chiastic structure of 2 Kgs 5:18 centers upon the expression "leaning on my arm" (נִשְׁעָן עַל־יָדִי) which identifies Naaman as the right-hand man of the Syrian king. The same phrase appears later in the

---

33. Nwaoru, "Story of Naaman," 37.

Elisha narrative to portray Naaman's counterpart in the Israelite army as "the captain on whose hand [the king] leaned [נִשְׁעָן עַל־יָדוֹ]" (7:2, 17).

In the context of fierce battle between the kings of Syria and Israel, the repeated phrase "leaning on the hand" (5:18; 7:2, 17) suggests a contrast between their respective commanders, or right-hand men (table 1).[34] The Syrian and Israelite commanders both have an encounter with the prophet Elisha. Both commanders initially doubt the word of the prophet (5:10–12, 7:1–2). Both stories feature lepers as protagonists (5:2, 7:3–10). Naaman the Syrian is healed (both physically and spiritually) because of his trust in the prophet's word. The commander of Israel, however, is trampled to death because of his unbelief (7:17–20). The contrast between their fates highlights the faith of Naaman the gentile military commander who trusts the Lord during a time when Israel's own military commander failed to trust God.

Table 1. Military Commanders of Syria and Israel in 2 Kgs 5 and 7

Feature	Syria's Commander (2 Kgs 5)	Israel's Commander (2 Kgs 7)
Name	Naaman (5:1)	Not mentioned
Relationship to King	Right-hand man (5:18; see also 5:1)	Right-hand man (7:2, 17)
Response to Elisha	Initial unbelief followed by faith (5:11–14)	Persistent unbelief (7:2)
Role of Lepers	Naaman's leprosy healed (5:14) and transferred to Gehazi (5:27)	Four lepers discover the abandoned Syrian camp (7:3–10)
Result	Healed physically and spiritually (5:14–19)	Trampled to death (7:17–20)

---

34. Maier points out that the Israelite king is healthy enough to tear his garments, which further suggests that the commander "on whose hand he leaned" is not meant in a literal sense (i.e., the commander is needed to support a king in ill health) but in a figurative sense (i.e., the commander is the king's right-hand man). Maier, "Naaman in Missiological Perspective," 188.

Overall, we can glean a few key points from the story of Naaman. Naaman's conversion shows that Israel's Lord is also the God of the gentiles. Although the Syrians are ostensibly the enemies of God's people, we surprisingly find that God is using their commander (5:1) and has compassion on his leprous condition (5:3). Moreover, Naaman's conversion is authentic even if his understanding of the Lord remains somewhat undeveloped. Naaman's dilemma is an example which shows us that "every faithful person who does not simply abandon the world is confronted by the wrenching issue of divided loyalties. There is no easy answer that works every time."[35] It is perhaps for these reasons that Naaman appears in a strategic place in the narrative of Luke–Acts.

Naaman in Luke–Acts

Outside of 2 Kgs 5, Naaman is mentioned only once in the rest of the Bible. Surely, the paucity of references to Naaman contributes to the obscurity of the Syrian commander to modern Bible readers. It is important to note, however, that the one place where Naaman appears has an outsized impact. This is because Naaman is featured as an example during Jesus' inaugural sermon at the Nazareth synagogue (Luke 4:16–30). For the purposes of our study, it is also significant that Luke is the only one of the four evangelists to mention Naaman. In this section, I will discuss the significance of Naaman's appearance in Luke's account. Although the Syrian is named only once in Luke–Acts, his story is echoed elsewhere in the narrative.

In Luke's Gospel, Jesus makes his first public appearance at the synagogue in Nazareth. On the Sabbath day, Jesus proclaims his Messianic identity by declaring that he is the fulfillment of the Old Testament Scriptures. With all eyes fixed on Jesus, he carefully selects a passage from Isaiah to demonstrate his salvific mission. At the end of his Sabbath speech, Jesus makes a surprising turn to predict his audience's rejection of his message and the positive reception of gentiles. Gentile inclusion, according to Jesus, is nothing new.

> And he said, "Truly I say to you, no prophet is acceptable in his hometown. But in truth, I tell you, there were many widows in Israel in the days of Elijah, when the heavens were shut up three years and six months, and a great famine came over all the land, and Elijah was sent to none of them but only to Zarephath, in the

---

35. Nelson, *First and Second Kings*, 183.

land of Sidon, to a woman who was a widow. And there were many lepers in Israel in the time of the prophet Elisha, and none of them was cleansed, but only Naaman the Syrian." (Luke 4:24–27)

Of all people mentioned in the Old Testament, why would Naaman be highlighted during this programmatic sermon at the start of Jesus' public ministry? Luke features the Syrian commander because he prefigures the centurions in Luke–Acts. The conversion of Naaman serves as a narrative pattern for the first centurions that appear in both the Gospel of Luke (Luke 7:1–10) and the book of Acts (Acts 10). A further discussion of these centurions will have to wait until chapter 4.

Conclusion

The Bible presents many examples of government officials who serve as proponents of God's purposes. Although we may typically think of Israel's rulers and government officials as the good guys, the Old Testament presents many foreign leaders as supporters of God's people and plans. In this chapter, I focused on two case studies: one from the time of Israel's exile and the other from the time of Israel's divided kingdom. Through the stories of Daniel and Naaman, we saw examples of how God can use government officials for his purposes.

Daniel and his companions are Israelites who become rulers within powerful gentile empires. Through their integrity and God-given wisdom, these young Hebrew men navigate the tensions of living within a pagan culture to become conduits for God's blessing to the nations whom they serve. Daniel's story demonstrates how God can place his own people as servants within hostile kingdoms. Through Daniel's example, we see how a Jewish person could acclimate into a gentile culture while remaining faithful to God. Importantly, Daniel is also supported by several other non-Jewish officials. Although some of these gentile officials are minor characters in the story, their actions lead to critical turning points in the lives of the Jewish protagonists. These minor characters include mid-level officials like Ashpenaz and Arioch in Daniel's story. Finally, we saw how foreign kings could come to acknowledge God's hand at work in the lives of Daniel and his companions. In some cases, these kings make stunning declarations of God's authority and eternal rule. Indeed, although these kings initially appeared as enemies of God's people and purposes, by the end of their stories, they look more and more like the good guys.

Naaman is a gentile military commander who converts to faith in Israel's God and prefigures the Roman officials that will be introduced throughout the narratives of Luke–Acts.[36] After experiencing a miraculous healing, Naaman faces an immediate dilemma. How would he continue serving the Syrian king while also remaining faithful to the God of Israel? Naaman's crisis shows the types of tensions that would typically be faced by believers who are embedded within an evil system. These are exactly the types of tensions that we will explore later in the book. But before we get ahead of ourselves, we must first ask the question, who was Luke–Acts written to? This is the topic we will address in the next chapter.

---

36. Richard Hays points out that Jesus' sermon at Nazareth "provocatively recounts Gentile-inclusive episodes from the stories of Elijah and Elisha . . . that prefigure the Gentile-inclusion controversies played out subsequently in the pages of Acts." Hays, *Echoes of Scripture*, 273–74. I believe Hays's observation can also be linked more broadly to the Gospel of Luke through the theme of the centurions.

3

Luke and His Audience

> It seemed good to me also, having followed all things closely for some time past, to write an orderly account for you, most excellent Theophilus, that you may have certainty concerning the things you have been taught.
>
> —Luke 1:3–4

Who was Theophilus? On the one hand, this may seem like an inconsequential question. After all, Theophilus's name appears only twice in the entire New Testament (Luke 1:3, Acts 1:1). As such, most readers gloss over his name when reading Luke and Acts. Loveday Alexander laments the indifference Christians have held towards Luke's reader: "Christian tradition has never, so far as I can tell, taken Theophilus seriously at all, even as a reader: there is no Saint Theophilus, no attempt to discover sanctified bones or to find him a place (like Onesimus) in the hierarchies of church history."[1] Since Christians have paid such little attention to Theophilus, some may question whether it is worthwhile to consider his identity. Yet, to read Luke–Acts well, the thoughtful reader ought to consider how the references to Theophilus shape our understanding of Luke's intended audience, the overall message of Luke–Acts, and the implications of Luke's message for Christians today.

---

1. Alexander, "What If Luke Had Never Met Theophilus?," 164.

In this chapter, I will argue that Luke's first reader, Theophilus, was most likely a high-ranking Roman official who was interested in the gospel message. I will build this argument in three steps. The first step will discuss the intended readers of Luke–Acts, arguing that Luke wrote for both a broad and narrow audience. The second step will discuss the prefaces to Luke and Acts and their significance for ascertaining Luke's audience. In the third step, I will discuss the identity of Theophilus to whom Luke dedicated his writings. At the end of the chapter, I will summarize my findings and explore implications for understanding Luke–Acts.

Luke's Audiences

The question of Theophilus's identity falls within a broader discussion about the intended audiences of the four Gospels. Did Luke write to a specific community, a general audience, or an individual? It turns out that not all of these categories are mutually exclusive.

Luke's Broad Audience

In his introductory essay to *The Gospels for All Christians*, Richard Bauckham argues that the Gospels were written for circulation among a general Christian audience. In this book, Bauckham and his colleagues contest the prevailing view (since the 1960s) that each Gospel author wrote to address the specific concerns of his own local Christian community.[2] In one article, Thompson argues that although early Christians lived in local communities, frequent travel and communication across communities facilitated the rapid distribution of Christian literature to new localities.[3] Moreover, the Gospel writers would have expected such distribution since their own ministries probably spanned multiple geographical regions.[4] Thus, rather than being written for a so-called "Lukan community," it is likely that Luke–Acts was intended for broad circulation among Christian readers.[5]

---

2. Bauckham, "For Whom Were Gospels Written?," 10–11. For examples of the "community audience" view of Luke, see Moxnes, "Social Context of Luke's Community"; Kilgallen, "Luke Wrote to Rome."

3. Thompson, "Holy Internet."

4. Bauckham, "For Whom Were Gospels Written?," 44.

5. The debate about Gospel audiences is not yet resolved. For two representative responses to Bauckham's view, see Esler, "Community and Gospel in Early Christianity";

Luke's Narrow Audience

By affirming Bauckham's thesis that the Gospels were written for distribution among Christians, it is not necessary to rule out the possibility of a Gospel also being addressed to a specific recipient. In the case of Luke's Gospel, the identification of a broad or narrow audience is not an either-or decision. As Isak du Plessis points out, Luke's Gospel should be treated somewhat differently than the other three canonical Gospels because Luke explicitly addresses an individual, Theophilus. In other words, while Luke's Gospel was likely intended to be circulated among a general audience, it was first addressed to a narrow audience.[6] Thus, while I agree with Bauckham that the Third Gospel was probably not written for a so-called "Lukan community," it is still important to recognize that Luke addressed his work to Theophilus. Luke evidently wrote first to Theophilus; however, the very fact that he took the time to write a book suggests that he expected his work to be circulated among "Greek-speaking Christians everywhere."[7]

Luke's Dual Audience

Luke wrote to a dual audience: first to Theophilus, and second to the wider Christian world.[8] The notion of a dual audience is consistent with what we know of book production in the ancient world. It was common for a recipient of a book to provide personal copies to friends who would then make their copies available for others to make additional copies.[9] The publication and circulation of a book would typically proceed among

---

Mitchell, "Patristic Counter-Evidence." In response to Esler's critique, Bauckham points out that "the question of the expected audience of a Gospel is a quite different question from that of the influence of the evangelist's local context on his writing" (Bauckham, "Response to Philip Esler," 249). As Mark Strauss points out, "the truth probably lies somewhere between two extremes" (Strauss, *Four Portraits, One Jesus*, 2nd ed., 39).

6. "As far as Luke is concerned one need, therefore, not really 'reconstruct' his first audience. . . . Even though it is most probable that Luke's Gospel was meant for a wider public/audience, it was in the first place directed to an individual—different from the other three Gospels." Du Plessis, "Lukan Audience," 259. See also Mitchell, "Patristic Counter-Evidence," 60–61.

7. Bauckham, "For Whom Were Gospels Written?," 30.

8. Craig Keener sees the audience of Acts as both Theophilus (Luke's literary patron) and the broader audiences who would gather to hear the reading of the book. Keener, *Acts*, 1:424.

9. Gamble, *Books and Readers*, 84–85.

the social networks of people interested in literature, who were typically upper-class individuals with the time and leisure to read.[10] If Theophilus was indeed Luke's patron, he would be expected to disseminate the work to a broader audience of readers.[11] In other words, the dedication to Theophilus would have likely provided a "more elevated audience for the book in addition to its normal networks of communication."[12] Later in this chapter, I will return to this discussion of Theophilus's identity. But first, let's take a closer look at the prefaces to Luke and Acts.

Prefaces to Luke and Acts

Each of the four canonical Gospels begins in a unique way. Matthew recounts Jesus' genealogy (Matt 1:1–17), Mark cites Old Testament prophecy (Mark 1:1–3), and John exalts Jesus as the eternal Word of God (John 1:1–18). Luke's Gospel begins with a preface (Luke 1:1–4) which is written in excellent Greek. The preface employs a careful sentence structure which stands in contrast to the more ordinary writing style of the rest of the book.[13] Luke's sequel, the book of Acts, begins with a brief preface that connects back to the preface of Luke's Gospel (Acts 1:1; see also Luke 1:3). In this section, I will briefly examine the prefaces to Luke and Acts.[14]

Similarities to Historical Documents

Scholars have long noted that Luke's prefaces show remarkable similarities to contemporary extrabiblical literature.[15] One notable example is Josephus's two-volume work *Against Apion*. Josephus's first volume of *Against Apion* begins with a longer preface that introduces both the first book and the entire two-volume work.[16] Although the preface to *Against Apion I* is significantly longer than Luke's preface, it contains several remarkable similarities, such as the naming of his recipient as "most excellent [κράτιστε]

---

10. Gamble, *Books and Readers*, 85.
11. Gamble, *Books and Readers*, 102.
12. Alexander, "Ancient Book Production," 104.
13. Marshall, *Gospel of Luke*, 39.
14. Here, I assume the unity of Luke–Acts. For a brief introduction to the topic, see Tannehill, *Narrative Unity of Luke–Acts*, 1:1–12.
15. Cadbury, "Preface of Luke," 506.
16. In *Against Apion*, Josephus defends the long history of the Jews against critics.

Epaphroditus," which bears striking resemblance to Luke's address to "most excellent [κράτιστε] Theophilus" (Luke 1:3).[17]

In a manner analogous to Acts 1:1, Josephus's *Against Apion II* begins with a brief recapitulation that connects his reader back to the preface of the first volume. Compare the opening lines of Josephus's and Luke's second volumes below:

> In the first volume of this work, my most esteemed [τιμιώτατέ] Epaphroditus, I demonstrated the antiquity of our race.[18]

> In the first book, O Theophilus, I have dealt with all that Jesus began to do and teach. (Acts 1:1)

In their second volumes, both Josephus and Luke address their recipient in a different way compared to the prefaces to their respective first volumes, where both authors used κράτιστε. Josephus switches to the adjective τιμιώτατέ at the opening of his second volume. It is likely that Josephus changes the epithet for the sake of variety, as he does once again at the end of *Against Apion* 2, where he addresses his reader simply by the name Epaphroditus without an adjectival modifier.[19] Luke, likewise, opts for variety by replacing the adjective κράτιστε with a simple vocative in Acts 1:1.

Similarities to Technical Literature

Since Cadbury's 1922 publication of a twenty page commentary on Luke 1:1–4, scholars have emphasized the continuity between Luke's preface and the prefaces to contemporary historical works such as Josephus's *Against Apion*.[20] In her extensive study on Luke's preface, Alexander challenges the consensus view by suggesting that Luke's preface more closely resembles the prefaces of contemporary technical (or scientific) literature than the prefaces of historical documents.[21] In making this comparison, Alexander

---

17. Josephus, *Ag. Ap.* 1.1 (LCL 162–63). Although Cadbury thinks it was unlikely that κράτιστε was always used in an official sense, he nevertheless believes that Epaphroditus was a government official (Cadbury, "Preface of Luke," 506). Barclay believes Epaphroditus was possibly a freedman who served as Josephus's literary patron. See John Barclay's commentary in Josephus, *Ag. Ap.* 1.1 (FJTC 3n3).

18. Josephus, *Ag. Ap.* 2.1 (LCL 292–93).

19. Josephus, *Ag. Ap.* 2.296. See also Barclay's translation note in Josephus, *Ag. Ap.* 2.1 (FJTC 169n1).

20. Cadbury, "Preface of Luke."

21. Alexander, *Preface to Luke's Gospel*. In her 1993 book, Alexander uses the

draws attention to technical treatises that were commonly used in schools of philosophy, medicine, rhetoric, mathematics, or a broad variety of other topics.[22] While technical treatises were written in a variety of forms to cover a broad range of subject matter, what set them apart was their function. Such literature often functioned as treatises to be presented in a lecture hall, or as handbooks to systematically explain a particular topic.[23]

By following the conventions of prefaces to technical literature, Luke 1:1–4 prepares the reader for what was to come in the rest of his Gospel.[24] Like contemporary technical literature, Luke's Gospel shares a respect for tradition, continuity with previous writers, and a lack of concern for originality.[25] By briefly mentioning his careful investigation of sources, Luke reassures his reader of the trustworthiness of his account (Luke 1:3–4).[26] Moreover, Luke's writing style was appropriate for the social and educational levels of most early Christians.[27] While some works of literature, such as epics or didactic poetry, were written in a high literary style, the Gospel of Luke and most of the New Testament writings were written in a "literate but not literary" style.[28] Alexander argues that these similarities to contemporary technical literature show that Luke wrote from within a Christian social context that resembled the philosophical schools of Greco-Roman society.[29]

---

terminology "scientific tradition" to refer to these technical treatises. In a later work, she clarifies that "technical literature" would have been a more suitable term. Alexander, *Acts*, 3.

22. Alexander, *Preface to Luke's Gospel*, 21–22, 211. See for example, Galen's *Method of Medicine*, esp. books 1–4.

23. Alexander, *Preface to Luke's Gospel*, 42–43.

24. Alexander questions whether Luke envisioned writing Acts as a companion volume at the time of composing his preface to Luke. Alexander, *Preface to Luke's Gospel*, 145–46. For a defense of the narrative unity of Luke and Acts, see Green, *Luke*, 6–10.

25. Alexander, *Preface to Luke's Gospel*, 205.

26. Alexander, *Preface to Luke's Gospel*, 206.

27. Alexander, *Preface to Luke's Gospel*, 210.

28. Alexander, *Preface to Luke's Gospel*, 48, 169–71, 210.

29. In the late second century, Galen would attack the rational basis for Christianity as a rival philosophical school that brought with it not only a body of traditional teachings but also an entire way of life. Wilken, *Christians as the Romans Saw Them*, 72–83.

For Alexander, the realm of technical literature may also help to shed light on the relationships between the canonical Gospels and their preceding oral traditions. Alexander, *Preface to Luke's Gospel*, 211–12.

In response to Alexander's landmark study, scholars point out similarities between ancient historical works such as Josephus's *Against Apion* and the technical literature studied by Alexander.[30] Thus, while Alexander astutely notices parallels between the prefaces to Luke's Gospel and technical treatises, others suggest that the same features are also present in prefaces to historical documents. Moreover, as Aune points out, Alexander's conclusions do not adequately account for the limited sample size of extant Greek manuscripts which may not represent the entire genre of historical literature during Luke's day.[31] Thus, while there is much to commend about Alexander's detailed study, her argument may draw too sharp of a distinction between the prefaces to historical and technical documents. Instead, it seems that Luke's preface may share similarities with both genres.

The similarities between Luke 1:1–4 and ancient technical literature can also be used to corroborate the traditional view that the Third Gospel was authored by "Luke the beloved physician" (Col 4:14; see also 2 Tim 4:11, Phlm 24).[32] It is worth noting that, for Alexander, "technical literature" could be used to communicate historically accurate accounts.[33] In fact, technical literature was meant to distill and convey true knowledge, including accurate biographical information about key individuals, to a wide range of people who were interested in a particular school of thought.[34] By following the customary practices of technical literature, Luke shows that his work was meant for broad dissemination, as was typically the case for literature belonging to a particular school of thought.[35] These findings support my argument that Luke had in mind a dual audience that encompassed both the elite of Roman society and a more general audience.

---

30. Josephus, *Ag. Ap.* 1.1 (FJTC 3n1).

31. Aune, "Luke 1.1–4."

32. Alexander, *Preface to Luke's Gospel*, 177. This point is also highlighted in Marshall's review of Alexander's work (Marshall, "Review of *The Preface to Luke's Gospel*"). For a defense of Luke the physician as the author of Luke–Acts, see Kuhn, *Elite Evangelist*, 1–9; Kuhn, *Kingdom*, xviii–xix.

33. Alexander, *Preface to Luke's Gospel*, 200–201.

34. Alexander, *Preface to Luke's Gospel*, 202–4.

35. Alexander, *Preface to Luke's Gospel*, 168–86; Alexander, *Acts*, 3–4, 231–52. Commenting on Luke's writing style, Alexander observes that Luke wrote in "standard educated *Koine*" rather than atticized Greek and that this "linguistic choice itself very clearly identifies Luke's writings as not belonging to the prestige literary registers for which atticizing (or at least classicizing) Greek was fast becoming the norm" during this period. Alexander, *Acts*, 251.

Luke's Stated Purpose for Writing

Aside from any similarities to contemporary literature, Luke's preface introduces his purpose for writing (Luke 1:3–4). Luke was aware of many existing narratives on the life of Jesus, including the accounts of eyewitnesses and ministers of the word (1:1–2). After following these things closely for some time, he set out to write an "orderly account" for "most excellent Theophilus" (1:3) so that his reader might "have certainty concerning the things [he had] been taught" (1:4). Thus, Luke's purpose was to craft a historically accurate account so that Theophilus would have assurance regarding what he had previously learned about Jesus.[36] Luke's naming of his recipient sets his work apart among the four canonical Gospels and invites us to explore the significance of Luke's first reader. The rest of this chapter will discuss the identity of Theophilus.

Who Was Theophilus?

While many readers give little thought to Theophilus's identity, scholars have made various attempts at identifying Theophilus. The various opinions can be grouped into two broad categories of viewing Theophilus as either a prototypical reader or a historical individual.

Theophilus as a Prototypical Reader

As early as Origen (AD 185–254) some have proposed that Theophilus was a symbolic name meant to represent any Christian reader. According to Origen's *Homilies on Luke*, "someone might think that Luke addressed the Gospel to a specific man named Theophilus. But, if you are the sort of people God can love, then all of you who hear us speaking are Theophiluses, and the Gospel is addressed to you."[37] Etymologically, "Theophilus" (θεόφιλος) combines two Greek words for "God" (θεός) and "friend" or "lover" (φίλος), leading Origen and others to take the name as representative of

---

36. Acts was likewise written as an accurate account of history. On the historical reliability of Acts, see Hemer, *Acts*, 101–58.

37. For an English translation, see Leinhard's Origen, *Homilies on Luke*, 9. The quoted line comes from *Homilies on Luke* 1.6 where he explains Luke 1:1–4. According to Mitchell, Origen held that Theophilus was Luke's original recipient while also believing that Theophilus can represent anyone who loves God. Mitchell, "Patristic Counter-Evidence," 60.

an individual "friend of God" or "lover of God."[38] Ambrose, thus, believed that Luke's Gospel was written to all who love God. In his *Exposition on the Gospel of Luke*, Ambrose explains, "So the Gospel was written to Theophilus, that is, to him whom God loves. If you love God, it was written to you."[39] Such a meaning would not be out of place in Luke since the word φίλος appears to be one of his favorites. As Hart points out, φίλος appears in Luke more frequently than in any other New Testament book.[40]

Naming theories abound, with others seeing Theophilus as a representative reader among Luke's target audience. The Greek etymology and Luke's emphasis on gentile inclusion have led some to conclude that Theophilus represented a gentile reader. While Theophilus was a common name that appeared in the papyri to refer to real people, some believe Luke used Theophilus as a generic name to represent his intended gentile audience.[41] Kilgallen, for example, suggests that Theophilus was a foil to represent a prototypical reader living in Rome.[42] Moxnes argues that Luke's intent was to reach an urban audience of mixed ethnic, cultural, and social backgrounds.[43] More recently, Beck contends that Theophilus was a symbolic name given to a gentile who feared God and was sympathetic to Judaism, much like the "God-fearing" centurions described in Luke's text.[44] These views share a common feature that Theophilus was not the real name of a historical individual.

---

38. In contrast, Alexander argues that if the name Theophilus was meant to represent a typical Christian, the correct adjective would have been *theophiles* (θεοφιλής). Alexander, *Preface to Luke's Gospel*, 188. For more on the adverbial form, see Cadbury, "Preface of Luke," 507–8.

39. Just, *Luke*, 4. Interestingly, while Ambrose served as a Roman official before being elected bishop of Milan, he did not seem to make much of Theophilus's "most excellent" title.

40. Hart, "Gospel of Luke," 337. The word φίλος appears twenty-nine times in the New Testament, including fifteen times in Luke (7:6, 34; 11:5 [twice], 6, 8; 12:4; 14:10, 12; 15:6, 9, 29; 16:9; 21:16; 23:12) and three times in Acts (10:24, 19:31, 27:3). The rest of its appearances are in John (six times), 3 John (two times), James (two times), and Matthew (one time).

41. Cadbury points out that the name Theophilus appears in a range of papyri including a first-century papyrus that refers to a politarch in Egypt (P.Oxy. 4.745) and a third-century-BC papyri referring to a Pisidian (P.Lille 27) and a Thessalian (P.Petr. 1.19.30). Cadbury, "Preface of Luke," 507. Head et al., "Papyrological Perspectives," 34.

42. Kilgallen, "Luke Wrote to Rome."

43. Moxnes, "Social Context of Luke's Community."

44. Beck, *Light to the Centurions*, 1–24.

Theophilus as a Historical Person

Others argue that Theophilus was a historical person.[45] In favor of this view, Alexander points out that the name Theophilus was used by historical individuals. Alexander's analysis suggests that texts were generally dedicated to real people, although whether the dedicatee actually read the texts was another question. Moreover, the existence of some fictional dedications in ancient texts does not mean that all dedicatees were fictitious; rather, the fictional cases were imitations of the common practice of dedicating texts to real people.[46]

Many hold that Theophilus was a historical individual while disagreeing on his identity. Brent argues that Theophilus lived in a context that exalted the imperial cult.[47] Arthur Just proposes that Theophilus was a catechumen from Philippi.[48] Others, following the tradition that Luke came from Antioch, believe that he wrote to a wealthy Christian named Theophilus of Antioch. An even bolder proposal comes from Streeter, who argues that Theophilus may have been a secret name for Titus Flavius Clemens, cousin of Emperor Domitian, who would have been interested in the faith of his Christian wife, Domitilla. Streeter suggests that Luke–Acts was written as a defense of Christianity to the Roman aristocracy.[49]

Scholars who view Theophilus as a historical person typically describe him using three categories: literary patron, Jewish reader, or Roman official. These three categories, while not mutually exclusive, will be described next. I will briefly survey the categories of literary patron and Jewish reader before devoting a longer section to the Roman official category.

Theophilus as a Literary Patron

Many recent scholars view Theophilus as Luke's literary patron.[50] As Gamble points out, the ancient world knew nothing of copyright laws

---

45. Fitzmyer, *Luke (I–IX)*, 299–300; Marshall, *Gospel of Luke*, 43; Stein, *Luke*, 66. Commenting on Luke 1:3, Erasmus takes Theophilus as "a person's proper name" (Kreitzer, *Luke*, 5).

46. Alexander, *Preface to Luke's Gospel*, 188.

47. Brent, "Luke–Acts."

48. Just, "Luke's Canonical Criterion."

49. Streeter, *Four Gospels*, 534–39. Several of the aforementioned views, and a few others, are summarized in Marx, "New Theophilus," 18.

50. Garland, *Luke*, 56; Marshall, *Gospel of Luke*, 43; Dunn, *Acts*, 10; Bock, *Luke*, 1:63.

that would provide financial benefit for authors. Thus, it was customary for authors to finance their books through the "patronage of wealthy or influential persons."[51] Alexander notes, however, that "the relationship between dedication and patronage is complex; not all dedicatees are patrons, and not all patrons receive a dedication."[52] Thus, while the dedication to Theophilus does not require him to be a patron, Alexander suggests that it is plausible that "Theophilus could well be such a patron" for Luke.[53]

Theophilus as a Jewish Reader

Others propose that Theophilus was Jewish. In support of this view, Alexander points out that while Theophilus was not a Roman name, the name was commonly used by Hellenized Jews.[54] Bengel suggests that the name "Theophilus" is a Greek translation of the Hebrew name יְדִידְיָה ("beloved of Yahweh"). Bengel then proposes that Theophilus was none other than the Jewish philosopher Philo of Alexandria, whose Hebrew name, יְדִידְיָה, could have been translated into Greek as "Theophilus."[55]

It is indeed possible that Theophilus was a Jewish reader since "the name Theophilus occurs frequently from the third century BC on for both Jews and Greeks."[56] Interestingly, Josephus's *Jewish Antiquities* mentions a Jewish high priest named Theophilus.[57] Citing Josephus, Anderson identifies Luke's reader with the Theophilus who served as Jewish high priest between the years AD 37 to 41.[58] For Anderson, identifying Theophilus as high priest suggests that Luke's Gospel was meant to be circulated among a Jewish audience. While Anderson's view is not the majority view, the existence of a high priest named Theophilus has been corroborated by archaeological evidence.[59]

---

51. Gamble, *Books and Readers*, 83.
52. Alexander, *Preface to Luke's Gospel*, 190.
53. Alexander, *Preface to Luke's Gospel*, 191.
54. Alexander, *Preface to Luke's Gospel*, 133. Among the examples cited by Alexander is the *Letter of Aristeas* 49. Wright, *Letter of Aristeas*, 166.
55. Marx, "New Theophilus," 18. Marx cites Bengel's *Ordo Temporum*.
56. Nolland, *Luke 1—9:20*, 10.
57. Josephus, *Ant.* 18.123–124, 19.297.
58. Anderson, "Theophilus."
59. Barag and Flusser, "Ossuary of Yehoḥanah."

Theophilus as a Roman Official

So far, none of the views mentioned above have dealt with a critical clue that Luke provides regarding Theophilus. Luke addresses his reader as "most excellent" (κράτιστε, Luke 1:3), a title that he uses elsewhere in Acts to address high-ranking officials.[60] Significantly, the adjective κράτιστος appears only four times in the New Testament, and all four of these appearances are found in Luke–Acts.[61] After Luke 1:3, the second time the term appears is in official correspondence from Claudius Lysias to "most excellent [κρατίστῳ] governor Felix" (Acts 23:26). Next, during Paul's trial, the spokesman, Tertullus, addresses the governor as "most excellent [κράτιστε] Felix" (Acts 24:3). The title appears for the fourth time on the lips of Paul, while on trial before Felix's successor, Porcius Festus. Standing before the governor, Paul employs the title "most excellent [κράτιστε] Festus" (Acts 26:25). Thus, although the title κράτιστος occurs only once in Luke, it appears three times in Acts, each time as an honorific title for a Roman governor.

Writing in the eleventh century, the Greek archbishop Theophylact of Ohrid argues that Theophilus was most likely a senator or ruler (based on the title κράτιστος) and that any God-loving reader was also a "Theophilus" (see Origen's view above).[62] Theophylact combines two of the theories on Theophilus, suggesting that he was a Roman official and that his name could also represent a prototypical reader. In his article from 1721, Heumann also contends that Theophilus was a Roman magistrate.[63] Cadbury's

---

60. The phrase "your Excellency" is a helpful modern English rendering that captures the sense of the word κράτιστε. Dillon, "Previewing Luke's Project," 217; Karris, *Luke, Artist and Theologian*, 8.

61. BDAG 565. In the Septuagint, κράτιστος appears eight times, usually referring to objects rather than people. The following is a list of those eight occurrences: "the best [κράτιστα] of the sheep" (1 Sam 15:15); "their best gifts [ταῖς κρατίσταις]" (2 Macc 3:2); "the chief [κρατίστους] young men" (2 Macc 4:12); "the bravest [κράτιστα] of the armed men" (3 Macc 1:2); the "best places [τοῖς κρατίστοις]" and "most excellent [κρατίστη] heritage" (Ps 16:6 ET / 15:6 LXX), "the best [κράτιστον] wine" (Ps 23:5 ET / 22:5 LXX), and "the chief [κράτιστον] of all these kingdoms" (Amos 6:2).

62. Von Soden, *Die Schriften des Neuen Testaments*, 324; Mitchell, "Patristic Counter-Evidence," 60–61. On the significance of Theophylact's commentaries, Brown writes, "Despite their eleventh-century date, the commentaries of Theophylact have often been accorded the same degree of respect as the writings of the earlier Greek fathers. Based on the commentaries of Chrysostom, but at the same time more concise and accessible, the work of Theophylact exercised a wide influence." Brown, "Gospel Commentary of Theophylact," 194.

63. Heumann, "Dissertatio de Theophilo."

1922 study on Luke's preface similarly concluded that Theophilus was likely a Roman official.⁶⁴ More recently, Dunn suggests that Theophilus was "a man of some rank and influence."⁶⁵ Marx goes even further to speculate that Theophilus was none other than King Agrippa II and that Acts was written in an effort to persuade Agrippa to become a Christian (see Acts 26:28).⁶⁶ Since Agrippa II was Jewish, Marx's suggestion combines the three views that Theophilus was a historical person, a Jewish reader, and a Roman official. Still others maintain that Theophilus was a Roman official, without attempting to further identify him.⁶⁷ Viewing Theophilus as a Roman official has the benefit of relying upon a clear literary argument based on the use of the word κράτιστος within the narrative of Luke–Acts.

Thus far, I have claimed that Theophilus was most likely a Roman official based upon the title "most excellent" (Luke 1:3), which is used to address Roman governors during Paul's trial narrative in Acts. There is, however, further literary evidence from Acts to support my view that Theophilus was a Roman official.

Significantly, the preface to Luke's Gospel (Luke 1:1–4) shares multiple lexical and thematic connections to the narrative of Paul's arrest and trial (Acts 21:26—26:32). In addition to the word "most excellent" (κράτιστος, Luke 1:3), variations of the words "accurate" (ἀκριβῶς, Luke 1:2) and "certainty" (ἀσφάλεια, Luke 1:3) also appear throughout Paul's trial narrative to emphasize the need for Roman officials to understand Paul's case with certainty and accuracy.⁶⁸ The importance of these repetitions is better appreciated when we consider how infrequently these words appear in the rest of Luke–Acts (see table 2). As discussed earlier, κράτιστος appears only four times in Luke–Acts and exclusively within Luke's preface and Paul's

---

64. Cadbury, "Preface of Luke," 505–7. Cadbury also acknowledges the possibility that Theophilus was not an official and that Luke used κράτιστος merely as a title of respect.

65. Dunn, *Acts*, 10.

66. Marx, "New Theophilus."

67. Others remain uncertain (though open to the possibility) that Theophilus was a Roman official. Bovon, *Luke 1:1—9:50*, 23; Fitzmyer, *Luke (I-IX)*, 300; Nolland, *Luke 1—9:20*, 10; Stein, *Luke*, 66.

68. Moreover, the Greek word for "servants" (ὑπηρέται, Luke 1:2) also appears with reference to Paul in his trial narrative where the apostle refers to himself as both "a servant [ὑπηρέτης] and a witness [μάρτυς]" (Acts 26:16). Du Plessis, "Once More," 265. Although du Plessis notes the repetition of these words in Luke's preface and Paul's trial narrative, he does not use these recurrences to support his claim that Theophilus was a Roman official.

trial narrative. Cognates of the word ἀκριβῶς appear a total of eight times, with six of these occurrences in the preface or trial narrative. Similarly, cognates of the word ἀσφάλεια occur eight times in Luke–Acts, with four of these appearances in Luke's preface or Paul's trial narrative. Overall, Luke's preface and Paul's arrest and trial account for only 8 percent of the total verses in Luke–Acts and yet contain 70 percent of the appearances of the words κράτιστος, ἀκριβῶς, and ἀσφάλεια (and their cognates).

Table 2. Links Between Luke's Preface and Paul's Trial Narrative

Word Group (Appearances in Luke–Acts)	Luke's Preface (Luke 1:1–4) 0.2 percent of 2151 verses	Paul's Trial (Acts 21:27—26:32) 7.7 percent of 2151 verses	Rest of Luke–Acts 92 percent of 2151 verses
κράτιστος most excellent (four times)	one time; Theophilus (1:3)	three times; Felix (23:26, 24:3) and Festus (26:25)	zero times
ἀκρίβεια, ἀκριβής, ἀκριβῶς exactly, accurately, closely (eight times)	one time; author (1:3)	five times; Lysias (23:15, 20), Felix (24:22), Paul (22:3, 26:5)	two times; Apollos (Acts 18:25, 26)
ἀσφάλεια, ἀσφαλής, ἀσφαλῶς, ἀσφαλίζω certainty, definite, to secure (eight times)	one time; Theophilus (1:4)	three times; Lysias (21:34, 22:30), Festus (25:26)	four times; Jesus (Acts 2:36), prison (Acts 5:23; 16:23, 24)
Total (twenty times)	three times; 15 percent of appearances	eleven times; 55 percent of appearances	six times; 30 percent of appearances

I contend that these lexical connections between Luke's preface and Paul's trial narrative are not accidental. Instead, they are literary signals demonstrating that Paul's climactic trial functions as a narrative fulfillment of Luke's stated purpose for writing. Just as Paul reasons with the Roman officials in Acts, so Luke wrote to Theophilus so that he might know the truth with accuracy and certainty.

A brief look at the use of cognates of ἀσφάλεια and ἀκριβῶς outside of Luke's preface and Paul's trial narrative will help to further illuminate Theophilus's need for understanding. Aside from three instances about securing a prison (Acts 5:23; 16:23, 24), the remaining three appearances of these words appear in connection with understanding the gospel. In Acts 2:36, the word ἀσφαλῶς is used by Peter to describe certainty in Jesus' lordship. Like the Israelites to whom Peter spoke, Theophilus also needs to "know [γινωσκέτω] for certain [ἀσφαλῶς] that God has made him both Lord and Christ, this Jesus whom you crucified" (Acts 2:36). In Acts 18:25–26, the words ἀκριβῶς and ἀκριβέστερον describe Apollos's growth in grasping the gospel. Although Apollos "taught accurately [ἀκριβῶς] the things concerning Jesus" (18:25), he needs further instruction so that he might know "the way of God more accurately [ἀκριβέστερον]" (18:26). Like Apollos who "had been instructed [κατηχημένος] in the way of the Lord" (18:25) but required additional teaching to increase his understanding, so also Theophilus needs the accounts of Luke–Acts to provide "certainty concerning the things [he] had been taught [κατηχήθης]" (Luke 1:4).[69]

To be clear, these types of connections between Luke's preface and the rest of Luke–Acts have been explored by some.[70] Nevertheless, most scholars do not leverage the results of such analysis to support the argument that Theophilus was a Roman official.[71] I believe, however, that these textual ties help to solidify the connection between Theophilus and

---

69. Du Plessis, "Once More," 269–70. Although the verb κατηχέω can mean "to be informed" or "to be told" as an outsider (Acts 21:21, 24), it can also mean "to be instructed" as one who is associated with the Christian community (Acts 18:25). Johnson prefers the latter meaning here (Johnson, *Luke*, 28). Due to the colocation of the words ἀκριβῶς and ἀκριβέστερον (cognates of the word ἀκριβῶς used in Luke 1:3) alongside the verb κατηχέω in Acts 18:25–26, I agree with Johnson that the stronger meaning "to be instructed" is preferred in Luke 1:3.

70. Cadbury, "Preface of Luke," 492–510; du Plessis, "Once More," 265–71; Strelan, "Note on Asphaleia," 169–70; Creamer et al., "Who Is Theophilus?," 5; Dillon, "Previewing Luke's Project," 224–27. In an insightful study, Alexander demonstrates the importance of considering not only Luke's preface (Luke 1:1–4) but also his narrative prologue (Luke 1:5–4:30) for understanding how the beginning of Luke's two-volume work pairs with its ending in Acts 28. Alexander, *Acts*, 207–29.

71. Cadbury suggests that Theophilus was "an influential non-Christian" but is tentative to affirm that Theophilus was a Roman official (Cadbury, "Preface of Luke," 510). Although du Plessis believes Theophilus was a Roman official, his analysis focuses more on Acts 18:25–26 than on Paul's trial narrative (du Plessis, "Once More," 269). My analysis expands upon du Plessis's work by placing more emphasis upon Paul's trial before Roman officials.

Roman officials in Luke–Acts. It is not an accident that 70 percent of the occurrences of the words κράτιστος, ἀκριβῶς, and ἀσφάλεια (and their cognates) appear in two relatively short passages that account for just 8 percent of the total verses in Luke–Acts. These verbal links between Luke's preface and Paul's trial remind the reader that Luke's goal in writing is to persuade a Roman official towards the faith.[72]

In the trial narrative, cognates of the words ἀσφάλεια and ἀκριβῶς repeatedly appear alongside verbs of knowing to describe various Roman officials' attempts to understand Paul's case.[73] Regardless of rank, each of these officials wants to gain a more accurate knowledge of Paul's life and message. The scene of Paul's arrest in Jerusalem features several attempts by the Roman commander Claudius Lysias to understand Paul's case. Amid a chaotic crowd of Jews, Lysias wants "to learn the facts" (γνῶναι τὸ ἀσφαλές, 21:34) about why the Jews oppose Paul. After allowing Paul to make a "defense" (ἀπολογία, 22:1) for himself and for the gospel, Lysias is still struggling "to know the real reason" (γνῶναι τὸ ἀσφαλές, 22:30) why the Jews are accusing him.[74] Recognizing the commander's desire for clarity, the Jews devise a plan to ambush Paul under the guise of wanting "to inquire somewhat more closely [διαγινώσκειν ἀκριβέστερον] about him" (23:15; see also 23:20). After the ambush plan is thwarted, Lysias sends Paul to Caesarea, where he must stand before Felix, the governor.

Like Lysias, Felix must examine Paul to "find out" (ἐπιγνῶναι, 24:8) the reason for his arrest. Unlike Lysias, however, Felix has "a rather accurate knowledge [ἀκριβέστερον εἰδὼς] of the Way" (24:22). Although Felix repeatedly hears Paul testify about Jesus, Felix defers the case to his successor, Porcius Festus (24:24–27). Like his predecessor, Festus finds nothing unlawful about Paul. But when Paul dramatically appeals to Caesar (25:11), Festus is left with a conundrum because he has "nothing definite to write [οὐ ἀσφαλές τι γράψαι] to [Caesar] about [Paul]" (25:26). Festus's words echo

---

72. The word ἀσφάλεια ("certainty") is emphasized as the final word of the preface to indicate Luke's goal of increasing Theophilus's confidence in the Christian faith (Luke 1:4). Bovon, *Luke 1:1—9:50*, 23; Creamer et al., "Who Is Theophilus?," 5.

73. These appearances echo the grouping of the same words alongside the verb "to know" (ἐπιγινώσκω) in Luke 1:4. During Paul's trial, verbs of knowing that appear in relation to Roman officials include γινώσκω (Acts 21:34, 22:30); διαγινώσκω (23:15); ἐπιγινώσκω (24:8); οἶδα (24:22); and ἐπίσταμαι (26:26). Trial before officials is an important motif in Luke–Acts. Neagoe, *Trial of the Gospel*, 4; Tajra, *Trial of St. Paul*, 197.

74. Fitzmyer renders ἀσφαλές as "the truth" in Acts 21:34 and 22:30. Fitzmyer, *Acts*, 716.

Luke's preface where the author declares his goal "to write" (γράψαι) an orderly account for Theophilus so that he might have "certainty" (ἀσφάλειαν) about the things he had been taught (Luke 1:3–4).

In response, Paul delivers one final speech before Festus, who is joined by King Agrippa and Bernice. In his speech, Paul uses words that cast him among the "eyewitnesses and ministers" (αὐτόπται καὶ ὑπηρέται, Luke 1:2) to whose testimony Luke adds his two-volume work. Standing as a "servant and witness" (ὑπηρέτην καὶ μάρτυρα) of the resurrected Christ whom he had "seen" (ὀφθήσομαί, 26:16), Paul gives a "true and rational" testimony to persuade "most excellent Festus" (κράτιστε Φῆστε, 26:25) and King Agrippa towards faith (26:27). Since King Agrippa already "knows [ἐπίσταται] about these things" (26:26), Paul's goal is to convince the king to believe the gospel (26:27).[75] These verbal echoes between Paul's trial and Luke's preface remind the reader that Luke is writing his two-volume work to a Roman official.

In summary, while the exact identity of Theophilus may not be possible to determine with absolute certainty, each of the proposals (prototypical reader, literary patron, Jewish reader, Roman official) discussed above lends interesting insights into reading Luke–Acts. I argue that Theophilus was a high-ranking Roman official who may have also functioned as Luke's literary patron. The attractiveness of this view is that it takes seriously the narrative context of Luke–Acts and assigns one consistent meaning to the word "most excellent" (κράτιστος) in all four of its occurrences in Luke–Acts.[76] If the honorific designation refers to Roman officials in the latter chapters of Acts (23:26, 24:3, 26:25), then the most natural reading would be to assign the same meaning to its appearance in Luke 1:3 to describe Theophilus.[77] In addition to the word κράτιστος, I also briefly mentioned other lexical and thematic threads (including the words ἀκριβῶς and ἀσφάλεια) that link Luke's preface to Paul's climactic trial before Roman

---

75. Although Acts 26:25–27 does not use the same key words as Luke's preface, its theme is quite similar.

76. Apart from these instances, the word is not used elsewhere in the entire New Testament.

77. It is worth noting that Luke does not use the "most excellent" title in the opening of Acts. This could be due to variations in writing style, similar to the variations observed in the ways Galen addresses his reader in the three volumes of his *Method of Medicine* (see discussion below). Alternatively, Bengel suggests, "the same title is not given to the same Theophilus in Acts i. 1, either because he was then in private life, or because his excellence and Luke's intimacy with him had increased." Bengel, *Gnomon of the New Testament*, 2:4.

officials. As a member of the Roman government, Theophilus was likely "either a Christian or a strong sympathizer" who had been previously taught about Jesus (Luke 1:4).[78] Although I take Theophilus to be a historical person, the name may have been a pseudonym to mask his true identity as an official. As will become clear later in this book, this conclusion would lead to significant insights regarding Luke's purposes for writing.

Answering Objections

Admittedly, this interpretation is not without its problems. Alexander points out three significant objections to the view that Theophilus was a Roman official. Before concluding this chapter, I will respond to her three strongest objections.

Objection 1: κράτιστος Does Not Always Refer to a Superior

Based on her survey of prefaces in ancient Greek literature, Alexander points out that the adjective κράτιστος does not always refer to a superior.[79] For example, in his fourteen-volume work *Method of Medicine*, Galen (AD 129 to 216/217) uses various descriptors to address his reader, Hieron. In the opening lines of the first three volumes, Galen addresses his reader as "my dearest [φίλτατε] Hieron" (1.1), "most excellent [κράτιστε] Hieron" (2.1), and "O Hieron" (3.1).[80] Since the term φίλτατε (1.1) is "often used in letters to address a person lower in rank than oneself," Alexander claims that Galen's use of κράτιστε (2.1) does not necessarily imply that Hieron was Galen's superior.[81] However, just because Galen used φίλτατε and κράτιστε interchangeably does not mean that Luke also used his terms with such flexibility. In other words, just because κράτιστος "is not a strict indicator of rank" does not mean that it can never function as an indicator of rank.[82] Indeed, the internal evidence of Luke–Acts shows consistent usage of κράτιστος to refer to a superior in all three of its appearances in Acts.

---

78. Dunn, *Acts*, 10.

79. Following a similar logic, Tannehill suggests that Theophilus was a person of high social standing although not necessarily a Roman official. Tannehill, *Luke*, 35.

80. Galen, *Method of Medicine* 1.1, 2.1, 3.1 (LCL 1:2–3, 122–23, 242–43).

81. Alexander, *Preface to Luke's Gospel*, 133.

82. Alexander, *Preface to Luke's Gospel*, 188.

Thus, without strong reason to think otherwise, the biblical reader would naturally expect κράτιστε to also refer to a superior in Luke 1:3.

Objection 2: Theophilus Was Not a Roman Name

Alexander mentions a second reason for rejecting the assumption that Theophilus was a Roman. Her second objection is that Theophilus was a Greek name, rather than a Roman name, used among Hellenistic Jews.[83] If Theophilus was not a Roman name, then how could Theophilus have been a Roman official? Since Alexander rightly insists that Theophilus was a historical person, the Greek name would seem to rule out the possibility that Luke's dedicatee was a Roman.[84] However, another possibility is that Luke used a pseudonym to address his reader. If Theophilus was indeed a Roman official who was sympathetic towards Christianity, it seems reasonable that he would want to mask his identity. As David Garland suggests, "it is possible that Theophilus, the friend of God, is an alias for a prominent Roman who needed to remain incognito."[85]

Objection 3: No Evidence of Theophilus's Conversion

Alexander's final argument against identifying Theophilus as a Roman official is that early Christian tradition does not mention the conversion of such a prominent person. In Alexander's view, this objection is a "more significant" issue than the prior two objections. Since early Christians delighted in recounting "the conversion of prominent members of society," Alexander thinks it unlikely that the historical records would have been silent on Theophilus's conversion.[86] However, the lack of historical evidence does not rule out the possibility of an unnamed Roman official who was covertly considering the Christian faith.[87] Indeed, it was very

---

83. Alexander, *Preface to Luke's Gospel*, 133. Tannehill, *Luke*, 35.

84. Alexander, *Preface to Luke's Gospel*, 188. Garland notes that if Theophilus was a fictitious reader, the adjective "most excellent" would seem out of place. Garland, *Luke*, 56.

85. Garland, *Luke*, 56.

86. Alexander, *Preface to Luke's Gospel*, 188.

87. During the third century, Tertullian describes unnamed Christian men and women who were known to Scapula—the proconsul—and other Roman officials. Tertullian, *To Scapula* 4–5 (*ANF* 3:107–8).

common for Christians in the early church to write to their civil authorities. Luke's address to a Roman official could have been a predecessor to the works of the second-century apologists.[88] Furthermore, my argument does not require that Theophilus was the real name of a public figure who was openly Christian. He could have been an official who was considering the claims of Christ, or a covert believer who chose to conceal his Christian identity for political or safety reasons.[89]

Conclusion

Who was Theophilus? Although the answer to this question is admittedly speculative, internal evidence within Luke–Acts suggests that Theophilus was a high-ranking Roman official who was considering the claims of Christianity. By analyzing connections between Luke's preface and Paul's trial narrative, we saw several instances where Roman officials sought to know the truth with accuracy and certainty. These examples reflect Luke's purpose for writing to Theophilus so that he might have certainty concerning the things he had been taught. At the same time, there is sufficient evidence that Luke–Acts was meant for more than just Theophilus's eyes alone. Instead, as Bauckham argues, Luke likely intended his text to be disseminated to a broad Christian readership. Theophilus would have been expected to serve as a patron, whether officially or otherwise, who could help to circulate the book to a wider audience, including those among the "literate or governing classes in some parts of the Empire."[90]

Despite the objections raised by Alexander, a close reading of Luke–Acts points towards identifying Theophilus as a high-ranking Roman official. Although the existence of conflicting historical evidence presents serious challenges to this view, I am choosing to weigh the internal evidence of Luke–Acts more heavily than the external evidence of ancient

---

88. Eusebius, *Ecclesiastical History* 4.3.1–2 (*NPNF*² 1:175); Aristides, *Apology* introduction (*ANF* 9:263); Justin Martyr, *First Apology* 1 (*ANF* 1:163); Justin Martyr, *Second Apology* 1 (*ANF* 1:188); Tertullian, *To Scapula* 1 (*ANF* 3:105); Tertullian, *Apology* 1.1 (*ANF* 3:17). In addition to the apology of Quadratus (cited first in the list above), the *Epistle to Diognetus* may be another example of an apology to a Roman official. Although little is known about the addressee, some have suggested that "most excellent Diognetus" (κράτιστε Διόγνητε, Diognetus 1.1) was a Roman official (Holmes, *Apostolic Fathers*, 688).

89. Creamer et al., "Who Is Theophilus?," 3.

90. Dunn, *Acts*, 10.

Greco-Roman literature. Not only are there valid answers to each of Alexander's objections, but the internal evidence of Luke–Acts also reveals a strong emphasis upon the Roman Empire and its centurions, among other officials. Such an emphasis is consistent with Luke's dedication to a Roman official. In the next chapter, I will look more closely at each of these centurions.

4

Centurions in Luke–Acts

> I tell you, not even in Israel have I found such faith.
>
> —LUKE 7:9

IN THE PREVIOUS CHAPTER, I argued that Theophilus was a high-ranking Roman official who was either a Christian sympathizer or convert. In this chapter, I will examine every instance where centurions appear in Luke–Acts. I will show that centurions play critical roles in Luke's narrative and represent the entryway for the gospel to reach the gentiles. At key junctures in the narrative, centurions facilitate the spread of the gospel across ethnic and geographic boundaries from Jerusalem to the end of the earth (Acts 1:8). Although some recent works on Luke–Acts have dealt with the role of centurions and soldiers, most authors give only passing attention to centurions. Given the relative paucity of scholarship on centurions in Luke–Acts, readers may be surprised to discover that centurions appear at five points in the narrative. Perhaps even more striking is that each of these centurions plays a positive role in the gospel's advance among all types of people. For example, centurions are the first gentile converts in both Luke's Gospel (Luke 7:1–10) and the book of Acts (Acts 10). Throughout the rest of Luke–Acts, centurions are unexpected proponents of the gospel during the crucifixion of Jesus and in the spread of the gospel from Jerusalem to the end of the earth. The positive role of so many centurions in Luke–Acts would have piqued the interest of the Roman official Theophilus, and we will look to potential implications of this in the next chapter. Before looking to the centurions in the present chapter, I will briefly situate this discussion within the broader conversation on Luke–Acts. I will consider three key areas: literary themes, prior work on centurions, and historical background related to centurions.

Themes of Luke–Acts

As a two-volume work, Luke and Acts exhibit a narrative unity around a common message.[1] Scholars have attempted to summarize the theology of Luke–Acts under an overarching theme such as salvation through Jesus (Marshall), the purpose of God (Tannehill), or gentile inclusion (Bock).[2] Since many have written on the theology of Luke and Acts, I will provide only a brief summary of two key themes relating to our study on Roman officials.[3] The two themes I will discuss in this section are (1) Jesus, the Savior for all kinds of people, and (2) geographical movement in Luke–Acts.

Jesus, the Savior for All Kinds of People

The Gospel of Luke is known for its emphasis on gentile inclusion. Luke's account highlights many instances where the gospel transcends ethnic boundaries and socioeconomic classes. From the outset of his account, Luke's Gospel consistently emphasizes the inclusion of the marginalized, including women (1:26–56, 2:36–38, 7:11–17, 8:1–3); shepherds (2:8–20); tax collectors (3:12–13, 5:27–32, 15:1–2, 18:9–14, 19:1–10); Roman soldiers (3:14); the poor (4:18, 6:20, 7:22); and the sick (4:18, 38–41; 6:17–19). Luke purposefully shows that the gospel is for all kinds of people—whether Jew or gentile, rich or poor, male or female, young or old, outsider or insider. Moreover, Luke's Gospel reverses expected norms by exalting the lowly and humbling the proud (1:52, 14:11, 18:14;

---

1. Tannehill, *Narrative Unity of Luke–Acts*, 1:xiii–xiv, 1–12.

2. Marshall, *Luke: Historian and Theologian*, 19; Tannehill, *Narrative Unity of Luke–Acts*, 1:xiii; Bock, *Luke*, 1:1. Others, such as Robert H. Stein, suggest that there is no single purpose that explains why Luke wrote his two-volume work (Stein, *Luke*, 35). Drawing the themes of Luke–Acts into a Trinitarian shape, Patrick Schreiner views the two-volume work as unfolding the Father's plan of salvation through faith in Jesus and the empowerment of the Holy Spirit (Schreiner, *Mission of the Triune God*, 16).

3. For a helpful study on the theology of Luke–Acts, see Bock, *Theology of Luke and Acts*.

see also 4:18, 6:20–26, 9:48, 13:30).[4] Nevertheless, while Luke's Gospel is known for its emphasis on the marginalized, it also features salvation of wealthy individuals (19:1–10; see also Acts 4:36–37) and people of high social status (8:3, 23:50).[5] As we will see later in this chapter, Luke–Acts demonstrates the gospel is also for Roman officials.

Geographical Movement in Luke–Acts

Geographical movement is another important theme that unites Luke and Acts. While Luke's Gospel emphasizes movement towards Jerusalem (Luke 9:51), the movement in Acts proceeds outward from Jerusalem to the end of the earth (Acts 1:8). Indeed, Luke's account of Jesus and the church is "a story full of purposeful movement."[6] To follow Jesus entails joining God's mission and going wherever he leads.[7]

Luke's Gospel: From Jerusalem to Jerusalem

Luke's narrative begins and ends in Jerusalem. At the beginning of the Gospel, Zechariah receives a prophetic message while fulfilling his priestly

---

4. One way Luke makes this emphasis is by constructing pairs of adjacent narratives that focus upon opposite types of people (Stein, *Luke*, 376n156). Stein lists the following pairs of narratives: Luke 1:5–25 and 1:26–38; 2:25–35 and 2:36–38; 4:31–37 and 4:38–39; 7:1–10 and 7:11–17; 8:26–39 and 8:40–56; 15:4–7 and 15:8–10. To Stein's list, I would also add Luke 7:36–49, which is a single narrative that juxtaposes the forgiven woman and Simon the Pharisee.

For example, Luke's birth narrative interweaves pericopes involving Mary (1:26–56, 2:1–21) and Zechariah (1:5–25, 57–80). While Stein points out Luke's tendency to pair narratives that juxtapose men and women, I believe that this pattern extends to other categories besides male and female. For example, Mary is not only a woman, but she is also a young person of unknown socioeconomic background (1:27). In contrast, Zechariah is an older man who is described as righteous, blameless, and of Aaronic lineage (1:5–7). By contrasting Mary's faith (1:44) with Zechariah's unbelief (1:20), Luke shows that the gospel is for all types of people, regardless of social status. For more examples of paired narratives featuring opposite types of people, compare the prayers of the persistent widow (18:2–7) and the penitent tax collector (18:9–14); the blind beggar (18:35–43) and rich Zacchaeus (19:1–10); the widow-devouring scribes (20:45–47) and the generous poor widow (21:1–4); and the resurrection sightings by the women (24:1–12) and the male disciples (24:13–35).

5. Edwards, *Luke*, 510.

6. Maddox, *Purpose of Luke–Acts*, 11.

7. Green, *Conversion in Luke–Acts*, 68–69.

duties at the temple (Luke 1:5–25). The Gospel ends with the disciples "continually in the temple blessing God" (24:53). In Jesus' childhood journey to Jerusalem, the highlight of the story is that Jesus remains in the temple after his family leaves (2:41–51). Indeed, Jesus' desire to remain "in [his] Father's house" (2:49) foreshadows his later journey where he resolutely "set his face to go to Jerusalem" (9:51).[8] A significant portion of the Gospel narrative (9:51—19:27) describes Jesus' journey towards the city where he will suffer, die, and be raised to life. In Jerusalem, Jesus also elucidates his stance towards Caesar (20:19–26) prior to standing on trial before Jewish and Roman officials (22:47—23:49).

Acts: From Jerusalem to the End of the Earth

Like its prequel, the book of Acts also begins in Jerusalem (Acts 1:4). Following his resurrection, Jesus commands his disciples to remain in the city until the Holy Spirit empowers them to be his "witnesses in Jerusalem and in all Judea and Samaria, and to the end of the earth" (1:8). Figuratively speaking, the gospel reaches "the end of the earth" when Paul arrives in Rome and preaches unhindered for two years (Acts 28:16–31). As is commonly recognized, Acts 1:8 forms the theme verse of the entire book. The geographical movement of the gospel brings the good news to the gentiles throughout the Roman Empire (Luke 2:32). At various stages of geographical expansion, the gospel encounters a mixed response of opposition and reception from the established leadership of that region. The final move towards Rome is initiated at Caesarea, when Paul appeals to the most powerful official of the empire, Caesar (Acts 25:8–12, 26:32). Despite being offered a chance to return to Jerusalem, Paul insists upon standing before Caesar (25:9–11). Later in this chapter, I will demonstrate the important roles of Roman centurions in bringing the gospel to the gentiles and to the heart of the Roman Empire.

---

8. As Richard Hays points out, the Jerusalem journey motif shows that Jesus is on a journey that is "neither aimless nor unmapped." Moreover, Luke calls his audience "to understand itself as *participating in a journey*, an exodus to a promised destination not yet reached. Such a journey entails suffering, risk, and sacrifice." Hays, *Moral Vision*, 134; emphasis original.

Prior Work on Centurions in Luke–Acts

Most scholars of Luke–Acts have paid relatively little attention to centurions. Perhaps it is because the Lukan corpus is so rich in theological themes that most general works on Luke–Acts make only passing references to centurions.[9] At the same time, some scholars have pointed out the unexpected positive role of centurions in Luke–Acts. Marguerat, for example, cites the "chain of centurions" as an example of Luke's use of narrative chains to show "the continuity and progression of the narrative."[10] Though Marguerat is right to point out the positive roles of centurions as men of exemplary faith and protectors of the apostle Paul, his discussion is limited to just one paragraph. In the conclusion to his article on God-fearers in Luke–Acts, de Boer points out that the God-fearers in Luke 7 and Acts 10 are both centurions and suggests that more work is needed to elucidate the significance of this observation.[11] More recently, Huttunen devotes ten pages to discussing the generally positive portrayal of soldiers in Luke–Acts.[12]

Fortunately, some Lukan scholars have begun to pay more attention to centurions. One natural place where centurions have been discussed is within the context of studies on gentiles or God-fearers within Luke–Acts.[13] Moreover, in recent years, a growing number of articles, monographs, and dissertations have focused upon centurions or soldiers in Luke–Acts. Some of these works focus on one or two specific passages (typically Luke 7:1–10, 23:47, or Acts 10:1—11:18).[14] Others situate centurions within the broader theme of the Roman Empire in Luke–Acts.[15]

I will briefly survey a few representative works before placing my contribution within the context of these prior works. Bruehler highlights several unexpected elements in Luke 7:1–10 and argues that the centurion

---

9. Esler, *Community and Gospel in Luke–Acts*, 36–38, 93–96, 202; Walton, "State They Were In," 19–23; Green, *Theology of the Gospel of Luke*, 8, 15, 63, 89–90, 105, 126; Green, *Conversion in Luke–Acts*, 49, 96; Marshall, *Luke: Historian and Theologian*, 140.

10. Marguerat, *First Christian Historian*, 52.

11. De Boer, "God-Fearers in Luke–Acts," 68.

12. Huttunen, "Brothers in Arms," 167–76.

13. Gerstmyer, "Gentiles in Luke–Acts"; de Boer, "God-Fearers in Luke–Acts," 51–52. Beck, *Light to the Centurions*, 23.

14. Bruehler, "Expecting the Unexpected"; Gagnon, "Double Delegation in Luke 7:1–10"; Easter, "Certainly This Man Was Righteous"; Howell, "Imperial Authority"; Flessen, *Exemplary Man*.

15. Kyrychenko, *Roman Army and the Expansion*; Yates, "Centurions in Luke/Acts"; Brink, "Unmet Expectations"; Beck, *Light to the Centurions*.

is presented as a forebear of gentile inclusion in Luke–Acts.[16] Focusing especially upon Luke 7:1–10 and Acts 10:1—11:18, Kyrychenko argues that centurions were viewed as the principal representatives of Roman power and that Luke portrays centurions as prototypical gentile believers in anticipation of Christian mission to the empire.[17] In her study on soldiers in Luke–Acts, Brink argues that Luke characterizes soldiers according to stereotypes but then contradicts those stereotypes by presenting the centurion of Capernaum (Luke 7:1–10) and Cornelius (Acts 10) as examples of military characters who were capable of repentance and discipleship.[18] Flessen studies Cornelius as a model male figure and argues for his importance in the author's rhetoric regarding gender and empire.[19] Howell sees Luke's "seemingly" positive portrayal of Cornelius as "rhetorical irony (i.e., applying to a character traits that are contrary to reality)" and stresses that his confession of Jesus as "Lord of All" (Acts 10:34) points Luke's reader (presumably a gentile authority or benefactor) to give allegiance to Jesus over the emperor.[20] As a final example, Zeichmann provides a helpful historical overview of the Roman military while identifying the positive role of soldiers in Luke–Acts.[21] Despite making helpful observations on the roles of centurions in the narrative, some of these scholars either believe Luke is covertly criticizing Rome (Howell) or do not hold firmly to the historical accuracy of Luke's accounts (Brink, Zeichmann).

---

16. Bruehler, "Expecting the Unexpected," 85–86.

17. Kyrychenko, *Roman Army and the Expansion*, 7.

18. Brink, "Unmet Expectations," 63–64. Brink focuses on the role of soldiers in the narrative and does not necessarily believe these soldiers were historical figures.

19. Flessen, *Exemplary Man*.

20. Howell, "Imperial Authority," 25, 45–46. Although Howell makes many helpful points, I remain unconvinced that Luke's positive characterization of Cornelius was meant as a veiled criticism of the centurion. While I agree with Howell that Luke's image of a "centurion noted for his generosity directly counters depictions of centurions in other literary texts," I disagree that "this must represent another instance of Lukan irony" that is intended as a "covert criticism" of Roman authorities (Howell, "Imperial Authority," 42–43). Moreover, the text emphasizes that Cornelius becomes a disciple regardless of his background prior to conversion (Acts 10:15, 44–48; 11:17–18).

21. Zeichmann, *Roman Army*, 75–92. Like Brink, Zeichmann at times too easily concedes Luke's historical accuracy. For example, he suggests that Luke fabricated certain details, such as Cornelius's and Julius's identification with the Italian and Augustan cohorts (Acts 10:1, 27:1) and Paul's Roman citizenship (21:39) (Zeichmann, *Roman Army*, 84, 86, 90). In Zeichmann's view, "Acts defies a 'realistic' reading" and instead shows signs of literary embellishment (Zeichmann, *Roman Army*, 91).

Though each makes their own unique contributions, none of the above works focuses on the significance of the centurions for Luke's reader, Theophilus.[22] Moreover, even scholars who make this connection are not necessarily convinced that Theophilus was a Roman official.[23] While drawing upon earlier works, I aim to make a new contribution by explicitly pulling together (1) the motif of centurions in Luke–Acts, (2) the significance of these centurions for Theophilus as a Roman official, and (3) implications for reading Luke–Acts in relation to the Roman Empire.[24] Moreover, I will uphold the historical reliability of Luke's accounts as I bring these three themes together.

Centurions in Luke–Acts: A Historical Sketch

The New Testament's portrayal of the military is complex and varied. This is due in part to the intricacies of the Roman Empire and the different administrative statuses granted to Galilee and Judaea during the times of Luke–Acts. Moreover, the military did not always consist of Roman citizens and sometimes included regional natives (such as Jews) who were working towards Roman citizenship. In this section, I will provide a brief overview of the military with a focus upon the regions of Galilee and Judaea featured in Luke–Acts. Along the way, I will argue that the centurions in Luke–Acts were most likely gentiles.[25]

Overview of the Military

Before we look more specifically at centurions, it is helpful to get an overview of the types of military forces who served in the Roman East during the

---

22. Howell's article seems to make this connection, though his discussion is naturally limited in scope due to length constraints of a typical journal article.

23. Witherington mentions that Theophilus would perhaps connect the centurion accounts of Luke 7 and Acts 10. However, while Witherington believes Theophilus was a person of high social status, he remains unconvinced that Theophilus was a Roman official. Witherington, *Acts*, 13–14, 347.

24. The current chapter focuses on centurions in Luke–Acts while the next chapter will cover the significance to Theophilus and implications for reading Luke–Acts in relation to the Roman Empire.

25. At first glance, one might think all Roman soldiers were gentiles. However, the military often included locals. Thus, in the regions of Galilee and Judaea, it was at least possible that some soldiers would be Jewish.

New Testament period. The military can be classified into four broad categories: legionaries, auxiliaries, royal forces, and the praetorian guard.[26] Of these categories, auxiliaries and royal forces are most relevant for our study of the types of soldiers that appear in Luke–Acts. To aid in understanding these soldiers, it is helpful to briefly describe all four groups.

Legionary soldiers were directly employed by Rome and were loyal to the emperor rather than any local kingdom. In AD 14, there were twenty-five legions based throughout the empire.[27] Legionaries were Roman citizens prior to their recruitment to the military and were generally stationed in major Roman provinces. Since Judaea did not become a major province until after the Jewish War, there were no Roman legionaries stationed in Judaea until around AD 66.

Auxiliary soldiers also served Rome, although auxiliaries were mostly non-citizens who would be granted Roman citizenship upon their discharge from military service.[28] Until around AD 70, most auxiliary soldiers were locals serving within their home province.[29] Auxiliaries were significantly less Romanized than legionaries and spoke local languages such as Aramaic, in addition to Greek and some Latin. Auxiliaries could either be stationed in major provinces alongside legionaries or in minor provinces such as pre-war Judaea, which did not have legionaries. Auxiliary units typically consisted of around five hundred soldiers and were commanded by officers of equestrian rank. The units came in three basic forms: infantry (*cohortes*), cavalry (*alae*), or a combination of both (*cohortes equitatae*).[30]

Royal forces did not directly serve Rome but were loyal to their local client king—for example, Antipas in Galilee and, prior to him, Herod the Great in Judaea. Though not official provinces of the empire, client kingdoms were allies of Rome located at the fringes of the empire. Soldiers in the royal forces helped secure the boundaries of the empire, but their

---

26. My descriptions of these four categories are largely based on Zeichmann's very helpful work. Zeichmann, *Roman Army*, 1–3.

27. By AD 200, the number of legions increased modestly to thirty-three. Campbell, *Romans and Their World*, 142–45.

28. Campbell, *Romans and Their World*, 150.

29. After a series of uprisings (including the Jewish War of AD 66 to 73), there was a concerted effort to relocate soldiers away from their home areas to mitigate ethnic uprisings. Zeichmann, *Roman Army*, 2.

30. Campbell, *Romans and Their World*, 147. Campbell notes that some auxiliaries had as many as one thousand men.

client kings lacked the authority to award them with Roman citizenship. Royal forces spoke the local languages of their region and had little vested interest in Roman culture.

The praetorian guard was a final group of elite soldiers who served as the emperor's personal military. They were a smaller group of soldiers and the only military group that served in the region of Italia. The praetorians guarded the emperor, performed ceremonial functions, and escorted the emperor when he left Rome. The praetorian soldiers enjoyed an easier lifestyle compared to legionaries, who were deployed to more distant lands.[31]

Administrative Regions and the Military

In Luke–Acts, centurions appear in Capernaum, Jerusalem, and Caesarea. Within this geographical region, different cities fell under different administrative jurisdictions.[32] During the time of Jesus' ministry, Capernaum belonged to the client kingdom of Galilee. Meanwhile, Jerusalem and Caesarea were part of Judaea, which was officially part of Rome (as an equestrian sub-province of Roman Syria) during much of the period covered by Luke–Acts.

Galilee

During the years of Jesus' ministry, the region of Galilee was a client kingdom under the tetrarch Herod Antipas, one of the sons of Herod the Great. The royal army of Galilee included a small number of soldiers inherited from the royal troops of Herod the Great, who had ruled the client kingdom of Judaea (which at the time included Galilee) from 37 BC to 4 BC. Roman auxiliaries did not serve in Galilee until AD 44.[33]

---

31. Campbell, *Romans and Their World*, 148.

32. In this section, I lean heavily upon Zeichmann's helpful chart which presents a timeline of the military in Palestine from 66 BC to AD 135, with a special focus on Capernaum. Zeichmann, *Roman Army*, 32–33.

33. Sherwin-White, *Roman Society and Roman Law*, 123–24.

Judaea[34]

Judaea was annexed by the Roman province of Syria and became an equestrian sub-province of Rome from AD 6 to 70 (except between AD 41–44 when Agrippa I ruled as a client king).[35] When Judaea was annexed by Rome in AD 6, the Judaean auxiliaries were formed from the royal forces of Herod Archelaus, whose army came from Herod the Great's royal forces. These forces included a mixture of Roman citizens and non-citizens, including some who served in exchange for citizenship rights.[36] The Judaean auxiliaries were comprised of five *cohortes* (infantry units) and one *ala* (cavalry unit).[37] These troops bore the name *Sebastenorum* because they were mainly recruited out of the Roman cities of Sebaste (formerly Samaria) and Caesarea. Since many Syrians lived in these cities, over time, most of the Judaean auxiliaries were ethnic Syrians who were culturally Hellenized.[38] The ethnic makeup of the auxiliaries is debated and seemed to include both gentiles and Jews. To complicate the ethnicity question even further, some of the Jewish auxiliaries apparently took Roman names upon enlisting, even if they were not citizens.[39] Judaean auxiliary soldiers held a wide variety of noncombat job duties, including civic construction (Luke 7:4–5) and arbitrating justice among local civilians (Luke 23:47).[40] Though there is evidence of extortion by soldiers (Luke 3:14), there are also reports of low-level officers serving as benefactors for their local communities (Luke 7:4–5).[41]

---

34. I use the Roman spelling "Judaea" to refer to the administrative region covering Judea, Idumaea, and Samaria (which included the cities of Jerusalem, Joppa, Caesarea, and Sebaste/Samaria) that came under Roman rule in AD 6. Cotton, "Roman Administration," 75.

35. Judaea briefly returned to being a client kingdom from AD 41 to 44 when Galilee and Betanaea were reunified with the Judaean kingdom under King Agrippa I. In AD 70, Judaea became a praetorian Roman province. Zeichmann, *Roman Army*, 32–33.

36. Zeichmann, *Roman Army*, 10–11.

37. Zeichmann, "Military Forces in Judaea," 95.

38. Josephus repeatedly suggests that the Judaean auxiliaries were mostly of Syrian descent. Zeichmann, *Roman Army*, 5; Zeichmann, "Military Forces in Judaea 6–130 CE," 95. In opposition to Josephus, Steve Mason, Jonathan Roth, and others suggest that the Judaean auxiliaries were mainly comprised of Jews and Samaritans. Zeichmann, *Roman Army*, 16n1.

39. Zeichmann, *Roman Army*, 6–7.

40. Zeichmann, *Roman Army*, 19–41.

41. Zeichmann, *Roman Army*, 28–29, 39.

Centurions in the Military

Centurions were officers in charge of about eighty soldiers who together formed the basic subunit of the legionaries or auxiliaries.[42] Centurions also served in the Herodian royal armies, which were organized in a similar manner as the Roman military.[43] In pre-war Judaea, centurions were expected to communicate in the local languages of their troops (Aramaic or Greek) and their superiors (Latin or Greek). A centurion would have typically climbed the ranks through personal achievement over a period of ten to twenty years, although a man of high social status could sometimes be directly appointed as a centurion. For most centurions, the promotion process was based on a variety of factors including personality, education, linguistic ability, relational skills, and socioeconomic background.[44] Centurions were typically experienced soldiers who earned relatively higher wages and had potential to rise through more senior ranks and then to civil administration.[45]

In his description of Herod the Great's funeral service, Josephus indicates that soldiers came from various ethnicities.[46] Moreover, since Luke–Acts describes centurions from various regions (Galilee, Jerusalem, Caesarea), we cannot automatically infer their gentile ethnicity based on their position as centurions. However, by combining historical studies with textual information within Luke–Acts, we have good reasons to believe that although some soldiers in the region were Jewish, the centurions portrayed in Luke–Acts were most likely gentiles. I will discuss their gentile identity on a case-by-case basis as we look to each centurion.

The Gospel for Roman Soldiers (Luke 3:14)

Before looking to the centurions in Luke–Acts, it will be helpful to examine one important verse that provides helpful background on Roman soldiers and the gospel. The passage recounts a conversation between John the

---

42. Zeichmann points out that though a centurion's subunit nominally consisted of one hundred men, in practice they often included around eighty soldiers. Zeichmann, *Roman Army*, 13.

43. Zeichmann, *Roman Army*, 13.

44. Zeichmann, *Roman Army*, 13–15.

45. Huttunen, "Brothers in Arms," 151.

46. Josephus, *Ant.* 17.198–199.

Baptist and various groups of Jews who came to receive his message, which is summed up as "a baptism of repentance for the forgiveness of sins" (Luke 3:3). After instructing tax collectors to avoid collecting more than their required amounts, John is approached by a group of Roman soldiers.

> Soldiers also asked him, "And we, what shall we do?" And he said to them, "Do not extort money from anyone by threats or by false accusation, and be content with your wages." (Luke 3:14)

Even though this verse does not directly mention centurions, Luke 3:14 provides a broad framework for how Roman soldiers—including centurions—could fit within the kingdom of God. Like tax collectors, Roman soldiers were known for their exploitation of the Jewish people. However, according to John, soldiers were not beyond the reach of the gospel. Surprisingly, Roman soldiers could join God's people by repenting and believing in the gospel. Importantly, Luke 3:14 provides a basis for soldiers converting to Christianity without necessarily leaving the military. The text does not call these soldiers to quit their jobs but rather to abandon the unethical aspects of their occupations. Rather than continuing to extort money, soldiers were to be content with their wages. In other words, Christian soldiers could demonstrate faith in Jesus by their high moral standards and fair treatment of others. Although Luke 3 does not give further details regarding the individual soldiers who received baptism, we soon meet a soldier who perfectly exemplifies John's message when we come to Luke 7.

Convert at Capernaum (Luke 7:1–10)

The centurion at Capernaum is the first gentile convert described in the Gospel of Luke. Up to this point in Luke's account, Jesus' ministry has been centered around the Galilee region where he preached in synagogues (Luke 4:15–37, 44; 6:6–11), exorcised demons (4:33–37, 41), healed the sick (4:37–40; 5:12–15, 17–26; 6:6–11), and called his first disciples (5:1–11, 27–32). Although Jesus' ministry began to draw people from as far as Tyre and Sidon (6:17), there have been no descriptions so far of individual gentile converts.[47] The centurion at Capernaum plays a critical role in the narrative as the firstfruit of the fulfillment of Simeon's prophecy of salvation to

---

47. In Joel Green's study of conversion in Luke–Acts, he chooses to begin with the call of the disciples in Luke 5:1–11, 27–32. Green, *Conversion in Luke–Acts*, 88–91.

the gentiles (2:32).[48] In addition, the centurion echoes the story of Naaman, whose conversion we studied in chapter 2.[49]

Luke indicates that the centurion is a gentile even though historians suggest that the Romans did not serve in Galilee until AD 44. Though there were probably few gentiles serving in Antipas's royal army in pre-war Galilee, nevertheless, Zeichmann affirms that "the situation is not difficult to imagine" and argues for the plausibility of a gentile centurion serving in Capernaum, which was located at an international border.[50] The centurion's non-Jewish ethnicity is emphasized by the Jewish elders, who attest that the centurion is "worthy" of Jesus' attention because "he loves our nation and . . . built us our synagogue" (7:4–5). The Jewish elders' emphasis on "our nation" implies that this centurion was not Jewish.[51] Despite being a gentile, the centurion had good rapport with the Jews and held sufficient social status to send a group of their leaders as his messengers.[52] The Jewish elders lauded the centurion for his role as a benefactor of their local synagogue.[53] While these local synagogue leaders claimed that the centurion was worthy of Jesus' help (7:4–5), the centurion's second envoy of friends pleaded his unworthiness to have Jesus come under his roof (7:6).[54] The narrative presents a contrast between the Jews' works-based approach to Jesus and the centurion's awareness that salvation is by grace. While the Jews point to the centurion's good works, Jesus points to the centurion's underlying faith

---

48. Edwards, *Luke*, 213.

49. Shelton, "Healing of Naaman"; Shelton, "Namaan and the Centurion"; Evans, "Elijah/Elisha Narratives," 80n24. On the comparison between Naaman and the centurion, Bruehler writes, "Luke's (gentile) centurion has more faith that anyone in Israel (7:9), and he needs no special exceptions granted to him like the one found in 2 Kings. The positive portrayal of the centurion exceeds even that of Naaman." Bruehler, "Expecting the Unexpected," 83.

50. Zeichmann, *Roman Army*, 67–68. While Zeichmann believes the interaction between Jesus and the centurion probably did occur, he nevertheless suggests that Luke may have fabricated parts of the story (Zeichmann, *Roman Army*, 78). For more on the centurion's gentile identity, see Bruehler, "Expecting the Unexpected," 76–77.

51. Tannehill, *Narrative Unity of Luke–Acts*, 1:114.

52. Luke Timothy Johnson points out that these were local Galilean elders (not elders who sat in the Sanhedrin) and that they were not sent under compulsion but as grateful patrons of the centurion (Johnson, *Luke*, 117). Darrell Bock emphasizes the centurion as an exemplar of respectful Jew-gentile relationships, an important theme in Lukan theology (Bock, *Luke*, 1:637).

53. Marshall, *Gospel of Luke*, 280; Johnson, *Luke*, 117.

54. Marshall, *Gospel of Luke*, 280.

as the matter of utmost importance.[55] The humble gentile centurion recognizes Jesus' authority (7:7–8), demonstrating a level of faith that Jesus had not found in Israel (7:9). Moreover, the centurion is an example of one who believes in Jesus without having seen him (1 Pet 1:8, John 20:29).[56]

The conversion of the centurion parallels Elisha's cleansing of Naaman the Syrian (Luke 4:27, 2 Kgs 5:1–27). Like the centurion, Naaman was a commander of a foreign army who was highly regarded by others. In addition to several similarities cited by James Edwards (both are gentiles, both have servants, both send emissaries, both change their minds), the centurion at Capernaum represents a striking contrast to Naaman.[57] In contrast to Naaman who became angry at Elisha for not coming to him, the centurion expresses his unworthiness for Jesus to come to him. Whereas Naaman sought to repay the prophet for his miraculous healing, the centurion approaches Jesus in humble faith rather than relying on his own merits.

Such exemplary faith is unexpectedly found in a gentile centurion. As Edwards points out, a centurion loyal to Herod Antipas would not automatically be considered a safe inquirer of Jesus (see Luke 3:19–20, 9:9, 13:31, 23:11).[58] While the centurion is the first gentile convert in Luke's Gospel, he is not the first soldier to appear in the narrative. As mentioned earlier, soldiers have already been portrayed positively, albeit indirectly, when John the Baptist exhorted repentant soldiers to change their lifestyle by not extorting others and being content with their wages (3:14).[59] Thus, the centurion represents one example of a soldier who embodied a repentant lifestyle.[60] Luke portrays him as a moral and sensitive man who cared

---

55. Marshall, *Gospel of Luke*, 277.

56. "Clearly this would encourage members of the Gentile churches who had not seen Jesus, but had received the gospel through Jewish messengers." Morris, *Luke*, 155. See also Marshall, *Gospel of Luke*, 278; Talbert, *Reading Luke*, 82.

57. Marshall, *Gospel of Luke*, 278. Marshall cites 2 Kgs 5:10 and Naaman's faith prior to seeing Elisha but does not draw out further parallels to the centurion. Although Edwards and Talbert point out similarities between Jesus' ministry and the Elijah/Elisha tradition, the following analysis of contrasts is my own. Edwards, *Luke*, 217; Talbert, *Reading Luke*, 81.

58. Edwards, *Luke*, 210.

59. Beck, *Light to the Centurions*, 170.

60. Green suggests that the centurion was converted prior to Luke 7:1–10 since he already embodies beliefs and practices consistent with Jesus' message. Whether the centurion was converted before or during the encounter described in Luke 7:1–10 does not affect my argument that he is the first gentile convert presented in Luke's narrative. See Green, *Conversion in Luke-Acts*, 49.

for his "dear" or "esteemed" servant (7:2).⁶¹ The centurion is respected by others in his local community, and his financial generosity towards the Jewish synagogue suggests that contentment—rather than extortion—was the pattern of his life. Like Jesus' first disciples, the centurion was a convert to the way of Christ, even if Luke did not explicitly narrate the exact moment of his repentance. The centurion at Capernaum is just the first among several centurions to appear in Luke's narrative.

Confession at Calvary (Luke 23:47)

The second centurion in Luke's Gospel appears at Jesus' crucifixion. It is plausible that the centurion at the cross would be a gentile since Roman auxiliaries had been in Judaea since AD 6.⁶² As was the case in Luke 7:1–10, this centurion is not the first soldier to appear in the immediate context (see 3:14). Just before his crucifixion, Jesus stood on trial and was mocked by Herod's soldiers (23:11). Moreover, as Jesus hung upon the cross, the soldiers mocked him, saying, "If you are the King of the Jews, save yourself!" (23:37). Based on these verses, it is likely that the centurion in charge of the crucifixion either participated in (or was at least complicit with) the ridicule of Jesus. The mockery of the soldiers called into question Jesus' messianic identity in ways that echoed Satan's wilderness temptations (see 4:3, 9). Given the circumstances, the reader would not expect to find support for Jesus in the centurion who oversaw the crucifixion.

Surprisingly, upon Jesus' death, it is the centurion who first recognizes Jesus' identity, declaring, "Certainly this man was righteous!" (δίκαιος, 23:47).⁶³ Though the word δίκαιος could be translated "innocent" (ESV, RSV), in this context, δίκαιος conveys the more theologically weighty notion of righteousness, which nonetheless includes innocence.⁶⁴ Thus, Luke por-

---

61. Bock, *Luke*, 1:636. Some have even suggested that the centurion had a homosexual relationship with his "dear" servant. For a helpful rebuttal from a historical perspective, see Zeichmann, *Roman Army*, 68–70, 78.

62. Kyrychenko, *Roman Army and the Expansion*, 144. Even if we admit a mixed military consisting of Jews, Samaritans, and Syrians, the military was becoming increasingly Syrian between the years of AD 6 to 70. Zeichmann, who believes that Jews and Samaritans likely formed the majority of Herod's royal army, also mentions the increased Syrian presence in Judaean auxiliaries during the time period leading up to the Jewish War (which began in AD 66). Zeichmann, *Roman Army*, 3–4.

63. Author's translation. See Garland, *Luke*, 929.

64. Johnson, *Luke*, 382; Bovon, *Luke 19:28—24:53*, 328. Robert Karris helpfully points

trays the centurion as the one who casts the final word on Jesus' life, declaring him to be righteous.[65] The centurion's words are significant because Jesus' righteousness becomes an important motif in the early church's evangelistic preaching in Acts. The centurion at the cross is the forerunner for Peter (Acts 3:14), Stephen (7:52), and Paul (22:14), who will also proclaim Jesus as "the righteous one."[66] The centurion's confession is important because it is the first instance in Luke–Acts where Jesus is called δίκαιος.[67]

The centurion's confession demonstrates a dramatic turn from mockery to faith. The centurion's response of praise (δοξάζω, Luke 23:47) is one of Luke's favorite ways of describing a person's positive response to divine activity and can be viewed here as the centurion's recognition of Jesus' divine identity. While the reader might expect one of Jesus' friends (see 23:49) to be the first to recognize the theological significance of the crucifixion, Luke instead shows that the centurion was the first person to give "praise to God for the way in which Jesus died."[68] As Garland suggests, the centurion's change of heart was an answer to Jesus' prayer on behalf of his executioners (23:34; see 6:28).[69]

Moreover, the centurion's confession initiates a movement of mourning among the crowd (Luke 23:47–48).[70] However, scholars dispute whether the crowds were repentant or merely remorseful.[71] In favor of the former view, the phrase "beating their breasts" (τύπτοντες τὰ στήθη, 23:48) is used elsewhere to indicate humble repentance (see 18:13).[72] Bock aptly suggests that the crowd was moved to contrition and that at least some among them

---

out that nowhere else in Luke–Acts does the word δίκαιος mean "innocent." For example, in the immediate literary context, Joseph is described as "righteous" (δίκαιος, 23:50) and the criminal on the cross describes himself as being punished "justly" (δικαίως, 23:41). Karris, "Lucan View of Jesus' Death," 66.

65. Kyrychenko, *Roman Army and the Expansion*, 149.

66. Easter, "Certainly This Man Was Righteous," 43–45. These verses account for three of the six of the occurrences of δίκαιος in Acts.

67. Easter, "Certainly This Man Was Righteous," 39.

68. Marshall, *Gospel of Luke*, 876. On δοξάζω, see Luke 2:20; 4:15; 5:25, 26; 7:16; 13:13; 17:15; 18:43; Acts 4:21; 11:18; 13:48; 21:20. Easter, "Certainly This Man Was Righteous," 51.

69. Garland, *Luke*, 929.

70. Tannehill, *Narrative Unity of Luke–Acts*, 1:273.

71. Marshall believes that the crowds were remorseful but not repentant (Marshall, *Gospel of Luke*, 877). Others see the remorse of the Jerusalem crowd as a precursor for their repentance at Pentecost (Johnson, *Luke*, 382).

72. Marshall, *Gospel of Luke*, 877; Johnson, *Luke*, 382.

may have been seeking gracious forgiveness for what they had done.[73] In response to Jesus' prayer and the centurion's declaration, the onlookers were moved toward a similar confession of Jesus' righteousness. Thus, the Roman centurion at the cross is significant because he is "one of the first characters to recognize this crucified Jesus as the Messiah."[74] The official at the cross exhibits the same type of faith as the centurion at Capernaum and becomes the first among many in Luke–Acts whose verbal proclamation leads others to believe in Jesus, the crucified (and soon to be risen) Lord.

Conversion of Cornelius (Acts 10:1–11:18)

Among the centurions in Luke–Acts, Cornelius receives the most attention in the narrative. As the first gentile convert in Acts, Cornelius plays a pivotal role in the spread of the gospel across geographic and ethnic boundaries (Acts 11:1, 18; see also 1:8).[75] In the prior chapters of Acts, the early church had begun in Jerusalem before persecution forced believers to scatter and bring the gospel to Judea and Samaria (8:1–25, 9:31). After the Holy Spirit's outpouring in Jerusalem (2:1–11) and Samaria (8:14–17), Cornelius and his family are the first gentiles to receive the Holy Spirit (10:45). Cornelius is the only gentile to receive a vision in Luke–Acts, and his conversion

---

73. Bock, *Luke*, 2:1865.

74. Easter, "Certainly This Man Was Righteous," 51.

75. Some scholars see the Ethiopian eunuch as the first gentile convert in Acts. However, even those scholars see the significance of Cornelius's conversion. Tannehill, for example, does not necessarily see Cornelius as the first gentile convert in Acts, but nevertheless considers his conversion a "breakthrough for Gentile mission" because "the conversion of the Ethiopian was a private and isolated event" that did not have as much of an impact on the following narrative—as Acts 15:7–11 makes clear (Tannehill, *Narrative Unity of Luke-Acts*, 2:137). I maintain, however, that Cornelius ought to be recognized as the first gentile convert in Acts. Although the Ethiopian eunuch is not ethnically Jewish, he would not have been seen as a pure gentile either since he follows Jewish practices (Acts 8:27–28). For more on the Ethiopian eunuch, see my discussion in chapter 5 and Bock's helpful analysis in Bock, *Acts*, 338.

Barrett argues that the Ethiopian eunuch and Cornelius were "neither born Jews nor proselytes but sympathetically interested in Judaism and its religion" (Barrett, *Acts*, 1:421). Commenting on Acts 10, Barrett explains, "The drift of the section as a whole, especially when it is viewed in the setting provided for it by Luke, is that the event marks a notable step in the extension of the Gospel to the world outside Judaism" (Barrett, *Acts*, 1:493). He continues, "One thing is clear: Luke intended his reader to understand that he was witnessing a decisive step, perhaps the decisive step, in the expansion of Christianity into the non-Jewish world" (Barrett, *Acts*, 1:495).

reflects the sovereign hand of God breaking through the resistance of both Peter and the Jerusalem church towards the gentiles.[76]

The significance of Cornelius's conversion is attested in the way that Luke draws out the story through reiteration.[77] No other gentile conversion account in Luke–Acts is told with such deliberate detail and repetition.[78] Similar to Luke's recounting of Paul's conversion, Cornelius's conversion is initially narrated from two perspectives (Peter's and Cornelius's, Acts 10:1–48) before being retold (11:4–18).[79] Moreover, the Cornelius account forms a "narrative chain" with the centurions at Capernaum (Luke 7:1–10) and Calvary (Luke 23:47).[80] Like the centurion at Capernaum, Cornelius's non-Jewish background is implied by his messengers, who describe their master as "well spoken of by the whole Jewish nation" (Acts 10:22; see also Luke 7:5).[81] Peter likewise implies that Cornelius is from "another nation" (10:28). Cornelius's gentile background is consistent with his residence at Caesarea, a Roman outpost whose populace was primarily gentile.[82] Though some Caesarean Jews served as Roman auxiliary soldiers, Luke

---

76. Gaventa, *Acts*, 162, 164. Cornelius's conversion also marks the ending of Peter's ministry, which is bookended by his two speeches about gentile inclusion (2:14–40, 15:7–11). Dupont points out that the Lukan writings highlight the theme of ethnic inclusion in the inaugural speeches and final declarations made by Jesus in the Gospel of Luke (Luke 4:25–27, 24:47) and by Peter (Acts 2:8–11, 17, 21, 38–39; 15:7–11) and Paul (13:38, 46; 28:28) in the book of Acts. Dupont, *Salvation of the Gentiles*, 22–25.

77. Gaventa, *Acts*, 162–63. Gaventa helpfully outlines Acts 10:1—11:18 as a sequence of four paired scenes. The first three pairs alternate between Cornelius and Peter by narrating their visions (10:1–8, Cornelius; 10:9–16, Peter), journey and welcome (10:17–23a, Cornelius; 10:23b–29, Peter), and speeches (10:30–33, Cornelius; 10:34–43, Peter). The fourth pair describes confirmation by the Holy Spirit (10:44–48) and the community (11:1–18).

78. Wilson, *Gentiles and the Gentile Mission*, 177.

79. Luke uses a similar scheme to emphasize the importance of Paul's conversion (Acts 9:1–19), which he initially narrates from two perspectives (Paul's and Ananias's) and later repeats two more times (22:6–21, 26:12–18). Both Paul's and Cornelius's conversions also feature the literary device of a double vision (Johnson, *Acts*, 182). Witherup provides an insightful discussion on the use of repetition in the accounts of Cornelius's conversion. Witherup, "Cornelius."

80. Marguerat, *First Christian Historian*, 52–53.

81. As mentioned in our earlier discussion, the centurion of Luke 7:1–10 recapitulates the story of Naaman in 2 Kgs 5. Thomas Brodie argues that the Cornelius account also echoes the Naaman story. Brodie, "Towards Unraveling the Rhetorical Imitation."

82. Johnson, *Acts*, 191.

repeatedly emphasizes that Cornelius was a gentile.[83] Furthermore, as a centurion belonging to the "Italian cohort" (10:1), Cornelius is portrayed as a representative of Rome.[84]

As we saw with the centurion at Capernaum (Luke 7:5), Cornelius's generosity towards "the people" (Acts 10:2) is consistent with the repentance and eschewal of extortion preached by John the Baptist (Luke 3:14).[85] Cornelius is described as a "devout man who feared God" and "prayed continually to God" (Acts 10:2). Though a gentile, Cornelius followed some Jewish practices, even if he was not circumcised (Acts 11:3) or converted to Judaism.[86] Cornelius is in fact the first among many Christian sympathizers whom Luke describes variously as God-fearers (13:16, 26), devout people (13:50; 17:4, 17), or worshipers of God (16:14, 18:7).[87] Thus, Cornelius represents a particular type of gentile whose sympathies towards Judaism have prepared them to receive the gospel message.[88]

The account of Acts 10 describes the conversion of Cornelius and not merely the Holy Spirit's coming upon one who had previously converted. Although Cornelius was a devout man, several features of the account point towards conversion, including Peter's evangelistic sermon (10:34–43), the response of water baptism (10:47–48), and the threefold emphasis on forgiveness (10:43), repentance (11:18), and salvation

---

83. Zeichmann, *Roman Army*, 5.

84. Although some scholars question whether Cornelius could have belonged to the "Italian cohort" (10:1), others have put forth plausible explanations for how the entire cohort (or just one of their centurions) could be present in Caesarea at this time. See Speidel, "Roman Army in Judaea," 237; Keener, *Acts*, 2:1737–42; Witherington, *Acts*, 347. Zeichmann, on the other hand, is not convinced that the Italian cohort was present in the region prior to AD 69 (when we have evidence of their presence in nearby Syria). Zeichmann suggests that Luke fabricated the details about the Italian cohort (10:1) and the Augustan cohort (27:1). Despite many strengths, one weakness of Zeichmann's work is his readiness to compromise at times on the historical accuracy of the biblical accounts, even when plausible alternative explanations exist. Zeichmann, *Roman Army*, 84, 90.

85. Both Johnson and Gaventa suggest that "the people" refers to Israel (see 2:47, 3:9, 6:8). Johnson, *Acts*, 182; Gaventa, *Acts*, 164.

86. Luke uses the word "proselytes" to refer to converts to Judaism (see 2:11, 6:5, 13:43). Gerstmyer, "Gentiles in Luke–Acts," 333; de Boer, "God-Fearers in Luke–Acts," 54–55.

87. Gaventa, *Acts*, 164; de Boer, "God-Fearers in Luke–Acts," 52–53. Scholars debate whether "God-fearer" was a technical term referring to gentiles who were sympathetic towards Judaism. In any case, as de Boer points out, gentile sympathizers are also attested by Philo and Josephus. De Boer, "God-Fearers in Luke–Acts," 58–59.

88. Gerstmyer, "Gentiles in Luke–Acts," 349.

(11:14). Moreover, the outpouring of the Holy Spirit upon Cornelius, his relatives, and his close friends (see 10:24) echoes Pentecost (10:47; see also 2:17).[89] This is clearly a watershed moment that Fitzmyer aptly calls a "Pentecost of the Gentiles."[90] In this case, the outpouring of the Spirit coincides with the moment of conversion.

The conversion of Cornelius also helps to mark a transition where Luke shifts his focus from Peter to Paul. Not long afterward, Peter is imprisoned (Acts 12:1–19) and fades into the background of the narrative. The next time Peter appears is at the Jerusalem Council where he affirms gentile inclusion by once again alluding to Cornelius's conversion (Acts 15:7–11). Starting in Acts 13, however, the focus of the narrative shifts towards Paul's ministry.

Conflict and Citizenship (Acts 21:27—23:35, 24:23)

After the conversion of Cornelius, the gospel continues to find reception among gentiles, including some who were previously sympathetic towards Judaism (Acts 13:12, 46–49; 14:1, 27; 16:14–15, 30–34; 17:12, 34). Nevertheless, people tend to have a polarized response to the gospel, and it is often the Jews (though sometimes gentiles also) who oppose the gospel (Acts 13:45; 14:2, 5, 19; 17:5; 18:12). As was the case with Jesus and the Jews (Luke 23:18–23), the mounting tensions between Paul and the Jews reach a tipping point as the scene shifts towards one final trip to Jerusalem.[91] Upon completing his missionary journeys throughout Asia Minor, Paul determines to go to Jerusalem, even if imprisonment and death await him there (Acts 21:13; cf. Luke 9:51). The gospel had reached people from many nations in Asia Minor, but before it could truly reach "the end of the earth" (Acts 1:8), Paul must pass through Jerusalem one final time.

It is during Paul's tense visit to Jerusalem that we encounter a collection of pericopes containing centurions (Acts 21:27—23:35, 24:23, 27:1–44).[92] Since some of these pericopes may deal with the same centurions, I will treat them together as a group. The auxiliary soldiers at Jerusalem were garrisoned at the Antonia Fortress near the northwest

---

89. Tannehill, *Narrative Unity of Luke-Acts*, 2:142–43.

90. Fitzmyer, *Acts*, 460.

91. Johnson, *Acts*, 382.

92. Regarding Acts 21:31, Johnson comments, "From this point on in the narrative Paul will have almost constant contact with the Roman military." Johnson, *Acts*, 382.

corner of the temple complex.⁹³ As in the case of the centurion at the cross (Luke 23:47), it is plausible that the centurions who interact with Paul in Jerusalem would be gentiles (Acts 21:27–36; 23:17, 23–35). Since Judaea was annexed by the Roman province of Syria in AD 6, the Roman auxiliaries in major cities like Jerusalem and Caesarea would have likely become increasingly Romanized (see Acts 22:28) in the ensuing decades. These centurions each play important protective roles for Paul, and we will now briefly look at each pericope in order.

Rescue by Binding (Acts 21:27–36)

Paul spends about one week in Jerusalem before the Jews from Asia come to stir up the crowds against him (Acts 21:27). The whole city is stirred up, and an angry mob drags Paul out of the temple and is seeking to kill him (21:30–31). When the commander of the military hears this, he takes soldiers and centurions to stop the crowds from beating Paul (21:32). The commander, whom we later learn is named Claudius Lysias (23:26), and his centurions play an important role in protecting Paul's life from the Jews throughout his time in Jerusalem (see 23:10).

Ironically, the way the centurions save Paul's life is by binding (δεθῆναι) him in chains and removing him from the mob (21:33). The actions of the centurions are significant because the verb "to bind" (δέομαι) plays an important role in the overall narrative of Paul's final visit to Jerusalem. At Ephesus, Paul informs the elders that he is "bound [δεδεμένος] by the Spirit" (20:22) to go to Jerusalem even though he knows that imprisonment awaits him there. During Paul's final stop in Caesarea, the local believers and Agabus dramatically attempt to dissuade Paul from going to Jerusalem, where he will be bound and delivered over to the gentiles (21:11, where δέομαι appears twice). Yet, Paul reaffirms that he is "ready not only to be bound [δεθῆναι], but even to die" (21:13) in Jerusalem for the sake of Christ. The binding of Paul by the centurions enables the fulfillment of Agabus's prophecy and creates an opportunity for Paul to preach the gospel in Aramaic to the Jews at Jerusalem (22:1–21). Paul's defense, however, is cut short when the mob is incited again and the tribune orders Paul to be brought back to the barracks to be examined by flogging (22:22–24).

---

93. Zeichmann, *Roman Army*, 86; Johnson, *Acts*, 382.

Asserting Citizenship Rights (Acts 22:25–26)

As the soldiers prepare to punish him, Paul initiates a conversation with their centurion supervisor (Acts 22:25). This centurion was likely among the centurions who earlier rescued Paul from the mob (21:32). Since we did not hear the voices of any of the centurions in the prior pericope, Acts 22:25–26 is the first instance where we hear directly from one of them. The conversation centers upon Paul's status as a Roman citizen, a point to which Paul had alluded in his earlier conversation with the commander (21:39; see also 16:37–39).[94] In contrast with his commander who ordered Paul to be flogged despite knowing that he was a citizen of Tarsus, the centurion immediately recognizes the impropriety of such punishment and raises the issue of Paul's citizenship to his commander (22:26). Lysias's subsequent letter to Felix conveniently omits Paul's near flogging, and Lysias claims that he rescued Paul upon learning of his Roman citizenship.[95] Unlike Lysias, who demonstrates the common "tendency of those in political power structures to shade the truth for self-protection," the centurion is portrayed in a wholly positive light.[96] Similar to the centurion at the cross who declares that Jesus is righteous (Luke 23:47), this centurion testifies that Paul is a Roman citizen.[97] The centurion's move triggers his commander to stop the flogging and to ensure a proper trial for Paul (Acts 22:27–30).[98] The centurion thus plays an important role in asserting Paul's citizenship rights, initiating a process that will culminate in Paul's appeal to Caesar and his trip to the heart of the empire (Acts 25:11–12).

Thwarting and Escorting (Acts 23:17, 23; 24:23)

In Acts 23:12–35, Paul's life is once again in danger. The narrative focuses upon the actions of unexpected characters—including a centurion—who

---

94. Johnson, *Acts*, 391–92.

95. Tannehill, *Narrative Unity of Luke-Acts*, 2:295. Later in the narrative, the commander will also evade direct responsibility by punting Paul's case to the governor (Acts 23:23–30). In Keener's view, Claudius Lysias is sympathetic but ultimately prefers politics over justice. Keener, *Acts*, 3:3339.

96. Tannehill, *Narrative Unity of Luke-Acts*, 2:295.

97. Keener, *Acts*, 3:3250.

98. In the ensuing conversation, we learn that the commander purchased his citizenship while Paul was born a citizen (Acts 22:28).

rescue Paul yet again.[99] After learning that Paul is a Roman citizen, the commander allows Paul to address the Jewish high priests and council (22:30). Paul's speech to the council leads to another uproar, and once again, the commander and his soldiers rescue the apostle (23:10). While Paul is being protected in the barracks, the Jews hatch a murder plot involving forty men (23:12–15). When Paul's nephew discovers the plot, the apostle calls a centurion to bring the young informant to Lysias the commander (23:17). Without knowing the reason for approaching the commander, the centurion complies with Paul's request.[100] Consistent with the rest of the centurions in Luke–Acts, this centurion responds favorably by escorting Paul's nephew to his commander.[101] Lysias reacts by immediately dispatching two of his centurions along with hundreds of troops to escort Paul towards Caesarea by night (23:23).[102] Due to the volatility of Paul's situation, Lysias sends an entourage to discreetly escort Paul to safety in Antipatris before some of the troops continue with Paul to complete their journey to Caesarea on the following day (23:31–32).[103]

After Paul's stay in Caesarea is extended, Felix puts him in custody under yet another centurion. Under orders from Felix, the centurion facilitates Paul's liberty to host visitors who help provide for his needs (24:23; cf. 21:7–14). As was the case with the previous centurions in Luke–Acts, this centurion plays a positive role in the narrative by granting Paul significant freedom while in custody. After two years in Caesarea under Felix (24:27), Paul stands before the new governor, Festus, who offers to send Paul back to Jerusalem (25:9). Rather than return to Jerusalem, Paul appeals to Caesar (25:11–12) and is heard by Agrippa (26:1–32) before being sent by boat towards Italy.

---

99. Tannehill, *Narrative Unity of Luke–Acts*, 2:293.

100. Keener, *Acts*, 3:3316.

101. Throughout this account, Paul's status was gradually elevated to the point where he could dispatch a centurion despite being a prisoner. Johnson, *Acts*, 404.

102. Zeichmann suggests that the number of troops would represent nearly half of the troops under Claudius Lysias's charge (Zeichmann, *Roman Army*, 89). Keener summarizes the case for the plausibility of this number of troops and suggests that the absence of the soldiers at Antonia would hardly be felt since they would only be away for one night (Keener, *Acts*, 3:3321–23).

103. Witherington, *Acts*, 697. Antipatris (Acts 23:31) was a site of Roman auxiliary barracks and would have been the logical place for the troops to stop to spend the night midway between Jerusalem and Caesarea. Located in predominantly gentile territory, it would be a safe place to leave behind the infantry. Hemer, *Acts*, 128; Keener, *Acts*, 1:205.

Capitulate or Capsize (Acts 27:1–44)

As in the pericope of Paul's rescue from ambush (Acts 23:12–35), Paul plays a less prominent role in Luke's description of his sea voyage. While Paul appears at critical moments in the narrative, other characters, including a centurion, play central roles in this pericope.[104] At the start of the sea voyage, Julius, a centurion of the Augustan cohort (σπείρης Σεβαστῆς), assumes custody over Paul and some other prisoners (27:1).[105] Julius's significance in the narrative is suggested by the fact that he is one of only two centurions (the other being Cornelius) who is named in Luke–Acts. Though we cannot be certain of his ethnicity, Julius's name and position would be fitting for a Roman.[106]

We quickly learn that "Julius treated Paul kindly" (φιλανθρώπως, 27:3), indicating that he is a man of good character. As Johnson points out, the adverb φιλανθρώπως and its cognate φιλανθρωπία (see Titus 3:4) rarely appear in the New Testament, although in Hellenistic literature the words frequently refer to people known for high ethics and civilized behavior.[107] Like the previous centurion at Caesarea (Acts 24:23), Julius permits Paul to visit his friends while their ship is at port in Sidon (27:3). A few stops later, the centurion transfers Paul, his travel companions (27:2), and the rest of the prisoners (27:1, 42) to another boat headed for Italy (27:6). As Paul advises the centurion, this latter part of their sea voyage will become dangerous (27:10). The friendly relationship of trust between Julius and Paul will play a vital role in keeping their ship from capsizing.[108]

Julius's favorable disposition towards Paul is consistent throughout the voyage with one exception, where he listens to the owner of the ship rather

---

104. Tannehill, *Narrative Unity of Luke–Acts*, 2:330.

105. The Augustan cohort is attested in Syria during the first century, though an auxiliary cohort could also bear the name as an honorific title. Another possibility is that Σεβαστῆς refers to a cohort under Agrippa I who derived its name from the city of Sebaste (Samaria). Johnson, *Acts*, 445.

106. The name "Julius" was common both to emperor Tiberius (whose name included "Julius" and who died in AD 16) and Gaius Caligula (also Julius, who died in AD 41) (Keener, *Acts*, 4:3571n138). Despite Julius's name, some scholars remain unconvinced that he was Roman. While I tend to think Julius was a Roman, there is, nevertheless, evidence that some Jews served in the Roman army at Caesarea (Zeichmann, *Roman Army*, 5).

107. Johnson, *Acts*, 445.

108. Tannehill, *Narrative Unity of Luke–Acts*, 2:331.

than heeding Paul's guidance (27:11).[109] When Paul's prediction proves true, the centurion changes his demeanor and listens to Paul. At a critical moment when the boat approaches a rocky shore, the situation becomes so dire that some sailors seek to escape in a smaller boat (27:30). At Paul's word, however, the centurion and soldiers remain in the boat, trusting that their lives will be spared because of their capitulation to Paul (27:31–32). Finally, after the boat shipwrecks upon the shore, Julius stops the soldiers from killing the prisoners because he wants to save Paul (27:43). Although Julius previously doubted Paul's predictions, by the end of the journey, the centurion trusts Paul and takes risky actions to save Paul's life.

"Salvation" (σῴζω in 27:20, 31 and σωτηρία in 27:34) is a key motif throughout the sea voyage narrative. Although referring to physical safety in this context, the motif ties the sea voyage into the broader theme of salvation in Luke–Acts.[110] For this reason, Tannehill sees a spiritual metaphor played out in the sea narrative. Paul and his companions comprise a small Christian contingent on the boat, but there is hope for all on the boat to be saved if they trust God's word spoken through Paul (27:25). The centurion plays a critical leadership role by ensuring different parties on the ship—soldiers, sailors, prisoners, and Christians—work together so that "dangers would be avoided and the ship would be finally saved."[111] In this way, Julius demonstrates how a Roman official could enable cooperation for the greater good in situations where Christians form a small minority of the overall population. Moreover, Julius facilitates Paul's safe journey towards Rome where he will fulfill the Lord's promise that his followers will be his witnesses to "the end of the earth" (1:8).

Conclusion

Centurions serve as proponents of the gospel throughout Luke–Acts. The centurion at Capernaum (Luke 7:1–10) is a forerunner for gentiles who humbly recognize their need for Jesus' salvation. By declaring "surely this

109. Among the centurions in Luke–Acts, Julius is the only one to be portrayed negatively, albeit briefly.

110. Johnson, *Acts*, 455; Marshall, *Luke: Historian and Theologian*, 94–102. Throughout Luke–Acts σῴζω and σωτηρία can refer to either physical healing or salvation from sin through repentance and faith in Jesus (Luke 1:77, Acts 2:21, 4:12, 16:30–31). The verb σῴζω often refers to physical healing in ways that are often closely related to spiritual salvation by faith (Luke 7:50; 8:12, 48, 50; Acts 4:9).

111. Tannehill, *Narrative Unity of Luke–Acts*, 2:338.

man was righteous" (Luke 23:47), the centurion at the cross initiates a movement of repentant mourning among the crowds. Moreover, the centurion at Calvary foreshadows Peter, Stephen, and Paul, who preach Jesus as the "righteous one" during key sermons in Acts. Cornelius (Acts 10:1—11:18) is a precursor of subsequent gentile God-fearers in Acts who also profess faith in Jesus.

Upon Paul's arrival in Jerusalem, centurions frequently serve as his protectors. These centurions help to thwart a murder plot and serve as an armed guard to escort Paul safely to his trial in Caesarea. Their presence in the narrative helps to show God's providential hand in leading Paul to "testify also in Rome" (Acts 23:11). By repeatedly saving Paul's life and asserting his citizenship rights, the Jerusalem centurions are instrumental to moving Paul along towards testifying before the "highest religious and political authorities of the region."[112] At Caesarea, the centurion in charge of Paul facilitates his liberty to receive guests (Acts 24:23). Finally, Julius plays a key role in preserving Paul's life and leading him safely to Rome while ensuring that both believers and the non-Christian majority work together for the common good (Acts 27:1–28).

---

112. Tannehill, *Narrative Unity of Luke–Acts*, 2:285.

5

Government Officials as the "Most Excellent" Proponents of the Gospel in Luke–Acts

> Render to Caesar the things that are Caesar's,
> and to God the things that are God's.
>
> —LUKE 20:25

> All the saints greet you, especially those
> of Caesar's household.
>
> —PHILIPPIANS 4:22

WRITING FROM PRISON, PAUL concludes his letter to believers in the Roman colony of Philippi (see Acts 16:12) with a special greeting from the household of the emperor. Ironically, although Paul is in chains (see also 2 Tim 2:9), the gospel has spread throughout the imperial guard (Phil 1:12–14) and even touched those closest to Caesar (4:22). But how did the gospel traverse from the ranks of the centurions to the elites of Caesar's household? The present chapter will help to address the gap between Caesar and the centurions by examining additional evidence from Luke–Acts.

In the previous two chapters, I argued that (1) Luke's first reader, Theophilus, was most likely a high-ranking Roman official who was sympathetic to the gospel and that (2) Luke consistently portrays centurions as supporters of the gospel's advance among gentiles in general, and especially among Roman authorities. In this chapter, I will draw these two strands together and explore their significance for readers of Luke-Acts. Why did Luke emphasize the positive role of centurions in his account to Theophilus? I will argue that Luke aimed to show Theophilus that embracing the gospel was a fitting and honorable path for a Roman official. For Theophilus, the centurions in the narrative would serve as excellent models of authorities who embraced the gospel (or supported the church) while remaining embedded in the Roman establishment. Aside from the centurions, does Luke-Acts describe other sympathetic officials?

The rest of this chapter will unfold as follows. First, I will begin by surveying the broader theme of the Roman Empire in Luke's writings. Next, I will present additional examples of authorities—including Romans and non-Romans—who become proponents of the gospel in Luke-Acts. Finally, I will explore the theme of supportive government officials during Paul's Roman imprisonment at the end of Acts.

Overview of the Roman Empire in Luke-Acts

Among the four Gospels, Luke's is the only one to mention a Roman emperor by name. Early in the narrative, Luke presents Jesus' birth in the context of Caesar Augustus (Luke 2:1), who ruled as emperor from 31 BC to AD 14. The beginning of John the Baptist's ministry is likewise placed during the rule of Tiberius Caesar (Luke 3:1; ruled AD 14–37).[1] Similarly, the book of Acts mentions Emperor Claudius by name (Acts 11:28, 18:2; ruled AD 41–54) and alludes to Emperors Caligula (ruled AD 37–41) and Nero (ruled AD 54–68) using the titles "Augustus" (25:21, 25; cf. 27:1) and "Caesar" (17:7; 25:8, 10, 11, 12, 21; 26:32; 27:24; 28:19).[2] Viewed as a whole, the entire narrative of Luke-Acts is framed in reference to the Roman emperors who appear at both the beginning (Luke 2:1, 3:1) and end (Acts 27:24, 28:19) of the two-volume work.[3]

---

1. Pinter, "Gospel of Luke," 104–5; Walton, "State They Were In," 16. Each of the Synoptic Gospels mentions Caesar in the encounter regarding taxes (Matt 22:17–21, Mark 12:14–17, Luke 20:22–25). The Gospels of Luke and John both mention Caesar on the lips of the Jews who accuse Jesus of being disloyal to Rome (Luke 23:2, John 19:12–15).

2. Robbins, "Luke-Acts," 206–7; Walton, "State They Were In," 16.

3. Alexander argues that Luke 1–4 and Acts 28 frame the entire narrative of

Along with the emperor, Luke's Gospel also mentions several other representatives of Rome. In some instances, Rome's agents are portrayed positively, while other cases seem to show that Rome was at odds with the early church.[4] As discussed in chapter 4, Roman centurions are consistently portrayed positively (Luke 7:1–10, 23:47) despite the poor reputation of Roman soldiers (3:14, 23:11). Similarly, we find positive examples of Roman tax collectors (5:27–28, 18:9–14, 19:1–10) despite their bad reputation (3:12, 5:30, 15:1, 18:11, 19:7). Among those in the empire's higher ranks, Herod the Tetrarch is hostile toward John the Baptist and Jesus (3:19–20, 9:7–9, 13:31) and Pilate is violent towards the Galileans (13:1, 23:1–25). While Roman officials are often depicted as neutral or positive, the Herodians in particular are portrayed more negatively.[5]

In Luke's Gospel, the most ambivalent portrayal of Roman rule occurs in Jesus' trial narrative. The trial shows both Roman support and opposition within a single passage.[6] Pontius Pilate provides a powerful picture of one Roman governor who finds no fault with Jesus. After sending him to be tried by Herod Antipas, Pilate proposes three times to the Jews that he will flog Jesus and send him away (Luke 23:4, 14, 22). Earlier in the narrative, Pilate sent Jesus to Herod Antipas, who likewise found no fault in him (23:15). Thus, on the one hand, Pilate sees Jesus' innocence and seeks to acquit him (23:4, 14, 22). On the other hand, Herod and his soldiers mock Jesus, and Pilate ultimately hands over Jesus for execution (23:24–25). While it is true that Pilate acted under pressure from the Jews, a legal system that punishes the innocent could hardly be worthy of endorsement.[7]

Such ambivalence towards Roman representatives continues in the narrative of Paul's trial described in the book of Acts.[8] After hearing Paul's

---

Luke–Acts. Alexander, *Acts*, 207–29.

4. Pinter, "Gospel of Luke," 104.

5. Richard Rackham points out an exception to Luke's negative portrayal of the Herods. "Of all these Herods, Agrippa II comes out the best" (Rackham, *Acts*, 458). Based on Rackham's comment, Marx argues that "Theophilus" was a pseudonym for Agrippa II (Marx, "New Theophilus," 19).

6. Philip Esler accounts for this ambivalence by suggesting that "Luke is differentiating between Pilate's questionable character and his role as arbiter of Roman law." Esler also points out that Luke, in contrast with Mark (see Mark 15:1–15) portrays Pilate in a relatively positive light, thus shifting more of the blame onto Herod and the Jewish leadership. Esler, *Community and Gospel in Luke-Acts*, 202–3.

7. Rowe, *World Upside Down*, 149; Walton, "State They Were In," 20, 22–23.

8. Harry Tajra explains the complexity of Luke's portrayal of Roman and Jewish authorities. "Luke tries hard to cast the Roman authorities in as favourable a light as

defense, Felix is indecisive (Acts 24:22), fearful (24:25), and wants a bribe (24:26). Similarly, Festus is passive (25:26–27) and, along with Agrippa, declares that Paul had done nothing wrong (26:31–32). Finally, Paul appeals to Caesar because he realizes that he has little chance for a fair trial before the Roman governors.[9] Overall, the narrative demonstrates the reasonableness of the Christian faith and Paul's innocence in the eyes of Roman officials.[10]

Elsewhere in Acts, Herod Agrippa I fiercely persecutes early Christian leaders (12:1–23), consistent with the antagonism of Herod Antipas in Luke's Gospel. Despite these negative examples, the book of Acts also presents several sympathetic Roman officials including Sergius Paulus, the proconsul of Paphos who becomes a believer (13:7), as well as the various centurions discussed in chapter 4 (10:1—11:18, 21:27—23:35, 24:23, 27:1–44). I will discuss Sergius Paulus in more detail later in this chapter.

Major Scholarly Views

Given the mixed portrayal of Rome in Luke's narrative, it is not surprising that scholars have debated the relationship between the church and the Roman Empire in Luke–Acts. I will now briefly mention a few major scholarly views before presenting my own view within the context of this broader conversation.[11] Until the late twentieth century, most scholars followed Heumann's view that Luke–Acts was written to a Roman official (Theophilus) as an *apologia pro ecclesia* to show that Christianity was politically harmless and to defend Christians against their Roman accusers.[12] In contrast, Walaskay inverts the apologetic view by reading Luke–Acts as a pro-Roman

---

possible. He can thereby demonstrate the inherent justice of the Roman system of law, which he sharply contrasts to the basic injustice and violence of Paul's Jewish foes (especially the Sadducaean wing of the Sanhedrin)." Tajra, *Trial of St. Paul*, 199.

9. In Tajra's view, "the appeal to Caesar is the central event on which Luke's whole account of Paul's legal history turns." Tajra, *Trial of St. Paul*, 197.

10. Rowe, *World Upside Down*, 136, 148.

11. For helpful surveys of major views see Walton, "State They Were In"; Pinter, "Gospel of Luke"; Rowe, *World Upside Down*, 3–4.

12. Heumann, "Dissertatio de Theophilo." For a brief summary of Heumann's argument, see Neagoe, *Trial of the Gospel*, 10. The Roman governor Pliny the Younger, writing around the year AD 112, provides evidence for accusations against Christians near Pontus (see 1 Pet 2:12). Wilken, *Christians as the Romans Saw Them*, 1–30.

document to teach Christians to integrate with the empire.[13] Rowe, on the other hand, argues that Luke wrote neither an apology for or against Rome, but instead sought to subvert the empire by presenting Christianity as an entirely different way of life. In Rowe's words, "Christianity is not a governmental takeover but an alternative and salvific way of life" that calls people to view the world based on Jesus' lordship.[14]

Walton helpfully summarizes five major perspectives on Luke's depiction of the relationship between Christians and the state.[15] According to Walton, most scholars view Luke–Acts as either (1) a political apology on behalf of the church addressed to Roman officials (Heumann), (2) an apology for Rome addressed to believers (Walaskay, Robbins), (3) legitimation for Romans to believe in Jesus (Esler, Witherington), (4) guidance for believers on trial for their beliefs (Cassidy), or (5) an apolitical work (Jervell).[16] To Walton's list of five views, one might add a sixth view: that Luke–Acts calls for allegiance to Jesus as Lord and subverts the Roman way of life (Rowe). The existence of such disparate views reflects the reality that Luke–Acts presents a mixed picture of the Roman Empire.

A Proposal

I agree with Rowe that Luke wrote to present an alternative way of life where Jesus is honored as Lord of all. However, while Rowe seems to make little of Theophilus, I believe that Luke–Acts was addressed to a Roman official to demonstrate how he could become a proponent for the gospel.[17] In this regard, my proposal resembles Philip Esler's "legitimation" view.[18] However,

---

13. Walaskay, *So We Came to Rome*, 15–37.

14. Rowe, *World Upside Down*, 136.

15. Walton, "State They Were In," 2–12.

16. Heumann, "Dissertatio de Theophilo"; Walaskay, *So We Came to Rome*; Robbins, "Luke–Acts"; Esler, *Community and Gospel in Luke–Acts*; Witherington, *Acts*, 37, 809–12; Cassidy, *Society and Politics*, 145–70; Jervell, *Acts of the Apostles*, 15–16, 100–106.

17. In Rowe's view, "Acts is best read as a document intended for Christians" rather than an apology for the church (Rowe, *World Upside Down*, 10). Rowe does not make much of Theophilus but remains agnostic about the reader, explaining, "We have no idea where Acts was written, or for whom, or at what particular time, or where it was to be sent" (Rowe, *World Upside Down*, 11).

18. In his study of Luke–Acts, Esler applies the sociological category of legitimation, which he defines as "the collection of ways in which an institution is explained and justified to its members." Luke's two-volume work legitimates the early Christian

I also differ from Esler in at least two areas. First, I uphold the historicity of Luke's narrative, including its recounting of Cornelius's conversion.[19] Second, I do not follow Esler's view that Luke wrote to one specific Christian community of Jews and gentiles that included Roman soldiers and administrators.[20] Instead, I follow Bauckham's argument that each Gospel was likely written for broad dissemination rather than for targeted communities of the early church.[21] Earlier, I argued that Luke wrote to a dual audience: first to Theophilus and second to a general population of Christian readers. Thus, I affirm (with Esler) that Luke wrote to a Roman official without assuming a Lukan community as his target audience (with Bauckham). Writing to a dual audience, Luke presents Jesus as the Savior for all types of people, including Jews and gentiles, the poor and rich, the sick and marginalized, and even Roman administrators and soldiers.

Roman Officials and Loyalty to Jesus

As Green argues, conversion in Luke–Acts entails an entire change of life direction.[22] However, new converts did not necessarily jettison all aspects of their pre-Christian lives. For example, when tax collectors and soldiers express repentance, John the Baptist instructs them not to leave their occupations but rather to remain in their roles while upholding God's righteous moral standards (Luke 3:12–14).[23] For these individuals, conversion meant pledging allegiance to Jesus without necessarily leaving their positions within the Roman establishment. Such a choice would inevitably create tension in the lives of Roman officials who turned to faith in Christ.

---

movement for its adherents in a similar way as the Declaration of Independence would have legitimated the American Revolution for the forefathers of the United States. Esler, *Community and Gospel in Luke–Acts*, 16–17.

19. Esler, *Community and Gospel in Luke–Acts*, 37, 95–96. See Steve Walton's rebuttal of Esler's view; Walton, "State They Were In," 8n18.

20. Esler, *Community and Gospel in Luke–Acts*, 16, 25–26, 210. Despite my quibbles with Esler, I nevertheless find his analysis very helpful and aligned with my views in many ways. As Esler admits, even if Luke wrote to a general audience, "that fact would not invalidate the methodology adopted in this book or the results produced by it." Esler, *Community and Gospel in Luke–Acts*, 26.

21. Bauckham, "For Whom Were Gospels Written?," 9–13.

22. Green, *Conversion in Luke–Acts*, 87–88.

23. Walton, "State They Were In," 20–21.

How could a Roman official remain loyal to Caesar while also serving God? This question is perhaps most succinctly addressed by Jesus' instructions to "render to Caesar the things that are Caesar's, and to God the things that are God's" (Luke 20:25). In his insightful response to the question of taxes, Jesus called for both respecting Rome ("render to Caesar the things that are Caesar's") while reserving ultimate loyalties for God ("and to God the things that are God's").[24] This teaching would provide a helpful paradigm for an individual embedded within the Roman establishment. Such a framework would be applicable for officials of all types, including those in higher ranks (like Theophilus), the lower-ranking centurions, and others in positions of authority within a non-Christian establishment.

The Gospel for Political Leaders in Luke–Acts

Throughout Acts, the gospel encounters Roman authorities in various ways. Tannehill explains,

> The narrator is not content to present the powerful effect of the Christian mission in the private lives of individuals. Its cultural and political effect is also important. This aspect comes to the fore as Paul confronts high authorities of Judaism and Rome. Those who control religious and political institutions must listen to Paul and respond in some way to him.[25]

In other words, the gospel confronts all types of authorities—Roman, Jewish, and otherwise—throughout Luke–Acts.[26] Jesus hints at this topic when he foretells that his disciples will be led away to testify to kings and governors on account of his name (Luke 21:12–13). This prediction is fulfilled in Acts when Peter and John (Acts 4:1–22, 17–42), Stephen (7:1–60), and Paul (23:1—26:32) testify before Jewish and Roman rulers.[27]

24. Walton, "State They Were In," 18–19.
25. Tannehill, *Narrative Unity of Luke–Acts*, 2:285.
26. For example, in Luke's Gospel, the account of the centurion in Luke 7:1–10 is echoed just one chapter later through Jesus' encounter with Jairus, a Jewish synagogue ruler. On behalf of his sick servant, the gentile centurion sends Jewish elders who proclaim his worthiness for having built their synagogue. Similarly, Jairus the synagogue ruler comes to ask Jesus to heal his sick daughter (Luke 8:41–42). Both Jairus and the centurion are men in positions of authority. Both are associated with the Jewish synagogue. Both request Jesus to heal someone dear to them. These parallels point to the necessity for those in authority (like Theophilus) to come to Jesus.
27. Tannehill, *Narrative Unity of Luke–Acts*, 2:290–91.

Is it enough for such rulers to hear the testimony of believers, or is conversion the end goal of such encounters? Several strands of evidence in Luke–Acts suggest that faithfulness to Christ is an appropriate, though not universal, response for high-ranking officials. I will now present these strands of evidence in order. If the gospel is indeed meant for all types of people—including rulers—we might expect Luke to mention believers demonstrating loyalty to God while holding positions of authority. While my focus so far has been on the Roman Empire, does Luke provide any evidence for believing officials serving in the governments of other nations? It turns out that he does. I will now discuss examples of believing officials from outside of the Roman Empire before citing examples of believers embedded within the empire.

Stephen's Speech (Acts 7:1–60)

While it is natural to focus on the Roman Empire in our analysis of government officials in Luke–Acts, the narrative also presents officials from other nations. One place where foreign officials appear is in Stephen's defense (Acts 7:1–60), which is both the longest speech in Acts and its most detailed retelling of Old Testament history.[28] Faced with the Jews' accusations of speaking "against this holy place and the law" (6:13), Stephen centers his defense around two key ideas. First, God's presence is not confined to a specific people or place (7:2–6, 10, 15, 22, 29, 30–31, 33–34, 36, 38, 44–45, 48–50). And second, Israel's history is marked by its repeated rejection of God's chosen servants (7:9, 27, 35, 39–40, 52) and defiance of his law (7:41–43, 51, 53).[29] Significantly, the majority of Stephen's speech illustrates these two themes through the lives of two Old Testament believers—Joseph (7:9–16) and Moses (7:17–43)—who both had close ties to the Egyptian government.

In response to charges of speaking against the temple (6:13), Stephen cites Joseph as a "godly man who was blessed and used by God *outside* the Promised Land."[30] What is not often discussed in analyses of Stephen's speech, however, is that Joseph is also the earliest biblical example of an Israelite who serves within a gentile government.[31] After being sold to Egypt,

---

28. Keener, *Acts*, 2:1330; Padilla, *Acts*, 161–62.
29. Keener, *Acts*, 2:1329; Padilla, *Acts*, 163–64.
30. Padilla, *Acts*, 163; emphasis original.
31. Earlier examples of sympathetic gentile officials include Abimelech and

God "gave him favor and wisdom before Pharaoh, king of Egypt, who made him ruler over Egypt and over all his household" (7:10). Even though Joseph is embedded within a seemingly evil empire, "God was with him" (7:10) and providentially enables Joseph to save many lives during a famine (7:11–14). The Joseph story demonstrates that God can direct his people to ascend the ranks of gentile governments to fulfill his own purposes.

In addition to holding office in Pharaoh's court, Joseph also thoroughly assimilates into Egyptian culture.[32] Joseph is completely integrated into Egyptian society such that he becomes unrecognizable to his own brothers until he "made himself known" during their "second visit" to Egypt (7:13).[33] Appearances are not always what they seem. Even though Joseph is an Israelite, he functions as a gentile official who leverages his political power to become a surprising supporter of God's people.[34] Through Joseph, we see that believing officials may sometimes choose to strategically conceal their identities. In summary, Joseph provides one type of example of how a faithful follower of the Lord may operate within a gentile government.[35]

The next section of Stephen's speech responds to the allegation of speaking against the Mosaic law (6:13–14) by turning the tables on the

---

Melchizedek. Later biblical examples of Israelites serving in gentile courts include Nehemiah, Mordecai, Esther, and Jehoiachin. Emadi, *From Prisoner to Prince*, 115–37; Chen, *Messianic Vision*, 96, 104; Chan, "Joseph and Jehoiachin," 569–72.

32. Joseph's cultural assimilation is indicated through his wearing Egyptian clothing (Gen 41:42), taking an Egyptian name (41:45), marrying an Egyptian wife (41:45), raising Hebrew-Egyptian children (48:9), and being embalmed according to Egyptian customs (50:26).

33. The Genesis narrative masterfully presents Joseph as an apparently antagonistic Egyptian official (Gen 42:7–17, 30; 44:4–15) who is simultaneously a supporter of God's people (42:25–28, 35; 43:16–34). Joseph's official position serves as a relational bridge between Egypt and Israel, enabling the two nations to become mutual blessings to one another (47:7, 10). Thus, Joseph's leadership role in Egypt becomes one means by which God begins to fulfill the Abrahamic covenant (12:3).

34. Several minor characters in the Joseph story illustrate additional ways that government officials may serve God's purposes, even if unintentionally. Throughout Joseph's story, God uses several Egyptian officials (Potiphar, the cupbearer, the baker, and the pharaoh) to shape the trajectory of Joseph's life. Although these Egyptian officials are not always intending to be friendly towards Joseph, their actions enable him to make an unexpected rise through the ranks of the Egyptian government. In this sense, these Egyptian officials foreshadow some of the ways in which Roman centurions supported Paul during the last third of the book of Acts.

35. Joseph also foreshadows Daniel, whose role in the Babylonian government we discussed in chapter 2. For more on parallels between Joseph and Daniel, see Henze, "Use of Scripture," 282–83; Hamilton, *With the Clouds of Heaven*, 229–32.

Jews and demonstrating Israel's rebellion against Moses and his law.[36] Although Moses is not a government official, he holds a privileged position within the Egyptian establishment. As an infant, Moses is adopted into the home of the pharaoh's daughter who "brought him up as her own son" (7:21).[37] Moses assimilates into Egyptian culture and is "instructed in all the wisdom of the Egyptians" (7:22; see also Dan 1:4).[38] Like Joseph, Moses overcomes the initial rejection of his own people and uses his position of leadership as "ruler and judge" (7:27, 35) to bring about deliverance for many (7:35–36).[39] Though Stephen's speech primarily emphasizes Israel's rejection of God's servants and law, it also demonstrates that God can raise up faithful leaders from within seemingly hostile governments.

The Ethiopian Eunuch (Acts 8:26–40)

The narrative of Acts turns from Stephen to Philip, the second minister mentioned in Acts 6:5.[40] Philip's ministry strategically advances the gospel into Samaria and the ends of the earth (see Acts 1:8).[41] The narrative recounts Philip bringing the gospel to Samaria (8:4–8) and Simon the magician's conversion (8:9–25) before focusing upon Philip's extended encounter with an official from a kingdom that neighbored the Roman Empire (8:26–40). Luke takes great care to identify the desert traveler in several different ways. He is "an Ethiopian, a eunuch, a court official of Candace, queen of the Ethiopians, who was in charge of all of her treasure" (8:27). Although the eunuch is probably not ethnically Jewish, he

---

36. Keener, *Acts*, 2:1329.

37. Keener, *Acts*, 2:1384–86.

38. Although Moses' Egyptian education is not mentioned in the Pentateuch, it is nevertheless plausible given his upbringing as a son of Pharaoh's daughter. The Egyptian education of Moses is mentioned in postbiblical Jewish sources such as Philo, *Mos.* 1.20–24. Keener, *Acts*, 2:1336, 1387–88.

39. Like Joseph, the people rejected Moses the first time, "but the second time he came to them they had no option but to accept him (as Joseph's brothers recognized him on the second occasion)." Bruce, *Acts*, 142.

40. Keener, *Acts*, 2:1464. On the ethnic identity of Samaritans, Keener points out that the Samaritans "were treated like Gentiles in some respects.... Nevertheless, most Jewish teachers did not regard Samaritans as fully Gentile" (Keener, *Acts*, 2:1491). Thus, the Samaritan mission should be viewed as a step towards gentile mission.

41. Keener, *Acts*, 2:1534.

is deeply influenced by Judaism (8:27–28).[42] After meeting Philip, the eunuch humbly admits his lack of understanding (8:31, 34), welcomes Philip to share "the good news about Jesus" (8:35), and immediately receives baptism (8:37). Though not purely a gentile, the Ethiopian eunuch becomes the first foreigner to convert in Acts.[43]

Significantly, the eunuch is also a high-ranking official in a renowned African kingdom.[44] The Ethiopians were known as "wealthy, wise and militarily mighty."[45] As Candace's treasurer, the eunuch is a man of significant influence who controls the royal funds.[46] Keener explains that although eunuchs were marginalized in Israel's worship (Deut 23:1), this eunuch's official status within a powerful kingdom makes him one of the most prominent individuals to appear in Luke–Acts.[47] Despite his high rank, the eunuch's humility foreshadows that of Cornelius, another government official who also readily receives baptism (8:37, 10:47–48).[48]

The eunuch's conversion also echoes the accounts of two other sympathetic African officials who appear earlier in the Bible. One such official

---

42. Bruce, *Acts*, 175. Bock suggests that the eunuch was likely "a Diaspora Jew or a Gentile who is already tied to Judaism, as his coming to Jerusalem and reading Isaiah suggest." Although his castration may have precluded him from becoming a full Jewish proselyte, he could have been "somewhere between one who has been merely exposed to Israel's God and may have respect for this deity and one who is fully circumcised. . . . As such, he would not be seen as a pure Gentile" (Bock, *Acts*, 338).

43. In chapter 4, I suggest that Cornelius is the first pure gentile convert in Acts. Other scholars, including Keener, argue that the Ethiopian eunuch is "the first fully Gentile Christian" in Acts (Keener, *Acts*, 2:1541). Nevertheless, for Keener, Cornelius still holds an important place in the narrative because his conversion causes the church to officially endorse gentile inclusion.

44. Keener summarizes the scholarly consensus on the official's home country: "The Greek title 'Ethiopia' technically included all of Africa south of Egypt, but the Candace's title has convinced nearly all scholars that the Nubian kingdom of Meroë is specifically in view here." Keener, *Acts*, 2:1550–51.

45. Smith, "Do You Understand," 64. Later in the same article, Smith cites verses from the LXX that mention the wealth of the Cushites (Isa 45:14, Dan 11:43; see also 1 Kgs 10:1–2). The most memorable of these passages is Ps 68:31, which says, "Nobles shall come from Egypt; Cush shall hasten to stretch out her hands to God." Smith, "Do You Understand," 67.

46. "Most scholars, including nearly all commentators on Acts, hold that 'Candace' (pronounced *kan-dakè*) was not the queen's name but her dynastic title, presumably comparable to 'Pharaoh' or 'Ptolemy.'" Keener, *Acts*, 2:1573.

47. Keener, *Acts*, 2:1571. Keener continues, "The official is a treasurer, and not merely of any kingdom or ruler but of the powerful Candace of Meroë."

48. Smith, "Do You Understand," 65.

is Ebed-melech (Jer 38:7–13), an Ethiopian eunuch who becomes "one of Jeremiah's only allies."[49] During a time of national and personal crisis, when the rest of Israel's officials turn against God's prophet (38:4–6), it is surprising to find an Ethiopian eunuch arise as a protagonist who boldly delivers Jeremiah from persecution by drawing him out of a cistern (38:7–13).[50] Ebed-melech's faithfulness foreshadows the conversion of the Ethiopian eunuch who serves in Candace's court.[51]

Secondly, the conversion of Candace's treasurer echoes the well-known encounter between Solomon and the Queen of Sheba (1 Kgs 10:1–13, 2 Chr 9:1–12). This connection is also reflected by Josephus, who claims that the Queen of Sheba rules over both Egypt and Ethiopia.[52] Like the eunuch, the Queen of Sheba is also a high-ranking African official who comes to Jerusalem and leaves praising Israel's God (1 Kgs 10:9, 2 Chr 9:8; see also Acts 8:39). These parallels are further strengthened when we note that Luke only uses the word "queen" (βασίλισσα) twice and exclusively in reference to "Candace, queen of the Ethiopians" (Acts 8:27) and the Queen of Sheba (Luke 11:31).[53] Although Luke's Gospel describes her as the "Queen of the South [βασίλισσα νότου]" (Luke 11:31) the mention of Solomon makes clear that the Queen of Sheba is in view (see Matt 12:42). Her affiliation with "the south" also links the Queen of Sheba to the worldwide reach of the gospel, which summons people "from east and west, and from north and south [νότου]" (Luke 13:29). Moreover, her coming "from the ends of the earth" (Luke 11:31) casts the Queen of Sheba as a narrative precursor to the spread of the gospel documented in Acts (see Acts 1:8).[54] The narrative resonance between Candace and the Queen of

49. Keener, *Acts*, 2:1540.

50. Keener, *Acts*, 2:1578–79.

51. "It is probably no coincidence that the only Cushite individual depicted in detail in the OT also is a eunuch" (Keener, *Acts*, 2:1540). Furthermore, the faith of both Ethiopian eunuchs fulfills Isaiah's prophecy that eunuchs and foreigners would be included among God's people (Isa 56:3–7). Notably, this prophecy comes shortly after the section of Isa 53 being read by the Ethiopian eunuch (Keener, *Acts*, 2:1590).

52. Josephus, *Ant.* 8.165; Smith, "Do You Understand," 64. Keener explains, "Josephus calls Saba (Sheba) Ethiopia's royal city, which he claims was later renamed Meroë." Keener, *Acts*, 2:1578 (see also Josephus, *Ant.* 2.249).

53. Bernice is another female ruler who appears in the narrative (Acts 25:13), though Luke does not use the word βασίλισσα to describe her.

54. Keener, *Acts*, 2:1578. Later Ethiopian tradition views Candace (Acts 8:27) as the same individual whom Jesus called the "Queen of the South" (Luke 11:31). Ullendorff's short study helps to sort out this confusion. Ullendorf, "Candace," 53–56.

Sheba and the repeated use of the word "queen" (βασίλισσα) suggests that Luke probably saw a connection between these two African rulers. Reading the Ethiopian eunuch's conversion against the backdrop of the Queen of Sheba reinforces to Luke's reader that government authorities of all nations can serve as surprising supporters of the gospel.

The Gaza Road encounter is an early example of how the gospel reached "the end of the earth" (Acts 1:8; see also Luke 11:31, 13:29) and impacted those in the upper echelons of various kingdoms. Just as Cornelius's conversion shows that the gospel is for Roman officials, so, too, the eunuch's conversion shows that the gospel is for Ethiopian officials. Smith insightfully explains,

> Both the Ethiopian and Cornelius exhibit the character of persons who are the best candidates for gaining insight, that is, persons, who, though already intelligent, take on the posture of humility in order to learn more or to be saved.[55]

In a similar vein, the next government official to receive the gospel in Acts is also an intelligent and humble man. As we move to Acts 13, we will also shift our focus back to Roman officials.

Sergius Paulus (Acts 13:4–12)

The opening scene of Paul's inaugural missionary journey features another sympathetic official, Sergius Paulus.[56] Although Acts 13 is recognized as a key transition from the ministry of Peter to that of Paul, the full implications of the Cyprus scene (13:4–12) have been underappreciated.[57] The title "proconsul" (ἀνθύπατος) identifies Sergius Paulus as a Roman magistrate "most likely of senatorial rank" who would typically be appointed to serve for a one-year term.[58] As a proconsul, Sergius Paulus is of significantly

---

55. Smith, "Do You Understand," 65.

56. Several inscriptions bearing the name Sergius Paulus have been found in Cyprus and Pisidian Antioch. Although the inscriptions may refer to the figure described in Acts 13, Bock concludes that "we are not sure if they do or, if so, which one does." Bock, *Acts*, 444.

57. Ehrensperger, "Meeting the Romans," 103.

58. Ehrensperger, "Meeting the Romans," 104. The word proconsul (ἀνθύπατος) appears only five times in the New Testament, exclusively in Acts (13:7, 8, 12; 18:12; 19:38). Following BDAG, Bock explains proconsuls were "Roman magistrates who headed the government in a senatorial province where no troops were required." Bock, *Acts*, 444; see

higher rank than the centurions whom we met in chapter 4. Moreover, Sergius Paulus is one of only two named proconsuls in Acts, with the second being Gallio (18:12), whom we will discuss later in this chapter.

Just as Luke presents centurions as the first gentile converts in both the Gospel of Luke and the book of Acts, so now he introduces a Roman proconsul as the first convert in Paul's ministry.[59] The official's association with "a certain magician, a Jewish false prophet named Bar-Jesus" (13:6; also known as Elymas, 13:8) indicates that Sergius Paulus is open to various religious traditions, including Judaism.[60] The proconsul's intellectual openness soon leads to an opportunity to hear the gospel. Luke describes Sergius Paulus as "a man of intelligence, who summoned Barnabas and Saul and sought to hear the word of God" (13:7). Upon their arrival, however, Elymas "opposed them" (13:8), leading to a confrontation that occurs in the presence of the proconsul. Faced with a choice between false prophecy and gospel truth, Sergius Paulus "sought to hear the word of God" despite the magician's attempts "to turn the proconsul away from the faith" (13:8).

Paul dramatically rebukes the false prophet, causing him to experience temporary blindness. As a result, the proconsul believes, "for he was astonished at the teaching of the Lord" (13:12). Ehrensperger insightfully points out that although Sergius Paulus witnesses a miraculous sign, the narrative "decisively" emphasizes "the διδαχή . . . as having the transformative impact" that leads the proconsul to faith.[61] She contends that, like Cornelius, the proconsul's connection to the Jewish tradition—albeit through a false prophet—prepares him for faith in Christ. Ehrensperger explains,

> Knowledge, specifically pre-knowledge, is necessary for a non-Jew to be able to make sense of this messianic message. It does not convince the magistrate out of the blue. The διδαχή is convincing within the context of knowledge about Jewish tradition he already had before. The magistrate, as a member of the elite, is depicted as recognizing the value of the teaching as something worthy of

---

also BDAG 82.

59. Significantly, Sergius Paulus is also named in the narrative. Thus, he also holds the distinction of being the first named convert in Paul's ministry.

60. Ehrensperger, "Meeting the Romans," 105. Barrett suggests that the magician "may perhaps be thought of as a court astrologer." Barrett, *Acts*, 1:614.

61. Ehrensperger, "Meeting the Romans," 109. Marshall explains, "The superior power associated with the *teaching* of the Christian missionaries astounded the proconsul to such an extent that he was prepared to believe their message." Marshall, *Acts*, 233; emphasis original.

his level of education. As noted, it is the teaching (διδαχή) that astonishes him, not the sign that Paul's words trigger as such.[62]

Furthermore, Ehrensperger reasons that as a proconsul, Sergius Paulus would have been expected to perform priestly duties for the Roman cult. Such obligations would be difficult to forsake during his appointed time in office. Thus, she sees the fact that no baptism is reported here as a reflection of a realistic accommodation made for a believer who holds such high status within the Roman government.[63]

The conversion of Sergius Paulus would send a powerful message to Luke's first reader, Theophilus. The gospel is more powerful than any other competing religious offering—whether magic, Jewish tradition, or the ideology of Rome.[64] Moreover, while we have previously seen lower-ranking centurions turn to Christ, Sergius Paulus represents the first convert among the upper echelon of the Roman government. As a noteworthy leader and "a man of intelligence" (13:7), Sergius Paulus lends credibility to the notion of a Roman magistrate becoming a believer. Moreover, our analysis of Luke–Acts reveals that he is one of five government officials to convert at prominent points in the narrative (table 3). These conversions show that the gospel is not just for the Jews or the common people of the empire; it is also for Romans, Ethiopians, and even for authorities like centurions, proconsuls, and members of the royal court.

---

62. Ehrensperger, "Meeting the Romans," 109–10.

63. Ehrensperger, "Meeting the Romans," 110. Others speculate that the proconsul's conversion may not have been genuine; Marshall, *Acts*, 233; Gerstmyer, "Gentiles in Luke–Acts," 579–80.

64. Ehrensperger, "Meeting the Romans," 111. Both Acts 8 and 13 feature a contrast between Christianity and magic. Just as the Ethiopian eunuch's conversion is preceded by the account of Simon the magician, so the conversion of Sergius Paulus is juxtaposed with the competing claims of Elymas the magician. Moreover, Luke's description of Bar-Jesus strings together five descriptors (13:6) in a way that also reminds us of the way the Ethiopian eunuch is introduced in 8:7 (Schnabel, *Acts*, 976).

Table 3. Government Officials Who Convert at Key Points in Luke–Acts

Passage	Person	Official Role	Narrative Role
Luke 7:1–10	Centurion at Capernaum	Roman centurion	First gentile convert in Luke
Luke 23:47	Centurion at the cross	Roman centurion	First to proclaim the crucified Jesus' righteousness
Acts 8:26–40	Ethiopian eunuch	Treasurer for queen of Ethiopia	First "gentile" convert in Acts[65]
Acts 10:1–48	Cornelius	Roman centurion	First gentile convert in Acts
Acts 13:6–12	Sergius Paulus	Roman proconsul	First gentile convert in Paul's ministry

Christians Associated with Herod Antipas (Luke 8:3, Acts 13:1)

For Roman officials who were sympathetic towards the gospel, it would be reassuring to know that they were not the only ones in their social circles who considered converting to Christianity. Thus, it is noteworthy that Luke also identifies two individual believers among the inner circle of Herod Antipas, a regional ruler (or "tetrarch") under Roman authority. In keeping with the Lukan theme of gender inclusion, one of these believers is a woman and the other is a man. Luke is the only evangelist who points out "Joanna, the wife of Chuza, Herod's household manager [ἐπιτρόπου Ἡρῴδου]" (Luke 8:3) among the women who supported Jesus' ministry.[66] Joanna models how someone can simultaneously be one of Jesus' closest

---

65. Although a foreigner, the Ethiopian eunuch's participation in Jewish worship indicates that he is not purely a gentile.

66. The word ἐπίτροπος appears only three times in the New Testament, denoting a manager or foreman (Matt 20:8) or steward (Gal 4:2). Morris explains, "The word translated *steward* may mean the manager of Herod's estates, or it may point to a political office" (Morris, *Luke*, 169). Though we cannot be sure of Chuza's position, he could have been "a highly placed individual within Herod's retinue, perhaps head of his estate" (BDAG 385).

followers while also being married to an associate of Herod, the ruler over Galilee (3:1, 19). Joanna's piety is evident in that she provides for Jesus and the disciples from her own means (8:3) and appears at Jesus' crucifixion (23:49), burial (23:55), and empty tomb (24:10). Joanna's simultaneous ties to Jesus and Herod are surprising given that this is the same Herod who executes John the Baptist (9:7–9) and wants to kill Jesus (13:31; see also 23:7–12).[67] Her connection to Herod's household shows that the gospel is already making inroads among the social circles of the elite ruling class even during the time of Jesus' Galilean ministry.[68]

In Acts 13, we learn of another believer who has an even deeper connection to Herod Antipas. One of the prophets and teachers in the church at Antioch is a man named Manaen who is described as σύντροφος of "Herod the Tetrarch" (13:1).[69] Although Antipas was exiled in AD 39 and replaced by Agrippa I (whom we meet in Acts 12:1–23), Manaen's Herodian connection suggests that he is a man of considerable social status.[70] The term σύντροφος indicates that Manaen is either "a lifelong friend of Herod" (ESV), "a member of the court of Herod" (RSV), or perhaps both.[71] Regardless of which interpretation is chosen, Manaen (like Joanna) serves as an early example of a believer who devoted himself to Christian ministry while also keeping close ties to a local authority under Roman jurisdiction. Like the Ethiopian eunuch, Manaen remains steadfast to his Christian faith while also having special access to the relational community of a powerful political ruler.[72] Although it is unclear whether Manaen became a Christian during or after the lifetime of Herod Antipas, his link to the Herodian court would have exposed him to the same types of elite social networks that Theophilus would have also been a part of. Furthermore, Manaen's ministry as a prophet and teacher shows that he is recognized alongside Barnabas and Saul as a leader of significant spiritual influence in the church at Antioch (13:1).

---

67. Levine and Witherington, *Luke*, 224.

68. Bock, *Luke*, 1:713.

69. Keener explains, "'Manaen' (Μαναήν) is the LXX name Μαναημ (2 Kgs 15:14–23; cf. Jos., *Ant.* 9.229–33)—that is, the Greek form of 'Menahem' ('Comforter')." Keener, *Acts*, 3:1988.

70. Keener points out, "This positive member of the Herodian circle contrasts starkly with the demise of a Herod just reported in Acts 12:23." Keener, *Acts*, 3:1988.

71. The story of Rehoboam illustrates the amount of influence that can be held by those who grow up with a ruler (1 Kgs 12:8, 10, 14). Bock, *Acts*, 439; Keener, *Acts*, 3:1988–90.

72. Keener, *Acts*, 3:1988.

A Fitting Ending: Paul in Rome
(Acts 28:16–31)

Fittingly, the book of Acts ends with Paul reaching the heart of the empire, Rome (28:16–31).[73] In the overall arc of the book of Acts, Paul's arrival in Rome demonstrates the spread of the gospel to "the end of the earth" in fulfillment of Acts 1:8. Interestingly, this final passage also contributes to our study of Roman authorities by mentioning two individuals whose positions span the spectrum from the lowest to the highest ranks of the empire.

In Rome, Paul is granted his own living quarters where he is guarded by a Roman soldier (28:16). Even though he is under the watchful eye of a Roman representative, Paul can freely proclaim the gospel "with all boldness and without hindrance" (28:31). In this soldier, we see a final depiction of the harmonious type of relationship that Roman authorities can have with believers. This unnamed soldier embodies the paradoxical way in which agents of Rome can become proponents of the gospel. Like the centurions whom we met earlier in the narrative, he models a type of relationship with Christians that is far from antagonistic. Instead, the soldier's leniency enables friends to supply Paul's needs and facilitates the spread of the gospel.[74] Although the Roman establishment appears to be an evil empire that persecutes Jesus and his followers, the soldier reminds us that individual Roman agents can surprisingly serve as proponents of the gospel. Thus, under the custody of a Roman soldier, Paul experiences a level of freedom that is unmatched in the rest of the book of Acts. This freedom, however, is met with a mixed response from his Jewish hearers (28:24). Although the Jews may "see but never perceive" (28:26), Paul declares that "this salvation of God has been sent to the Gentiles" and that "they will listen" (28:28).

The ending of Acts leaves the reader in suspense. As Paul boldly shares the gospel with visitors, he awaits his opportunity to stand before the most powerful ruler of all, Caesar (28:19; see also 25:8–12, 26:32). How would the emperor respond to Paul's case? If we learned anything from

---

73. "Paul's ministry of welcoming and proclaiming is no longer being done in a Roman colony such as Philippi. It is no longer being done in a provincial capital such as Ephesus. It is no longer being done in a governor's province praetorium in Caesarea. Nothing less than the capital of the empire is now Paul's location." Cassidy, "Paul's Proclamation," 147. For more on the ending of Acts, see Troftgruben, *Conclusion Unhindered*, 114–43; Puskas, *Conclusion of Luke-Acts*, 106–35; Alexander, *Acts*, 207–29.

74. Rapske, *Paul in Roman Custody*, 182; Skinner, *Locating Paul*, 164–66.

Paul's appearances before Roman governors (24:10–21, 26:2–29), we can be assured that Paul would eagerly seize any opportunity to testify before the emperor concerning the good news of "the resurrection of the dead" (24:21). Although Luke does not give further details regarding Caesar, Paul's epistolary reference to "the saints . . . of Caesar's household" (Phil 4:22) indicates that the gospel reached the emperor's closest confidants.

Conclusion

In this chapter, I supported my main argument concerning centurions by presenting a broader range of evidence from the rest of Luke–Acts. Through several examples in Acts, we saw that Luke's attention towards government authorities was not limited to Roman centurions. In addition to the centurions whom we met earlier in this book, Luke demonstrates that believing officials were found in other cultural contexts including Egypt and Ethiopia. Within the Roman establishment, we met Christian converts including the proconsul Sergius Paulus, as well as Joanna and Manaen who were closely connected with Herod Antipas. Overall, we found that Luke–Acts presents a variety of government authorities who either become believers or supporters of Christians.

Acts concludes with Paul witnessing in Rome under the custody of a Roman soldier as he awaits his hearing before Caesar. Though the narrative ends, Paul's reference to believers within Caesar's household in Phil 4:22 shows that the gospel made significant inroads among the Roman establishment. These unnamed converts within Caesar's household demonstrate that some elites in the empire were turning to Christ. Since believers existed among Caesar's inner circle, it is likely that the emperor would have heard the gospel as well. Indeed, the gospel was not only for Theophilus and the centurions, but for Caesar, and everyone else in the Roman establishment. Nevertheless, as Rowe points out, the gospel was not so much about government takeover as it was about an alternative way of life marked by loyalty to Christ above all.[75] In the next chapter, we will turn our attention to the relationship between the gospel and Roman authorities in early church history beyond the narrative of Luke–Acts.

---

75. Rowe, *World Upside Down*, 136.

6

Roman Officials as Proponents of the Gospel in Early Church History

> Gaianus, also called Porphyrius, centurion, our brother, has made the pavement at his own expense as an act of liberality.
>
> —THE GAIANUS INSCRIPTION (C. AD 230)[1]

> The State is filled with Christians.... Both sexes, every age and condition, even high rank, are passing over to the profession of the Christian faith.
>
> —TERTULLIAN (C. AD 197)[2]

AT AN ANCIENT CROSSROADS between Capernaum and Caesarea—the two locations where the first centurion converts appear in Luke and Acts—archaeologists excavating ancient Megiddo uncovered the mosaic floor of one of the earliest known Christian meeting places.[3] This mosaic—which

---

1. Tepper and Di Segni, *Christian Prayer Hall*, 34.
2. Tertullian, *Apology* 1 (*ANF* 3:17).
3. Tepper and Di Segni, *Christian Prayer Hall*, 50. Tepper and Di Segni date the ancient prayer hall at Megiddo around the year AD 230, placing it in the same time period as the Dura-Europos Church, which is widely known as the oldest Christian church. The Dura-Europos Church is typically dated between the years AD 233 to 256 (González, *Story of Christianity*, 1:111; Angelo and Silver, "Debating the Domus Ecclesiae," 267). Other scholars question such an early dating of the Megiddo prayer hall, suggesting that

some date to the third century—includes an inscription commemorating a centurion named Gaianus, who commissioned the flooring at his own expense. The inscription refers to Gaianus as "our brother," suggesting a friendly relationship between the centurion and the believers in Megiddo. Although scholars differ on the exact nature of his connection to the local believers, the inscription indicates that Gaianus was at least a friend—if not a member—of the church.[4] Regardless of whether the centurion was a believer or a nonbelieving patron, the Gaianus Inscription provides a striking example of a local Roman official who was sympathetic towards the early church. Indeed, Gaianus's support for local Christians reminds us of the centurion convert who built the Capernaum synagogue (Luke 7:5) and Cornelius who "gave alms generously to the people" (Acts 10:2). The Gaianus Inscription provides an important link from the centurion protagonists in Luke–Acts to similar government authorities in early church history under Roman rule.[5]

In this chapter, and the next, we will trace the theme of supportive government officials from the pages of Luke–Acts into church history. Chapter 6 will make a more direct connection to Luke–Acts by focusing on the first few centuries of church history under the Roman Empire. Chapter 7 will extend our analysis to another cultural and historical context by examining the theme of supportive government officials during fourteen hundred years of Chinese history. In both chapters, I will survey key historical data with the goal of demonstrating typical issues that arise when officials serving an "evil empire" seek to either embrace the gospel or treat Christians favorably. The benefit of examining these two cultural contexts—Roman and Chinese—is that each one will act as a lens to highlight different sets of issues that arose in our earlier analyses of sympathetic government authorities in the Bible.

The goal of this chapter is to answer a few related questions. How did Roman authorities view Christians in the early centuries of church history? What historical evidence is there for believers serving within the Roman establishment? If believers could make positive contributions

---

it was either built in the third century or it was a Roman building that was later adapted for Christian use after Constantine's Edict of Milan in AD 313 (Adams, "Ancient Church at Megiddo," 65–66).

4. Adams maintains that Gaianus was a believer, while Runesson argues that Gaianus was merely a patron rather than a member of the church. Adams, "Ancient Church at Megiddo," 64–66; Runesson, "Centurions in the Jesus Movement?," 144–49.

5. Runesson, "Centurions in the Jesus Movement?"

to society, what tensions would be felt by an individual who remained embedded within the Roman establishment? To address these issues, I will survey several cases where Christians served within the Roman government, including during times of state persecution. In some instances, believers served the empire as soldiers, centurions, or magistrates. Other times, disciples of Christ would face unresolvable tensions that precluded them from serving God while maintaining loyalty to Rome. Throughout this chapter, the issue of military service will provide a critical point of convergence between our study of centurions and the potential for Christian influence upon the Roman Empire.

This chapter is divided into five parts that unfold in roughly chronological order. First, I will provide an overview of how Roman officials viewed Christians. Second, I will demonstrate how apologists defended the faith before officials by highlighting the church's positive contributions to Roman society, especially through the involvement of Christians in the military. The third section discusses the problematic religious implications of military service, drawing especially upon Tertullian's analysis of the limits of loyalty to Rome and its emperor. In the fourth part, we will assess a situation that Tertullian probably never envisioned—the Christianization of a Roman emperor. Finally, we will look to Augustine's "two cities" model as an overall framework for understanding how believers can broadly approach the topic of serving within an evil empire.

Roman Officials' Ambivalence Towards Christians

Earlier in this book, I argued that Luke–Acts was written to Theophilus, who was most likely a high-ranking Roman official. Though we know little about Theophilus, several encounters within Luke's narrative reflect the overall ambivalence with which Roman magistrates viewed Jesus and his followers. In this section, I aim to paint a broader picture of Roman officials' views of Christians. Outside of the New Testament, the earliest glimpse of Christianity from the perspective of a Roman magistrate comes through the letters of Pliny the Younger, a governor in Asia Minor during the early second century. Writing in the year AD 112, Pliny's perception of the church is reflected in a letter that he sent to Emperor Trajan where he assesses the economic struggles of Bithynia and Pontus. Looking to mitigate potential causes of social unrest, Trajan tasked Pliny with the job of dissolving any political clubs in the region.⁶ When Pliny arrives in coastal Pontus, he is approached by local citizens who complain that Christians had stopped making sacrifices, bringing economic loss upon local merchants (see also Acts 19:24–27).⁷ In *Epistle* 10.96, Pliny reports to Trajan that he does not know why believers are being charged, other than for bearing "the mere name of Christian."⁸ He finds no guilt in them since all they do is gather for worship and live virtuous lives.⁹ In response, Trajan advises Pliny not to seek out Christians but to test all who are brought to him by examining their loyalty to Roman gods. Anyone who agrees to pray to Roman gods could be released from punishment. Emperor Trajan's desire to treat Christians fairly is reflected in his reply to Pliny:

> You have followed the right course of procedure, my dear Pliny, in your examination of the cases of persons charged with being Christians, for it is impossible to lay down a general rule to a fixed formula. These people must not be hunted out; if they are brought before you and the charge against them is proved, they must be punished, but in the case of anyone who denies that he is a Christian, and makes it clear that he is not by offering prayers to our gods, he is to be pardoned as a result of his repentance however suspect his past conduct may be.¹⁰

Trajan's advice reveals one of the deepest points of contention between the church and Roman society. To what extent could a believer express loyalty to Rome and its idolatrous practices while also remaining firm in their faith? This is a topic that we will revisit in our discussion of military service. But for now, let's continue our survey of Roman perspectives on Christians.

Opponents of Christianity often caricatured it as a religion for the uneducated rather than the Roman elite. Writing around AD 185, the Greek philosopher Celsus argues that Christianity is popular "in the lower classes . . . because of its vulgarity and the illiteracy of its adherents."¹¹ According to Celsus, the church thrived among the "ignorant" and there

---

6. Wilken, *Christians as the Romans Saw Them*, 10.

7. Wilken, *Christians as the Romans Saw Them*, 15.

8. Pliny the Younger, *Epistle* 10.96 (Radice, 293).

9. Wilken, *Christians as the Romans Saw Them*, 22.

10. Pliny the Younger, *Epistle* 10.97 (Radice, 295). Following Trajan's custom, his letter of reply to Pliny was included in Pliny's collection of correspondence.

11. Celsus, *On the True Doctrine*, 57. See also Origen, *Against Celsus* 1.27 (*ANF* 4:408).

were "few moderate, reasonable, and intelligent people" who believed in the message of Jesus.[12] Moreover, Celsus argues that if everyone converted, then the Roman Empire would be overturned because believers shunned civic duty.[13] As I showed earlier, Luke–Acts offers a powerful defense against Celsus's critiques by detailing the conversions of intelligent Roman officials such as the centurion at Capernaum, Cornelius, and Sergius Paulus. Nevertheless, though Celsus overstates his case at times, he rightly identifies the tension that early Christians faced as dual citizens of the Roman Empire and the kingdom of God.[14] How did the early church deal with the difficulties raised by their critics?

Defending the Faith Before Roman Officials

Just as Jesus and Paul testified before Roman magistrates in Luke–Acts, so also several early apologists devoted themselves to the task of upholding the rationality of the gospel within Roman society. In response to their critics, the apologists wrote several letters appealing to Roman magistrates to provide religious protection. Starting in the early second century, Quadratus and Aristides addressed their apologies to Emperor Hadrian.[15] Similarly, Athenagoras's *Plea for Christians* (c. AD 177) was written to Emperor Marcus Aurelius and his son Commodus.[16] Justin Martyr wrote his *First Apology* to Emperor Antoninus Pius and his *Second Apology* to the Roman senate.[17] In northern Africa, Tertullian addressed his *Apology* (c. AD 197) to the senatorial class and his work *To Scapula* (c. AD 212) to the local proconsul at Carthage.[18]

---

12. Celsus, *On the True Doctrine*, 57. See also Origen, *Against Celsus* 1.27 (*ANF* 4:408).

13. Celsus, *On the True Doctrine*, 124. See also Origen, *Against Celsus* 8.68 (*ANF* 4:665–66).

14. Harnack, *Militia Christi*, 72–73.

15. Eusebius, *Ecclesiastical History* 4.3.1–3 (*NPNF*² 1:175); Aristides, *Apology* introduction (*ANF* 9:263).

16. Athenagoras, *Plea for Christians* introduction (*ANF* 2:129). Swift, *Early Fathers*, 35.

17. Justin Martyr, *First Apology* 1 (*ANF* 1:163); Justin Martyr, *Second Apology* 1 (*ANF* 1:188).

18. Tertullian, *Apology* 1 (*ANF* 3:17). Often tailoring his arguments to the needs of the moment, Tertullian's writings were polemical, while at times seemingly inconsistent and ambiguous (Swift, *Early Fathers*, 38). For a brief overview of Tertullian's life, see

In his letter *To Scapula*, Tertullian of Carthage (c. AD 160 to c. 220) defends his fellow believers against state persecution by demonstrating that they were upright citizens. Significantly, his letter also suggests that some believers at Carthage hold high positions in the government and are personally known to the proconsul. If Scapula were to execute all Christians of Carthage, he would be decimating "a multitude" of good people including his own "relatives and companions" and "men of your own order, and noble ladies, and all the leading persons of the city." Indeed, Tertullian argues, "Spare yourself, if not us poor Christians! Spare Carthage, if not yourself!"[19] Tertullian's appeal to the proconsul suggests that the gospel had won converts among Roman elites and rulers in third-century Carthage, just as it had in the first-century narratives of Luke–Acts. These elite converts remind us of the Ethiopian eunuch (Acts 8:26–40), the proconsul Sergius Paulus (Acts 13:4–12), and the believers among the inner circle of Herod Antipas (Luke 8:3, Acts 13:1).

Though not always explicitly seeking to convert their government leaders, the early apologists often connect their rational defenses for the gospel with the positive contributions that believers had on Roman society. Justin Martyr is one such apologist who leverages Christian moral conduct to exhort Roman officials to consider the credibility of the gospel. Justin argues that believers are known for upright behavior, despite being wrongfully accused as evildoers.[20] For Justin, the testimony of changed lives is itself a powerful apologetic, since "we who formerly delighted in fornication ... now embrace chastity alone," and "we who valued above all things the acquisition of wealth and possessions, now bring what we have into a common stock, and communicate to everyone in need."[21] Thus, believers, "more than all other men," ought to be viewed as "helpers and allies in promoting peace" because of their ethical lifestyles.[22] In Justin's words, Christians worship God alone while "in other things we gladly serve you, acknowledging you as kings and rulers of men" (see Luke 20:25).[23]

Litfin, "Tertullian of Carthage," 85–101; Tertullian and Minucius Felix, *Apologetical Works and Octavius*, vii.

19. Tertullian, *To Scapula* 5 (ANF 3:107–8).
20. Justin Martyr, *First Apology* 7 (ANF 1:165).
21. Justin Martyr, *First Apology* 14 (ANF 1:167).
22. Justin Martyr, *First Apology* 12 (ANF 1:166).
23. Justin Martyr, *First Apology* 17 (ANF 1:168).

One important way that some early believers demonstrated allegiance to Rome was through military service. Perhaps the most significant report of early Christians serving in the Roman military comes from the account of the Twelfth Legion (*Legio XII Fulminata*) which was based in Cappadocia during the rule of Marcus Aurelius (AD 161–180).[24] While fighting against the Quadi, a group of soldiers prayed for divine help and received a miraculous answer.[25] A thunderstorm arose, providing much-needed hydration to the beleaguered Roman troops and scattering the enemy forces.[26] According to Tertullian, this "well-known" event was one among many examples of the positive impact that believers had on Roman society.[27] The account of the Thundering Legion demonstrates that after the time of the New Testament, some Christians continued to serve in the Roman military, in the vein of John the Baptist's instructions to soldiers in Luke 3:14. By choosing to remain embedded within the Roman army, these believers left a lasting impression upon the emperor.

The Twelfth Legion caused Marcus Aurelius to hold a more positive view of the early church. In Tertullian's *Apology* to the senate, he mentions that Marcus Aurelius was a "protector" of Christians, partly because he remembered the effective prayers of the Thundering Legion.[28] In his list of the church's contributions to Roman society, Tertullian includes "We serve with you in the army!"[29] Writing to Scapula, the proconsul of Carthage, Tertullian explains, "A Christian is enemy to none, least of all to the

---

24. By the year 200, the Roman military had thirty-three legions stationed in nineteen provinces. These legions were typically identified by number and name. For a brief summary, see Campbell, *Romans and Their World*, 142–46.

25. The account of the "Thundering Legion" is recorded by Tertullian and the fourth-century church historian Eusebius. Eusebius, *Ecclesiastical History* 5.5 (*NPNF*[2] 1:220).

26. For this reason, the Twelfth Legion was also known as the "Thundering Legion."

27. Tertullian, *To Scapula* 4 (*ANF* 3:107). Though some dispute the details of the miraculous account, what is not disputed is the existence of a sizeable group of Christians serving in the Twelfth Legion. The presence of Christians in the Twelfth is supported by the fact that this legion was based in Melitene, which was near the Christian center of Edessa. Though we cannot be certain whether the soldiers converted while serving in the army or prior to enlisting, it is plausible that the soldiers would have heard the gospel through Christians living in the region of Edessa. Harnack points out that "the royal house of Edessa became Christian around the year 200, and already in the course of the third century, Christianity had penetrated Armenia." Harnack, *Militia Christi*, 74n8.

28. Tertullian, *Apology* 5 (*ANF* 3:22).

29. Tertullian, *Apology* 42 (*ANF* 3:49). Harnack, *Militia Christi*, 75. Here, I follow Harnack's rendering of the phrase that Schaff translates as "we fight with you" in *ANF*.

Emperor of Rome, whom he knows to be appointed by his God, and so cannot but love and honor."[30] While Tertullian was not always in favor of military service, these examples from his earlier writings show the positive impact believers could have upon the Roman establishment. Though not necessarily officials, the Thundering Legion shows how some in the early church demonstrated loyalty to Rome while also giving their highest allegiance to God.

The Limits of Loyalty to Rome

Following in the footsteps of the centurion converts in Luke–Acts, the Thundering Legion reflects the reality that some Christian soldiers chose to remain in the Roman military. However, there would inevitably be times when believers found themselves at odds with military culture. Helgeland explains that while separating religion from politics is a relatively recent development in Western societies, "the Roman world did not separate them: there was one world ruled by many gods."[31] The military, which was an integral part of Roman rule, was thus closely bound to the imperial cult through a system of rites.[32] The official aspects of the Roman army religion encompassed the following: consecrated symbols called "standards"; a sacred oath to the emperor as a rite of initiation; a liturgical calendar centered around prayers and sacrifices to Roman gods and emperors; and traditional ceremonies performed in sacred spaces within the military camp.[33] Despite the all-inclusive nature of Roman army religion, soldiers were unofficially allowed to hold their own religious beliefs if they did not disrupt the peace or promote what the Romans considered immoral.[34] Indeed, until Diocletian's Great Persecution in AD 303, the Roman army included many Christians who could navigate the religious obligations of the imperial cult.[35]

30. Tertullian, *To Scapula* 2 (*ANF* 3:105).

31. Helgeland, "Roman Army Religion," 1471.

32. Helgeland asserts that the Roman army was a "high-status organization" (Helgeland, "Roman Army Religion," 1471). The question of status is debatable since most auxiliaries were slaves and other non-citizens (Swift, *Early Fathers*, 26–27).

33. Helgeland, "Roman Army Religion," 1473–96, 1500–1504.

34. The worship of Mithra was the most famous of the unofficial religions practiced by Roman soldiers. Another well-known cult is the worship of Jupiter Dolichenus. Beyond these two, there were a countless number of other unofficial religions practiced by soldiers. Helgeland, "Roman Army Religion," 1497–500.

35. Helgeland, "Roman Army Religion," 1496–97.

The army was less accommodating, however, towards believers who openly objected to Roman religious practices.[36] For this type of soldier, life within the Roman establishment could come with intense pressures, especially during ceremonial events. This was because the Roman military was a symbol of the emperor's power.[37] Thus, military service became a place where believers had to navigate the tensions inherent in Jesus' twofold exhortation to "render to Caesar the things that are Caesar's, and to God the things that are God's" (Luke 20:25).[38] The tension between Caesar and God was inescapable for those wishing to engage with Roman society.[39] Indeed, when we look at early church history, we find Christians considering to what degree they could serve Rome while remaining faithful to Christ.

Eusebius reports one memorable incident involving Marinus of Caesarea, a devout soldier who was about to be promoted to the rank of centurion.[40] According to Musurillo, Marinus was likely a Roman legionary in *Legio X Fretensis*, which was stationed near Palestine around AD 260.[41] Eusebius recounts that Marinus "was honored for his military deeds, and illustrious by virtue of family and wealth."[42] When a position for centurion became available, Marinus was nominated for the role. However, as Marinus was about to receive the vine branch—a symbol conferred upon centurions—one of his rivals "came before the tribunal and claimed that it was not legal, according to ancient laws, for him to receive the Roman

---

36. Helgeland argues that as long as a Christian did not take the initiative to complain about Roman religion, they were generally not punished for their private beliefs. "Under these conditions it may actually have been safer for Christians in the army than in civilian society." Helgeland, "Roman Army Religion," 1497.

37. Rowe, *World Upside Down*, 107.

38. Elsewhere in the New Testament, this dual command is framed as a call to "fear God" and "honor the king" (1 Peter 2:17 NIV).

39. In Tertullian's day, soldiers were expected to participate in idolatry and burn incense to the emperor. See Tertullian, *On Idolatry* 17 (ANF 3:71–72) and Tertullian, *On the Crown* 11 (ANF 3:100). With the rise of Constantine, military service was no longer intertwined with emperor worship. However, even after the issue of idolatry was resolved, the tension between serving God and empire still remained (Swift, *Early Fathers*, 25). For more on the role of religion in the Roman army, see Helgeland, "Roman Army Religion."

40. Eusebius, *Ecclesiastical History* 7.15.1–5 (NPNF² 1:303). Marinus is one of several soldiers mentioned in Eusebius's Christian martyrdom accounts. Swift cautions, "Although the *Acts* of these Martyrs have to be evaluated with great care, they provide valuable insights into the problems faced by at least some Christians during the period before Constantine when they attempted to serve both God and Caesar." Swift, *Early Fathers*, 71.

41. Musurillo, *Acts of the Christian Martyrs*, xxxvi.

42. Eusebius, *Ecclesiastical History* 7.15.1 (NPNF² 1:303).

dignity, as he was a Christian and did not sacrifice to the emperors."[43] Marinus was questioned before the tribunal and given three hours to recant. After conferring with the local bishop, Marinus returned to the tribunal with a settled conviction to stand firm for his faith. Instead of being promoted to centurion, Marinus was immediately taken aside to be "beheaded for his testimony to Christ."[44]

Perhaps the greatest test of loyalty to Rome came when soldiers were commanded to persecute fellow believers. Eusebius describes two such incidents during the Decian persecution in Alexandria. In one case, a Christian soldier named Besas was executed after he resisted orders to persecute a group of believers.[45] In another instance, a squad of soldiers sided with believers who were on trial for their faith.[46] According to von Harnack, "it is certain that the whole little band of soldiers were Christians, or sympathizers, who in the critical moment came forth on the side of the Christians" whom they had been commanded to persecute. These episodes suggest the gospel had spread widely among the Alexandrian unit as early as AD 250 and show "how determined these Christian soldiers were to place their religion above military discipline."[47] Such loyalty is indeed what we might expect of a follower of Christ embedded in the Roman military.

Similar accounts of courage amid persecution are also attested by Tertullian. Although Tertullian's earlier *Apology* cast a positive light upon military service, his later writings display "a progressive hostility toward the Roman government."[48] Tertullian's *On the Crown* begins by recounting a bold stand taken by one soldier.[49] While the rest of his unit was wearing laurel crowns and lining up to receive awards of recognition, one Christian soldier walked with his crown in hand. The soldier, though not the only believer of the group, refused to wear the laurel crown out of loyalty to Christ. As a result of his defiance, he was ridiculed and put in prison to await martyrdom.

Tertullian defends the soldier's refusal to wear the crown from cultural and biblical perspectives. In pagan literature, the crown's purpose is

---

43. Eusebius, *Ecclesiastical History* 7.15.2 (*NPNF*² 1:303).
44. Eusebius, *Ecclesiastical History* 7.15.1 (*NPNF*² 1:303).
45. Eusebius, *Ecclesiastical History* 6.41.16 (*NPNF*² 1:284).
46. Eusebius, *Ecclesiastical History* 6.41.22 (*NPNF*² 1:285).
47. Harnack, *Militia Christi*, 91.
48. Helgeland, "Christians and the Roman Army," 150.
49. Tertullian, *On the Crown* (*ANF* 3:93–103).

to honor "those whom the world has believed to be gods." Thus, he argues that it is "abundantly clear how foreign to us we should judge the custom of the crowned head."[50] In other words, a Christian must never wear an earthly crown because "this attire belongs to idols, both from the history of its origins and from its use by false religion."[51]

Arguing from Scripture, Tertullian contends that God's people did not wear earthly crowns. Tertullian asks, "What patriarch, what prophet, what Levite, or priest, or ruler, or at a later period what apostle, or preacher of the gospel, or bishop, do you ever find the wearer of a crown?"[52] Indeed, only Jesus wore an earthly crown, and that was a crown of thorns designed by Roman soldiers to mock the Messiah.[53] Believers are to renounce their crowns just as the elders cast their crowns before the throne of God (Rev 4:10).

For Tertullian, wearing the laurel crown was just one among many military duties that conflicted with loyalty to Christ.[54] For instance, a Christian soldier would be punished for refusing "to burn incense to an idol." In addition, there were "many other offenses that are involved in the performances of camp offices, which we must hold to involve a transgression of God's law."[55]

About fourteen years after his *Apology*, Tertullian's treatise *On Idolatry* argues that believers ought not serve in the military since doing so would require taking up a sword to kill others.[56] Tertullian's pacifism is reflected in his rhetorical question, "Shall it be held lawful to make an occupation of the sword, when the Lord proclaims that he who uses the sword shall perish by the sword?"[57] For Tertullian, Jesus' command to "put away the sword" at Gethsemane (Matt 26:52) set a paradigm for the entire Christian life. Tertullian explains, "The Lord, by taking away Peter's sword, disarmed every soldier thereafter. We are not allowed to wear any uniform that symbolizes a sinful act."[58] Thus, believers must not "take part in the battle" or commit

---

50. Tertullian, *On the Crown* 7 (ANF 3:97).
51. Tertullian, *On the Crown* 10 (ANF 3:99).
52. Tertullian, *On the Crown* 9 (ANF 3:98).
53. Tertullian, *On the Crown* 14 (ANF 3:102).
54. Tertullian, *On Idolatry* 17 (ANF 3:71–72).
55. Tertullian, *On the Crown* 11 (ANF 3:100).
56. Helgeland, "Christians and the Roman Army," 150.
57. Tertullian, *On the Crown* 11 (ANF 3:99).
58. Tertullian, *On Idolatry* 19 (ANF 3:73).

violence using "the chain, and the prison, and the torture, and the punishment" that belong to Rome.[59]

Upon closer analysis, Tertullian's commitment to nonviolence may have lacked the biblical and theological depth that he displayed in his views on loyalty and idolatry.[60] For example, was Jesus' guidance at Gethsemane meant to set a paradigm for all situations, including the affairs of the government? If God gave the sword into the hands of earthly rulers, was it wrong for a Christian to serve society as a soldier (see Luke 3:14) or as a God-appointed earthy ruler (see Rom 13:1–7)? To be fair, in some of his writings, Tertullian shows awareness of the centurion converts in Luke–Acts and John the Baptist's instruction to soldiers (Luke 3:14).[61] Yet, he nevertheless uses Gethsemane as an overriding paradigm to argue against Christian military service.

Nevertheless, Tertullian was not the only voice to promote pacifism. Hippolytus's *Apostolic Tradition*, for example, provides a glimpse into Christian practices during the third century. In one section, we read, "A soldier in the lower ranks shall kill no one. . . . A catechumen or a member of the faithful who wants to join the army should be dismissed because he has shown contempt for God."[62] Though the *Apostolic Tradition* shares Tertullian's nonviolent stance, the very existence of these instructions "probably indicates that a growing number of men were somehow finding army life compatible with Christianity, and an absolute requirement that they desert was out of the question."[63] Those who found military life compatible with their faith perhaps anticipated concepts that would be stated more clearly by Augustine during the fourth century. But before we turn to Augustine, we must look to perhaps the most significant and controversial of all Christian government officials in the Roman era.

A Christianized Emperor

Connecting back to our study of Luke–Acts, if Luke indeed wrote to encourage a Roman magistrate to embrace the gospel, this goal was seemingly realized in the conversion of Constantine. With the rise of Constantine,

---

59. Tertullian, *On the Crown* 11 (*ANF* 3:99).
60. Swift, *Early Fathers*, 19–24.
61. Tertullian, *On the Crown* 11 (*ANF* 3:100).
62. Hippolytus, *Apostolic Tradition* 16.11 (Swift, *Early Fathers*, 47).
63. Swift, *Early Fathers*, 47.

the church would experience a level of religious freedom that it had never seen before. Constantine came to power during a time of political instability where various leaders ruled over different parts of the empire. Around AD 295, Diocletian, whose wife and daughter were believers, began purging the military of all Christians.[64] In AD 303, Diocletian ordered believers to be removed from positions of responsibility within the empire.[65] Many were martyred during Diocletian's Great Persecution, which continued until his successor, Galerius, issued the Edict of Toleration (AD 311) that turned the tides of the greatest period of persecution known to the early church.[66] In the next year, Constantine began to expand his rule following an important military victory at Rome.

Just as Marcus Aurelius saw God's power through the Thundering Legion, so Constantine's life would be marked by a supernatural experience in his battle at the Milvian Bridge. As Constantine prepared to march upon Rome, he famously instructed his troops to use a standard on their shield that resembled a Christian symbol. At the Battle of the Milvian Bridge (AD 312), Constantine defeated his rival Maxentius, and this incident became a critical moment in his journey of faith. Soon, Constantine's Edict of Milan (AD 313) would build upon the Edict of Toleration to further reinforce the end of state-sponsored persecution.[67] In AD 324, Constantine defeated another rival, Licinius, and became sole emperor over the entire Roman Empire.[68]

Several aspects of Constantine's policies reflect his attempts to Christianize the law. For example, he abolished practices that he viewed as dishonorable towards humanity such as crucifixion, disfiguring of the human face, and casting criminals to the beasts at gladiatorial games.[69] In other ways, however, Constantine's policies were typical of the times. Commenting on the character of Constantine's legislation, MacMullen points out, "He rarely approaches a problem as a Christian, rather as a whole man of the fourth century, of whatever religion."[70] Even though Constantine dif-

---

64. González, *Story of Christianity*, 1:119–20; Helgeland, "Christians and the Roman Army," 159.

65. González, *Story of Christianity*, 1:121.

66. Eusebius, *Ecclesiastical History* 8.17.6–10 (*NPNF*² 1:339–40).

67. González, *Story of Christianity*, 1:124–26.

68. Kreider, *Patient Ferment*, 245.

69. Barnes, *Constantine and Eusebius*, 51; Kreider, *Patient Ferment*, 263.

70. MacMullen, *Constantine*, 195.

fered from his predecessors because of his conversion, MacMullen claims that "the moral teachings of Christ had wrought no radical revolution" on most of his policies.[71] Significantly, Constantine was a military man both before and after his conversion. Starting at the Milvian Bridge, his adaptation of a Christian symbol as an army emblem and his attribution of victory to God's power reflect that he "clearly did not regard [Christianity] as a pacifist faith."[72] Thus, MacMullen describes Constantine as a violent ruler whose legacy was that of developing "a more truly Christian posture of active aggression."[73] Despite his shortcomings, Constantine left an enduring impact on the church's relationship with Roman society.

Constantine's support for the church was one of the most visible aspects of his legislation. Military martyrdoms ceased.[74] Soldiers were granted leave on Sundays to participate in worship services.[75] Believers were appointed to high positions in the government.[76] Imperial funds were disbursed to construct, enlarge, and beautify church buildings.[77] Some such building projects involved ornate decorations with "total disregard of cost."[78] Pilgrimage sites were restored as landmarks throughout the Holy Land. Property that was confiscated during Diocletian's persecution was returned to the church. Clergy and churches were granted legal privileges, food allowances, and exemptions from some taxes and civic obligations.[79] In Constantine, the church now had a ruler who "offered not only tolerance but alliance."[80]

On the surface, the emperor's support would seem to be a tremendous benefit for the church. However, in Constantine, we find that government support can be a double-edged sword that can have both helpful and harmful effects on spiritual vitality. Persecution and martyrdom were displaced

---

71. MacMullen, *Constantine*, 203.

72. Shean, *Soldiering for God*, 369.

73. MacMullen, *Christianizing the Roman Empire*, 50.

74. Helgeland, "Christians and the Roman Army," 163.

75. Barnes, *Constantine and Eusebius*, 48.

76. González, *Story of Christianity*, 1:140. Even so, however, MacMullen notes that "two-thirds of his government at the top were non-Christian." MacMullen, *Christianizing the Roman Empire*, 47.

77. Barnes, *Constantine and Eusebius*, 49.

78. MacMullen, *Constantine*, 235.

79. MacMullen, *Christianizing the Roman Empire*, 49; González, *Story of Christianity*, 1:142.

80. MacMullen, *Constantine*, 236.

by comfort and political power. Informal congregational worship in private homes was replaced by more institutionalized worship services held in beautiful buildings.[81] Increased wealth brought new dangers such as temptations to grasp position and power.[82] In many cases, one could legitimately question whether a new convert was motivated to follow the suffering Messiah or drawn to the status and influence that came along with being part of the church.[83] The sheer number of people flocking into churches meant that there was less time to catechize and disciple new believers.[84] Government officials in particular were tacitly incentivized to convert since "there was a clear if not very aggressive preference for Christians in office; and office was sought for material reward."[85]

Although Constantine seems to epitomize the Lukan theme of government officials as supporters of the gospel, many have debated the exact nature of the emperor's conversion.[86] In MacMullen's assessment,

> Few of the essential elements of Christian belief interested Constantine very much—neither God's mercy nor man's sinfulness, neither damnation nor salvation, neither brotherly love nor, needless to say, humility. Ardent in his convictions, he remained nevertheless oblivious to their moral implications.[87]

How could the emperor lack so many typical signs of a believer? It is important to note that while new converts typically went through a long period of catechesis, Constantine never submitted to such a discipleship process. In MacMullen's words, the emperor was "decidedly a Christian—on his own terms."[88] For example, even after his conversion, Constantine continued partaking in "pagan rites in which no Christian would participate."[89] Without any formal accountability, his syncretistic practices were unhindered by the repercussions that could have come if he placed himself under the authority of church leaders. Moreover, Constantine was not technically a Christian until he received baptism on his

---

81. González, *Story of Christianity*, 1:143–44.
82. González, *Story of Christianity*, 1:143.
83. MacMullen, *Christianizing the Roman Empire*, 114–15.
84. González, *Story of Christianity*, 1:144.
85. MacMullen, *Christianizing the Roman Empire*, 56.
86. Kreider, *Patient Ferment*, 251; Shean, *Soldiering for God*, 370.
87. MacMullen, *Constantine*, 239.
88. MacMullen, *Constantine*, 113.
89. González, *Story of Christianity*, 1:138.

deathbed in AD 337.[90] Thus, contemporary believers would have viewed the emperor as one who was "friendly or even inclined to become a Christian, but who had not taken the decisive step."[91]

Despite his sincerity, Constantine, like any other new believer, was a man in need of discipleship. Like Theophilus, he required further Christian instruction to gain clarity and certainty concerning the things he had been taught (Luke 1:3). Like Namaan, he needed guidance to navigate the pressures faced by a new convert who was also a powerful official in a pagan society (2 Kgs 5:18). Given his military background, Constantine was accustomed to a lifestyle marked more by harshness than humility, and more by pagan rites than Christian worship.[92] His lack of catechesis combined with the political pressures of being an emperor likely contributed to an underdeveloped spiritual life. If one thing is clear, Constantine "was a sincere believer in the power of Christ" which he had experienced at the Milvian Bridge.[93] At the risk of oversimplification, the logic of his conversion was that if God could deliver him from his enemies, then he would become a loyal lifelong servant to the Lord.[94] As a result, the emperor understood "the Christian God was a very powerful being who would support him as long as he favored the faithful" in his policies.[95] Although Constantine's faith was not developed to its fullest potential during his rule as emperor, he nevertheless left an enduring legacy upon both the church and the empire. It would take a few more decades for one of the early church's sharpest minds to develop a more comprehensive framework to help Christians conceptualize their relationship to the Roman Empire.

---

90. Thus, Kreider contends that Constantine did not become a believer until his deathbed, after going through a twenty-five year process of conversion. Kreider, *Patient Ferment*, 251, 273–74.

91. González, *Story of Christianity*, 1:138. He continues to explain that while some criticize Constantine for converting to gain political power among Christians, this is an anachronistic argument that reflects more upon modern Western society than the realities of Roman culture. Since most Christians came from the lower classes, the emperor had little to gain by securing their support. González, *Story of Christianity*, 1:138–39.

92. Kreider, *Patient Ferment*, 256.

93. González, *Story of Christianity*, 1:139.

94. MacMullen, *Christianizing the Roman Empire*, 43.

95. González, *Story of Christianity*, 1:139.

Augustine's Dual Citizenship Model

Constantine's conversion caused believers to reflect in new ways upon a question that has repeatedly surfaced in our study of supportive government authorities in Luke–Acts and early church history. That question is, How could a believer work out the tensions of serving in the Roman establishment while also remaining faithful to God? Earlier in this chapter, we saw how Tertullian sometimes drew sharp distinctions between serving God and empire. However, the thought of a Christianized emperor was a prospect that Tertullian had not considered.[96] Rome's newfound tolerance for Christianity meant that civil servants generally faced less religious persecution than in Tertullian's day. However, even as concerns of idolatry subsided, the broader issues of loyalty and pacifism remained.

Compared to Tertullian, Augustine (AD 354–430) benefited from two additional centuries of development in Christian thought. A prolific writer, Augustine was an influential early Christian voice on many topics, including civil authority, military service, and just war.[97] In the rest of this chapter, I will draw especially upon Augustine's dual citizenship model of understanding the role of believers within broader society. Augustine's thinking in this area centers around his conceptualization of two cities—one of God and the other of man—as developed in his *City of God* and related works. Thus, we will first look to his *City of God* before looking to letter 189 to Boniface, a Christian magistrate who exemplified many of the ideals that Augustine put forth.

Augustine's *City of God* casts a vision for how believers should relate to society using the framework of two cities: the earthly city of man and the heavenly city of God. The earthly city represents sinful humanity in rebellion against God while the heavenly city represents believers who belong to God's new humanity. Currently, the two cities are mingled together and await their final separation at Jesus' second coming.[98] As dual citizens, Christians belong to the city of God even though their present lives are embedded within the earthly city of man. Since the welfare of the two cities is inextricably linked during the current age, believers should

---

96. Swift, *Early Fathers*, 30, 81. On the implausibility of a Christian serving in the military, Tertullian writes, "Shall he carry a flag, too hostile to Christ? And shall he ask a watchword from the emperor who has already received one from God?" Tertullian, *On the Crown* 11 (*ANF* 3:100).

97. Swift, *Early Fathers*, 110.

98. Augustine, *Expositions on the Psalms* 62.4 (*NPNF*[1] 8:253).

seek the peace of the earthly city where they now dwell (see Jer 29:7).[99] As Augustine explains, "it is to our advantage that there be such peace in this life. For, as long as the two cities are mingled together, we can make use of the peace of Babylon."[100] This means that Christians, though living as exiles in the world (1 Pet 1:1), ought to strive for a well-ordered government that promotes the common good.[101]

Alluding to Cain's murder of Abel, Augustine recounts that the "city of man was first founded by a fratricide who was moved by envy to kill his brother, a man who, in his pilgrimage on earth, was a citizen of the City of God."[102] Following the path of Cain, sinful rulers rise up against others because of their "lust for domination" over others. This "lust for power harasses and afflicts the human race with serious evils."[103] Thus, when evil rulers conquer other nations, their "victory can be mortally poisoned by pride."[104] Since it is better to be ruled by the just than by evildoers, "when victory goes to the side that had a juster cause it is surely a matter for human rejoicing, and the peace is one to be welcomed." Thus, counterintuitively, Augustine argues that "the purpose even of war is peace."[105]

How might Augustine's dual citizenship framework apply more specifically to the life of a soldier or official? To answer this question, we look to Augustine's letter addressed to Boniface, a Christian who served as a Roman general and administrator.[106] Characteristic of Augustine, the letter

---

99. "Both types of homes and their masters have this in common, that they must use things essential to this mortal life. But the respective purposes to which they put them are characteristic and very different. So, too, the earthly city which does not live by faith seeks only an earthly peace, and limits the goal of its peace, of its harmony of authority and obedience among its citizens, to the voluntary and collective attainment of objectives necessary to mortal existence. The heavenly City, meanwhile—or, rather, that part that is on pilgrimage in mortal life and lives by faith—must use this earthly peace until such time as our mortality which needs such peace has passed away." Augustine, *City of God* 19.17 (Honan and Walsh, 226).

100. Augustine, *City of God* 19.26 (Honan and Walsh, 245).

101. Augustine, *City of God* 15.4 (Walsh and Monahan, 419). Swift, *Early Fathers*, 112–13.

102. Augustine, *City of God* 15.5 (Walsh and Monahan, 420).

103. Augustine, *City of God* 3.14 (Zema and Walsh, 149–50).

104. Augustine, *City of God* 15.4 (Walsh and Monahan, 419).

105. Augustine, *City of God* 15.4 (Walsh and Monahan, 420).

106. Augustine, *Letters* 189 (*NPNF*[1] 1:552–54). In letter 220, Augustine mentions that "Boniface had become Count of the Empire and of Africa, and had been placed in command in Africa with so large an army and so great authority." Augustine, *Letters*

opens with a call to love God and neighbor—and to work out this love within the context of Boniface's earthly occupation. Throughout the letter, Augustine encourages his friend to honor God through his role as a Roman official. Augustine's exhortation, "Do not think that it is impossible for any one to please God while engaged in military service," forms an overall summary statement as he recalls the biblical accounts of David, the centurion converts in Luke–Acts (Luke 7:1–10, Acts 10:1—11:18), and John the Baptist's instructions to the soldiers (Luke 3:14).[107]

In an interesting intertwining of categories, Augustine applies the Pauline concept of varying gifts in the church (1 Cor 7:7) to the different occupations held by individual believers. Comparing civilians and soldiers, Augustine describes that "some fight for you against invisible enemies by prayer, while you strive for them against visible barbarians by fighting." For Augustine, a Christian ought not to isolate himself from the complexities of life "in the midst of the erring and the godless." As citizens of the kingdom of heaven, "we should not wish to live before the time with the holy and upright only, that we may deserve to receive this reward in its own time."[108] Separation from evildoers is rightly meant for the afterlife as an incentive for those who endure faithfully during the age when the cities of God and man are intermingled.

Clearly, a Christian who serves in the Roman government or military would often face the tensions of living in a sinful world. One of the most difficult issues a believer would face was the prospect of war and violence. In Augustine's view, war is a necessary part of life in a fallen world. In a similar vein as his *City of God*, Augustine encourages Boniface to "hold fast to peace" and to wage war only "as the result of necessity." Echoing *City of God* 15.14, Augustine points out that even if war is necessary, the goal of war is to bring peace. Thus, Augustine exhorts his friend to be "a peacemaker even while you make war, that by your victory you may lead those whom you defeat to know the desirability of peace."[109]

Augustine contends that those serving in the military or positions of authority must ensure that their lust for domination is kept in check. This

---

220.7 (*NPNF*[1] 1:574). On this basis, Swift identifies Boniface as a Roman general (Swift, *Early Fathers*, 114) while Parsons identifies Boniface as a "Count or Governor in Africa under Honorius and Placidia" (see Parsons's translation of *Letters*, 266n1).

107. Augustine, *Letters* 189.4 (*NPNF*[1] 1:553).
108. Augustine, *Letters* 189.5 (Parsons, 269).
109. Augustine, *Letters* 189.6 (Parsons, 269).

is because "lust for power harasses and afflicts the human race with serious evils."[110] Thus, soldiers engage in war not to dominate others, but only as a last resort to promote the cause of peace.[111] If the need arises to kill an enemy, Augustine counsels Boniface to "let it be necessity, not choice, that kills your warring enemy."[112] Such guidance for Boniface reflects a significant point of divergence compared to Tertullian's pacifism. Drawing upon John the Baptist's instructions to the soldiers (Luke 3:14), Augustine suggests that when soldiers use force "as part of their military duty they are not guilty of homicide but are administering the law" and "that they are not avenging private wrongs but protecting the safety of the state."[113] Above all, the inner attitude of love for God and others must be the driving force for all outward behaviors, especially for Christian officials.[114]

---

110. Augustine, *City of God* 3.14 (Zema and Walsh, 150). Lust for power is a common theme in Augustine's writings.

111. In another letter, Augustine describes that war is to be used as a last resort, while diplomatic conflict resolution is to be preferred. "Preventing war through persuasion and seeking or attaining peace through peaceful means rather than through war are more glorious things than slaying men with the sword." Augustine, *Letters* 229.2 (Swift, *Early Fathers*, 115).

112. Augustine, *Letters* 189.6 (Parsons, 269).

113. Augustine, *Against Faustus* 22.74 (Swift, *Early Fathers*, 127).

114. Overall, Augustine's insights on love are very helpful. However, he was sometimes prone to overemphasizing inner attitudes while downplaying the importance of outward actions. Such dichotomizing appears subtly in his analysis of Jesus' instruction to patiently turn the other cheek (Matt 5:39). For Augustine, "these precepts pertain rather to the inward disposition of the heart than to the actions which are done in the sight of men." Augustine, *Letters* 138.13 (*NPNF*[1] 1:485).

Such de-emphasis on outward actions—when taken to the extreme—could lead to harmful results, especially in his dealings with those whom he perceived to be heretics (Kreider, *Patient Ferment*, 283). Although not a civic official, Augustine leveraged his church leadership role to influence state policies in his fight against doctrinal error within the church.

"Augustine was able to deploy 'love' to justify strong-armed policies—state-imposed fines, confiscating, and exile—that seemed necessary" for preserving the doctrinal purity of the church (Kreider, *Patient Ferment*, 285). Augustine rationalized such harsh treatment of heretics since he believed it was fundamentally motivated by love for his enemies, whose deepest need was to be steered away from theological error. Just as "a certain benevolent severity" is necessary to discipline one's own children, so a similar severity can be enacted upon one's enemies, as long as it is motivated by love. Augustine, *Letters* 138.14 (*NPNF*[1] 1:485); Kreider, *Patient Ferment*, 291.

In his dealings with the Donatists, Augustine justified the use of force in the name of bringing spiritual benefit (Augustine, *Letters* 93.1–2, 9 [*NPNF*[1] 1:382, 385]; Green, *Augustine of Hippo*, 141–43). By replacing the early church's hallmark of "patient ferment"

A Christian serving in the Roman establishment ought to be marked by integrity, even in dealing with his enemies. Augustine calls Boniface to keep any promises made towards enemies: "When your word is pledged, it must be kept even with the enemy against whom you wage war."[115] Moreover, Boniface is to show mercy to his defeated enemies because "mercy is due him who is defeated or captured, especially where no disturbance of peace is to be feared."[116] Above all, the integrity of a Christian soldier involves not only his combat life but also his inward love for God, as exhibited through attitudes of sobriety, moderation, and freedom from greed. Among these, the absence of greed, says Augustine, is the true mark of "a manly Christian."[117] The conclusion to Augustine's letter portrays Boniface as an exemplar of the above traits. Overall, letter 189 presents Boniface as a faithful believer who served as a high-ranking military official, akin to a fourth-century Cornelius.

Conclusion

In this chapter, I situated the discussion on Theophilus and the centurions within the broader context of early church history under the Roman Empire. Since Luke–Acts presents the conversion of officials without discussing their subsequent lives as disciples, the witness of early church history helps us to appreciate—and grapple with—the types of issues that arise when believers serve within an evil empire. By examining several examples between the second and fifth centuries, we saw how the early church interacted thoughtfully with Roman rulers who were often ambivalent towards the faith.

---

amid persecution with "impatient force" to impose right beliefs upon others, Augustine's approach to doctrinal conflict set a dangerous precedent for future generations. Thus, Augustine's brilliant "two cities" model became marred by the impression that Christianity is a violent religion and that "Christian mission—however loving its professed intentions—is essentially an exercise in imperialism." Kreider, *Patient Ferment*, 296.

115. Augustine, *Letters* 189.6 (Parsons, 269).
116. Augustine, *Letters* 189.6 (Parsons, 270).
117. Augustine, *Letters* 189.7 (Parsons, 270).

Extending upon my earlier analysis of centurions in Luke–Acts, I traced the thread of Christians serving in the Roman military into the early centuries of church history. I focused on the topic of military service for two reasons: (1) continuity with the theme of centurions in Luke–Acts and (2) to understand how the early church understood their relationship with the Roman Empire. While the church fathers held varying positions regarding military service, they were generally seeking to navigate the tensions inherent in Jesus' twofold exhortation to "render to Caesar the things that are Caesar's, and to God the things that are God's" (Luke 20:25). Several historical accounts demonstrate the positive impact of Christian soldiers and the limits of their loyalty to Rome. Indeed, many believers who served in the Roman establishment faced tensions between their loyalties to Christ and the Roman Empire. In this chapter, I demonstrated the types of pressures that Christians faced related to idolatry, violence, and religious persecution.

If Luke wrote to encourage a Roman official to embrace the gospel, this goal would have seemed to be realized in the person of Constantine. However, the story of Constantine reminds us that the conversion of high-ranking officials can come with much complexity. Constantine's rule brought state support and improved legal protection for the church. However, along with such support came unintended consequences that sometimes hindered the church's spiritual vitality.

In the fourth century, Augustine's *City of God* and letter 189 present a dual citizenship model that can help guide an individual who seeks to remain faithful to Christ while also serving in political leadership. Without downplaying the tensions involved in serving God and Rome, Augustine's approach helps to chart a course for how a government official might serve as a proponent of the gospel while serving within an evil empire.

7

Government Officials as Proponents of the Gospel in Chinese History

> Send me a hundred men skilled in your religion who before these idolaters may be able to reprove what they do.... When we shall see this we shall condemn them and their religion; and so I shall be baptized, and when I shall be baptized all my barons and great men will be baptized, and their subjects will receive baptism, and so there will be more Christians here than there are in your parts.
>
> —Emperor Kublai Khan's message to the pope, delivered via Marco Polo (c. AD 1265/1266)[1]

IN A QUIET COURTYARD near the base of a mountain on the outskirts of Beijing lie the ruins of an old religious site with a fascinating history. The Fangshan Cross Temple is one of three early Christian relics in the Beijing area that have survived centuries of political changes in China.[2] Although the Cross Temple was used by Buddhists at some point, stone carvings decorated with crosses and an ancient Syriac inscription—"those who look to him are radiant" (Ps 34:5)—indicate that the building was once

---

1. Moule, "Marco Polo's Description," 136–37.
2. The other two are a Ming dynasty inscription also located in Fangshan and a copy of a Syrian hymn discovered near Beijing University. Tang and Zhang, "Fangshan Cross Temple," 82.

associated with Christianity.³ While scholars debate the chronology, many believe the Cross Temple was used by Christians during the Yuan dynasty (1271–1368) or perhaps the Tang dynasty (618–907).⁴ Regardless of which date is correct, the Cross Temple attests to Christianity's long history in a land known for its resistance towards outside religions. How did Christianity reach Beijing so many centuries ago? And what role did government officials play in the spread of the gospel in China? This chapter will explore the surprising role that officials have played in the story of Christianity in China.

In his *History of Christianity in Asia*, Samuel Moffett insightfully explains that political rulers generally take one of three approaches in dealing with minority movements such as Christianity. They can join the movement, eliminate it, or control it.⁵ To Moffett's helpful taxonomy, I suggest that some officials find ways to support the Christian movement, even if they choose not to join or control it.⁶ This chapter builds on the previous one by providing additional historical examples of officials who served within hostile governments while also supporting God's purposes. Some of these officials professed to be believers, while others did not.⁷ While the previous chapter focused on the Roman Empire, this chapter

---

3. Tang and Zhang, "Fangshan Cross Temple," 82–84.

4. Tang and Zhang, "Fangshan Cross Temple," 88–92.

5. In a discussion of Christianity's encounters with the Sassanid Empire in sixth-century Persia, Moffett writes the following: "The choices open to a political leader facing the growth of a potentially dangerous movement were three. He could join the movement, as the Shah Kavadh had for a time done with the Mazdakians, he could eliminate it, as Chosroes himself had done with the same Mazdakians later, or, better yet, he could control it." Moffett, *Beginnings to 1500*, 231. In this case Chosroes I chose the third option (which, according to Moffett, was the best option), to control the Christians by appointing his personal physician, Joseph, a Christian, as the patriarch over the church.

6. In addition, officials can also go back and forth between positions of persecution and support, as was the case with Nebuchadnezzar.

7. As a side note, my purpose is not so much to examine the orthodoxy or personal theology of the officials who claim to be Christian. I acknowledge that upon close examination, some of those who claim Christianity could be seen as holding beliefs that are beyond the bounds of orthodox Christian faith. Generally, I will take an official's profession of faith at face value and recognize that a Christian political leader will typically encounter particularly challenging circumstances often fraught with tension and competing priorities. As we saw in the biblical example of Naaman, such individuals are often caught within situations of intense pressure where they face choices that sometimes threaten to compromise their consciences. Moreover, a newly converted Christian official would also need time to mature in their theology and practice.

will cover a broad range of sympathetic government officials across centuries of Chinese history.

The reasons for looking to China are threefold. First, China provides a complementary cultural and historical context compared to Rome. Many of our examples from the Roman Empire demonstrated a range of responses related to the tensions faced by Christians serving in the military. As we broaden our perspective beyond the Roman era, we will meet a variety of individuals who navigated similar tensions in different ways. A second reason for studying China is its significance in world affairs throughout history. Understanding China's history will help us to better grasp the situations of a significant population of Christians worldwide. Finally, China is commonly considered a country that is hostile towards Christianity. Without denying the realities of government persecution, I aim to show another side of the story by focusing on government officials who have become surprising supporters of the gospel throughout China's history.

The rest of this chapter will cover the roles of government officials as proponents of the gospel during five distinct eras of Chinese history: the Tang dynasty (618–907), the Yuan dynasty (1271–1368), the late Ming dynasty (1368–1644) and early Qing dynasty (1644–1912), the Republican era (1912–1949), and the Communist era (1949 to present). During each of these time periods, I will introduce individuals whose experiences reflect the diversity of ways in which officials can help Christians to operate within seemingly evil empires. Through these examples, I aim to show that even when a government appears to be hostile towards believers, there can sometimes be rays of hope that are manifested through the lives of individual officials who remain embedded in the overall system. Like the centurions in Luke–Acts, these government officials can become surprising proponents of God's plans and people in large or small ways.

Government Officials as Proponents of the Gospel During the Tang Dynasty (618–907): Beginnings

In 1623, a large black limestone was uncovered outside of Xian, the ancient capital of China. The stone, measuring nine feet tall and over three feet wide, is beautifully inscribed with a cross arising from a lotus leaf, along with a detailed inscription describing the earliest known arrival of Christianity in China. The Xian Stele monument is dated to the year 781 and commemorates the spread of the gospel along the Old Silk Road to the capital of China during the preceding century and a half.[8] Although Christianity had faced hurdles in China, its arrival from Syria was being commemorated by the emperor during a short-lived season of religious tolerance. Hundreds of words written mostly in Chinese (with some Syriac) recount the basic Christian message along with several key events surrounding the arrival of Christianity in China.

China was in its golden age. The Tang dynasty (618–907) was flourishing under its second emperor, Taizong. In the year 635, a Persian traveler named Alopen brought Christianity to China for the first time. It was an ideal time for the gospel to reach the Chinese. Ten years earlier or fifty years later, and Christianity would not have stood a chance. The first Tang emperor, Gaozu (ruled 618–626), was a committed Confucian who expelled Buddhism because he viewed it as a Western imposition upon Chinese culture. If he rejected Buddhism as too Western, Christianity surely would not have survived under his regime. But Emperor Gaozu's son, Taizong (ruled 626–649), was a different type of ruler. Taizong promoted a policy of religious tolerance, aiming for a balance between China's three major religions: Buddhism, Taoism, and Confucianism. In the year 635, Emperor Taizong welcomed the arrival of Christianity in China. Three years later, he would commission the building of the first known Chinese Christian church. The church was funded by the imperial treasury and built in Xian, which was the largest city in the world at the time.[9]

The Xian Stele recounts Emperor Taizong's reception of the Christian message brought by Alopen from Persia. The stele's inscription describes the emperor's friendliness towards Alopen in this way:

> Taizong, a cultured emperor . . . sent his minister of state, Duke Fang Xuanling, to receive him in the western suburbs and to bring him in with a warm welcome. After his scriptures were translated in the royal library, the palace officials investigated their teaching.

---

8. The stele is now displayed along with other cultural relics in the Stele Forest Museum in Xian, China. The monument is sometimes called the Chang'an Stele, reflecting the ancient name of the modern city Xian in central China. Another name for the monument is the Nestorian Stele, reflecting the widely held view that the earliest Christians to reach China were Nestorian. Upon closer examination, however, the theological views reflected in the Xian Stele and other early Chinese Christian manuscripts found from Dunhuang suggest that the believers were not Nestorian in their beliefs. Moffett, *Beginnings to 1500*, 306–12.

9. Moffett, *Beginnings to 1500*, 291–93.

After thoroughly understanding it to be suitable and true, special permission was given for its propagation.[10]

From this description, we learn that the earliest Christians in China did not merely breach the margins of Chinese society. The gospel message was welcomed by Emperor Taizong himself, who sent his secretary of state to receive Alopen and to facilitate the translation of the Bible into the Chinese language. Soon, the Bible was added to the imperial library.[11] Although the emperor did not necessarily become a believer, he endorsed the building of a church and the propagation of the gospel throughout his kingdom. In this sense, Taizong reminds us of King Cyrus of Persia, whose edict provided the protection needed for Israel to rebuild the temple (2 Chr 36:22–23, Ezra 1:1–4).

The Xian Stele also recounts several other government officials who became proponents of the gospel. One important official was Duke Guo Ziyi, known as the greatest general of this era for his role in overturning the An Lushan revolt of 756. Though Guo probably did not become a Christian, he became a great friend of the church and provided the military protection that the church needed.[12] The stele commemorates the duke's friendly relationship with the church using these words: "Duke Guo Ziyi, Secondary Minister of State and Prince of Fanyang . . . exerts himself for the Luminous community in the virtuous distribution of his wealth."[13]

Another important government official named Yisi was both a Christian leader and a general in the Chinese army.[14] The stele devotes a lengthy section to Yisi, describing him as both a "Deputy Military Commander" and a "priest; naturally mild and graciously disposed, [who] has learned the Way and follows it diligently."[15] The stele mentions several titles that Yisi bore showing that he was recognized as a political leader as well as a man of character. Yisi was a key assistant to Duke Guo in overturning the An Lushan rebellion and used his wealth to support the church, of which he

---

10. Thompson, *Jingjiao*, 213–14.

11. Moffett, *Beginnings to 1500*, 293. Taizong was known as both a warrior and an avid learner, with a library that contained over two hundred thousand volumes beside his palace.

12. Moffett, *Beginnings to 1500*, 299–300.

13. Thompson, *Jingjiao*, 223–24.

14. Unlike Guo Ziyi, whose name is known from other Chinese literature, Yisi's name is known to us only in the Xian Stele. Yin, "Institution of Chongfu Si," 112–13.

15. Thompson, *Jingjiao*, 222–23.

was a member. Although ethnically Persian, Yisi served as both a Chinese general and a Christian clergyman.[16] In the examples of Yisi and Duke Guo, we see Christianity's impact on officials within the Tang dynasty.[17]

It should be noted that Christianity remained a small movement among a culture that was dominated by Buddhism, Taoism, and Confucianism. Nevertheless, given the inroads that the gospel made among various government officials, it would not be accurate to characterize Christianity as a marginalized movement. Glen Thompson summarizes, "While [Christianity] always remained on the margins of Chinese life and culture, it was never totally marginalized. Most Chinese living in this period may never have known that [Christianity] existed, yet many highly placed government and military officials not only knew of it but appreciated the talents and integrity of some of its adherents."[18]

The Christian movement would decline during the later Tang era. Waves of persecution led to the destruction of the historic church building at Xian and increasing pressure upon Christians.[19] The An Lushan rebellion of 765 weakened the Tang dynasty, leading to its gradual decline. As the empire weakened in political power, it also became less tolerant of foreign religions, including Christianity. The Tang dynasty fell in 907 and so ended

---

16. Max Deeg proposes a probable lineage for Yisi, tracing three generations from Yisi's father, to Yisi, to Yisi's son Adam (whose Chinese name was Jingjing). Yisi's son Adam was the author of the text inscribed on the Xian Stele. Deeg writes, "It is quite probably that the father of Yisi was a North-Iranian refugee from Balkh whose skills had been appreciated in China where he could climb the social ladder without difficulties. His son Adam/Jingjing then may have been born or at least raised and have received a full Chinese education considering the high position of his father at court and in administration—which also would help to understand why he could act in the style of a fully educated *literati* in composing the stele text." Deeg, "Belligerent Priest," 114.

17. Deeg argues that the Xian Stele was meant as "a piece of religious rhetoric and propaganda aimed at securing the support of official Tang China for a Church, which compared for instance with Manichaeism, claimed a rather successful history in the realm of the Tang by bringing forward the eulogized biographical sketch of its most prominent representative," (i.e., Yisi). Deeg, "Belligerent Priest," 119.

18. Thompson, *Jingjiao*, 155. Thompson's original quote uses the word "Jingjiao," which was the Chinese term used to describe Syrian Christians during this time.

19. In the late seventh century, the Tang emperor was usurped by Empress Wu (690–705), who sought to stamp out Christianity as part of her pro-Buddhist policies. Under Empress Wu, Christians were persecuted and the historic church building at Xian was destroyed (Moffett, *Beginnings to 1500*, 293–95). Another wave of persecution came under Emperor Wuzong (840–846). As part of his pro-Taoist policies, Wuzong issued decrees in 843 and 845 against non-Chinese religions including Buddhism, Manichaeism, Zoroastrianism, and Christianity (Moffett, *Beginnings to 1500*, 303–4).

what Moffett calls "the greatest dynasty China has ever known, protector of religious liberties and for the most part the friend of Christians."[20] The empire that welcomed Christianity to China for the first time was now ousted, and, along with it, the Chinese Christian church virtually disappeared. On the apparent collapse of Christianity after the Tang dynasty, Moffett writes,

> The decisive factor was neither religious persecution, nor theological compromise, nor even its foreignness, but rather the fall of an imperial house on which the church had too long relied for its patronage and protection. Dependence on government is a dangerous and uncertain foundation for Christian survival.[21]

Although the Tang dynasty had ended, the story of Christianity in China was only just beginning. It would take many centuries before Christians would once again have an opportunity to influence the Chinese imperial courts. Nevertheless, the seeds of the gospel had already spread to other parts of China.[22] Those seeds would blossom in later centuries under government officials who would once again lend their support to Christianity.

Government Officials as Proponents of the Gospel During the Yuan Dynasty (1271–1368): Faith Under Mongol Rule

Following the Tang dynasty, China entered a period of political fragmentation, during which various smaller regimes ruled over different regions of the former empire. After a few centuries, political stability would come through the rise of a powerful foreign invader. This up-and-coming political superpower came from the northern regions beyond the Great Wall.

20. Moffett, *Beginnings to 1500*, 314.

21. Moffett, *Beginnings to 1500*, 313.

22. In 2006, another stone inscription, known as the Luoyang Stele, was unearthed in Luoyang, about 350 kilometers east of Xian. This inscription is inscribed with a cross, contains a Christian theological discourse, and names several individuals. According to the inscription, the Luoyang Stele is dated to the year 814 or 815 (Tang, "Preliminary Study," 110).

Another set of Christian manuscripts was found along with a trove of religious documents in the Dunhuang Caves, located 1,700 kilometers northwest of Xian. These manuscripts are traditionally dated as early as the seventh or eighth century, with some manuscripts dated to the tenth or eleventh century. On the traditional dating, see Moffett, *Beginnings to 1500*, 305. Jianqiang Sun challenges the traditional dating but still places some of the most important manuscripts in the years 745 and 1020 (Sun, "Re-Dating," 227). Generally, these dates suggest the continued presence of Christians in China for at least a few centuries after Alopen's arrival in 635.

Led by Genghis Khan, the Mongols took over China and conquered a vast swath of land encompassing Persia, central Asia, and southern Russia. In a stunning turn of events, all of China was now under the authority of its enemies. In Chinese historical narratives, the Mongol Empire is often portrayed as a destructive and foreign force—arguably their closest equivalent to an "evil empire." Yet within this apparently evil empire, shoots of Christian hope would sprout.

After Genghis Khan died, his kingdom was divided among his descendants. Genghis Khan's grandson, Kublai Khan, established the Yuan dynasty (1271–1368), initiating a century when the Mongols ruled over all of China. During this era, China became more integrated into international trade networks and exposed to a broader range of foreign ideas and cultures.

Kublai Khan's influential mother, Sorkaktani Beki, was a Christian who came from the Kerait people.[23] After her husband (a son of Genghis Khan) died, the widowed Sorkaktani successfully raised her four sons to become Mongol rulers over different regions of Genghis Khan's kingdom. Although Sorkaktani died before seeing the pinnacle of her son Kublai's rule in China, she was posthumously granted the title "empress" to recognize her influence upon the Yuan dynasty.[24] Sorkaktani was a committed Christian, but she also promoted religious tolerance towards Buddhists, Taoists, and Muslims.[25] Her pluralistic approach to religion left an enduring influence upon her son Kublai, even if he did not convert to his mother's faith. As Moffett points out, "Like his mother Kublai Khan was a friend of the Christians, but unlike her he was not a Christian himself."[26]

With the rise of the Mongols, Christianity would make its mark upon the highest government officials in China. Marco Polo, the famous Venetian merchant who came to China via the Old Silk Road, reported that Christians held official positions in Kublai Khan's imperial court. Around the year 1265 or 1266, Kublai sent Marco Polo back to Venice with a letter requesting the pope to send up to one hundred missionaries to China. Marco Polo records this bold invitation from the emperor to the pope:

---

23. Li, "Sorkaktani Beki," 350–51. The Kerait people were Christians whose spiritual lineage traced back to the Church of the East (sometimes called "Nestorian"). In China, this strand of Christianity was known by the names Jingjiao (景教) during the Tang dynasty and Yelikewen Jiao (也裡可溫教) during the Yuan dynasty.

24. Moffett, *Beginnings to 1500*, 443.

25. Rossabi, *Khubilai Khan*, 12–14.

26. Moffett, *Beginnings to 1500*, 444.

> Send as many as one hundred wise men of the Christian religion and who should know also the seven arts and who should know well how to argue and to show plainly to the idolaters and to the other classes of people that all their [religion is] erroneous . . . and who should know well how to show clearly by reason that the Christian religion is better than theirs.[27]

Significantly, Kublai Khan asks the pontiff to send Christians to convince the emperor of the legitimacy of their faith. If convinced, Kublai vows that he, his nobles, and his people would be baptized "so that the Christians in these parts will exceed in number those who inhabit your own country."[28] Although Kublai's interests in the Christian faith may have been tainted by his desires to make political alliances and glean from "the seven arts" of Western knowledge, his request was nevertheless met with a disappointing response. Rather than sending a hundred missionaries, Pope Gregory X initially sent only two Dominicans. Even more tragically, when these two missionaries encountered war in Central Asia during their eastward voyage, both men turned back on their journey before even reaching China.[29] Thus, although Kublai Khan was sympathetic towards Christianity, he ultimately remained unconvinced of its claims and never became a believer.[30]

Even though the Mongol emperor did not convert to Christianity, Kublai Khan welcomed several Christians to serve in his imperial court. Under Mongol rulers, believers held highly visible government positions, including roles as royal physicians and political advisors. One such high-ranking official was Mar Sargis, a Christian governor in the Zhenjiang

---

27. Moule, *Christians in China*, 129. According to Moffett, the "seven arts" could refer to Western science and learning. Moffett, *Beginnings to 1500*, 446.

28. Polo, *Travels of Marco Polo*, 160.

29. Moffett, *Beginnings to 1500*, 446; Moule, *Christians in China*, 130.

30. Moule, *Christians in China*, 136–37; Polo, *Travels of Marco Polo*, 159–60. Marco Polo recounts the emperor's interests in supernatural miracles as one reason that kept Kublai Khan from embracing Christianity as his own. When asked why he did not become a Christian, Kublai Khan cites his fascination with other religions whose adherents performed miraculous deeds such as supernaturally filling his cups with something to drink or controlling bad weather through their incantations. In the Christians, however, he saw no such miraculous deeds. Marco Polo records the following explanation from Kublai Khan: "Should I become a convert to the faith of Christ, and profess myself a Christian, the nobles of my court and other persons who do not incline to that religion will ask me what sufficient motives have caused me to receive baptism, and to embrace Christianity. 'What extraordinary powers,' they will say, 'what miracles have been displayed by its ministers?'" Polo, *Travels of Marco Polo*, 160.

district, located along the Yangtze River between Nanjing and Shanghai.[31] He was a descendant of a line of Persian Christian physicians who had served the Mongol court since the time of Genghis Khan. Around the year 1279, Mar Sargis established seven Christian monasteries in the Zhenjiang area, a reflection of the growing Christian influence under Mongol rule.[32] One official record from this region identifies about 200 Christians among a population of 13,500 inhabitants. Although Christians represent only a small percentage in this record, the statistics may understate the impact of Christianity in the region. A closer look at this official registry suggests that many of these 200 Christians were members of the government elite and that the total number of believers in the region may have been much higher.[33] Overall, the story of Mar Sargis illustrates how one local Christian official fostered the flourishing of the Christian faith during Mongol rule in China. After the time of Mar Sargis, the Christian community near Zhenjiang continued to benefit from a succession of Christian governors and assistant governors who were appointed by Kublai Khan.[34]

Perhaps the most visible Christian official of this time was Aixue, a Christian who originally came from Syria.[35] A longtime associate of Kublai Khan, Aixue was appointed by the Mongol emperor to oversee the government offices of astronomy and medicine. In 1273, Aixue was promoted to oversee a newly formed Bureau of Medicine. In the ensuing years, Aixue was sent abroad to negotiate foreign affairs on behalf of Kublai Khan. After completing his stint in diplomatic duties, Aixue returned to the imperial court where he was quickly promoted to become director of the Palace Library in 1287. Then, in 1289, Aixue was appointed as head over a new

---

31. His Chinese name is Ma Xuelijisi (馬薛裡吉思). Moule, *Christians in China*, 145–65.

32. Moffett, *Beginnings to 1500*, 448.

33. In this region, Christians were known by the name Yelikewen. The population statistics come from Thompson, who believes that most of these 200 Christians were members of the government elite. Almost all of the listed believers had foreign names, which suggests that (1) Christians comprised a significant percentage of the foreign population and (2) any local Christian converts may not have been included in this count (Thompson, *Jingjiao*, 171). Moffett, likely referring to the broader region around Zhenjiang, cites a total population between 400,000 to 700,000, including about 2,400 Christians (Moffett, *Beginnings to 1500*, 448).

34. Moffett, *Beginnings to 1500*, 448.

35. Moule, *Christians in China*, 228–29; Thompson, *Jingjiao*, 172. His Chinese name is 薆薛.

government office to oversee Christians across China.³⁶ In one sense, this form of government oversight elevated Christianity's status by granting it the official recognition long bestowed on most major religions in China. Moreover, there is no indication of whether Christians of the time felt negatively about this form of government oversight.³⁷

Before concluding our discussion of Christian officials under the Yuan dynasty, it will be helpful to look at two notable encounters involving Kublai Khan and Christian officials who sought to usurp his power. Although Kublai was generally supportive of Christians, it seems that not all Christians returned the favor. The first incident occurred early in Kublai's career, before he established the Yuan dynasty. Between the years 1260 to 1264, Kublai battled for control of China against his younger brother, Arikbuka, who was more inclined to his mother's, Sorkaktani's, Christian faith than Kublai was.³⁸ Although the conflict was likely more motivated by politics than religion, it was a precursor for another more serious incident where a Christian military leader was defeated by Kublai. Towards the latter years of his reign, Kublai Khan struggled to control the peoples living near the fringes of his empire. One of the most intense revolts was led by a Christian prince named Naian, a younger relative of Kublai Khan.³⁹ Naian assembled a huge army and rode into battle under the banner of the cross. However, unlike Constantine, who claimed victory by the cross, Naian was crushed in battle by Kublai's forces. When the victorious Mongols began to mock the defeated Christians, Kublai reproved his own men, saying that the Christian God vindicated him in battle by defeating his disloyal subjects who allied themselves with Naian.⁴⁰

In the defeat of Naian we are reminded that, unlike the Roman Empire, "Asia never produced a Constantine."⁴¹ Despite the emperor's request

---

36. This was called the Office of the Chongfu (崇福司) (Yin, "Institution of Chongfu Si," 316–19). According to the official *History of the Yuan Dynasty*, this newly formed office comprised about twenty officials spanning several ranks of Chinese government bureaucracy. The relevant section comes from book 89 of the official Yuan history (called the *Yuan Shi*, 元史), as cited and translated by Yin, "Institution of Chongfu Si," 312–13. In the ensuing few decades, the office was briefly elevated to become a "department" (*yuan*, 院) before reverting to become an "office" (*si*, 司) again (Thompson, *Jingjiao*, 174).

37. Thompson, *Jingjiao*, 175.
38. Moffett, *Beginnings to 1500*, 444.
39. Moffett, *Beginnings to 1500*, 455.
40. Moule, "Marco Polo's Description," 134–35; Moffett, *Beginnings to 1500*, 455–56.
41. Moffett, *Beginnings to 1500*, 455.

for missionaries and support for religious pluralism, Kublai never converted to Christianity. The usurpers Arikbuka or Naian were unable to bring China under a Christian ruler by defeating Kublai. Christianity in China would slowly blossom, rooted in soil far from the structures of Western Christendom. As we will see, Christianity in China would develop nonetheless, albeit along a different trajectory than it did in the Roman Empire.

With the fall of Mongolian rule in China, so too the church's strength declined much as it did after the Tang dynasty. The Mongol-led Yuan dynasty was replaced by the China-centered Ming dynasty (1368–1644). China reverted to its more isolationist tendencies and distanced itself from foreign influence. However, towards the end of the Ming dynasty, Christianity once again made an impression upon China's government officials.

Government Officials as Proponents of the Gospel During the Late Ming Dynasty (1368–1644) and Early Qing Dynasty (1644–1912): Jesuits in the Imperial Court

Christianity had already begun to take root in China under the Tang and Yuan Dynasties. At least three distinguishing features arise from our analysis of Christianity under those two dynasties. First, most Christians in China were foreigners rather than Han Chinese. Second, government officials played an important role in supporting the growth of Christianity in China. Third, Chinese Christianity lost significant momentum with the decline of the Tang and Yuan Dynasties that supported believers. For these reasons, the Chinese generally viewed Christianity as "a foreign religion protected and supported by a foreign government."[42] The Jesuit missionaries endeavored to change these perceptions.[43] In 1583, Italian Jesuits established a mission base outside of Guangzhou, a major city in southern

---

42. Moffett, *Beginnings to 1500*, 474.

43. Andrew Walls points out the formative role that Jesuit missionaries had on subsequent Protestant missions. Walls argues that the story of Western Christian missions is essentially a single story, even if some of those missionaries were Protestant and others Catholic. Walls writes, "The history of Western Christian missions is a single story, at least from the early sixteenth century. The Reformation complicates the story of missions, but it does not determine it. The roots of the work of the most adamantly Protestant missionaries lie in the work of Francis Xavier and Matteo Ricci and Pedro de Gante. In the non-Western world the attribute that first identifies Western missionaries is not that they are Catholic or Protestant, but that they are Western." Walls, *Cross-Cultural Process*, 49.

China. Among these early Jesuits in China was a bright young man named Matteo Ricci, who quickly became the leader of the group.[44]

A key part of Ricci's strategy was to engage locals through their interest in Western science and learning. This approach brought Ricci into the heart of Chinese elite culture. However, by 1585, the Jesuits had seen only twenty converts. Since the general population remained unreceptive to the gospel, Ricci became convinced that the only way for the Jesuit mission to succeed in China would be to gain the favor and approval of the emperor in Beijing.[45] Though Ricci may not have seen it this way, his ambition to reach the emperor would define the course of his life—much like Paul's dramatic appeal to Caesar, to which Festus replied, "To Caesar you have appealed; to Caesar you shall go" (Acts 25:12). Ricci spent more than a decade gradually moving towards the northern capital of Beijing. When Ricci finally reached Beijing, his request for an audience with the emperor was denied—likely due to interference from palace eunuchs, who controlled access to the throne. Ricci died in 1610 and, notably, was buried in Beijing at a cemetery donated by the emperor—an extraordinary honor for a foreigner at the time.[46] Despite never meeting the emperor, Ricci laid the groundwork for future Jesuits to gain entry to the imperial court. Notably, he also moved the Jesuit mission base to the southern capital of Nanjing, located roughly halfway between Guangzhou and Beijing. There, Ricci discipled several prominent Chinese scholars who influenced the government and intellectual life in the late Ming dynasty.[47]

The most influential of these Chinese elites was a man named Xu Guangxi, who was converted by the Jesuits and baptized as Paul Hsu.[48] Under Ricci's mentorship, Xu passed increasingly higher levels of academic

---

44. Three key leaders in the early Jesuit mission to China were Matteo Ricci, Alessandro Valignano, and Michele Ruggieri. After studying the recent history of Catholic missions in Asia, Valignano shaped the strategy of their Chinese mission in three ways. First, the Jesuits distanced themselves from Western colonial trade, which was seen as a hindrance to evangelism. Second, they abandoned oppressive tactics such as were used in the Inquisition, which had been applied in India in 1560. Third, the Jesuits adapted themselves to the local culture by embracing Chinese language, literature, and clothing. Eventually, however, Ricci became the leader of the Jesuit mission in China. Moffett, *1500–1900*, 106–7.

45. Moffett, *1500–1900*, 109.

46. Moffett, *1500–1900*, 113–14.

47. Moffett, *1500–1900*, 110–11.

48. Yang, "Hsu Kuang-Chi"; China Group, "Xu Guangqi"; Moffett, *1500–1900*, 111–12.

examinations, enabling him to ascend the ranks of the Chinese government. In 1603, Xu was admitted to the imperial Hanlin Academy and eventually became a top advisor of the emperor. While serving the emperor, Xu leveraged his government position to protect the Jesuit mission in China. In 1616, a high official in Nanjing initiated the first general persecution of Christians in China.[49] Although the Jesuits suffered some losses during this time, Xu's written appeal to Emperor Wan Li (ruled 1572–1620) defended the Jesuits from further setbacks.[50] Just as Daniel distinguished himself in the Babylonian court, Xu Guangxi became known for his expertise in Western mathematics, astronomy, and geography. In 1611, shortly after Ricci's death, the Muslim mathematicians in charge of the imperial calendar made a serious error in their prediction of an eclipse. Xu seized this opportunity and called upon a few of his Jesuit scholarly colleagues to correct the error.[51] From then on, a succession of Jesuit scientists were recognized as the emperor's trusted scientific advisors.

One of these scientists was a talented young Jesuit scholar named John Adam Schall von Bell. During his upbringing in Germany, Adam Schall was inspired by Matteo Ricci and learned the sciences in preparation to become a Jesuit missionary to China. In 1623, Schall began to serve alongside Xu in the imperial court to apply his knowledge of astronomy. While laboring as an astronomer, Schall also evangelized eunuchs and concubines, eventually leading as many as fifty concubines and forty eunuchs to convert by the year 1640.[52] Schall's position in the government also enabled the Jesuits to maintain their influence during the turbulent transition from the Ming dynasty to the Qing dynasty, which was established by the Manchu people of northeastern China.

As the Qing dynasty came to power, Jesuits continued leveraging their scientific expertise to sustain influence at the highest levels of the imperial court.[53] The Jesuits' expertise in astronomy was highly appreciated by the

---

49. Shen Que (沈㴿), an official in the influential Board of Rites, accused the Jesuits of having wrong motives for being in China. He pressured the emperor into signing an edict against the Catholics that led to Jesuits being arrested, humiliated, and expelled from China. Among those targeted were two Jesuit priests who corrected the calendar following the Muslim miscalculation in 1611. Moffett, *1500–1900*, 115; China Group, "Xu Guangqi."

50. China Group, "Xu Guangqi"; Moffett, *1500–1900*, 115–16.

51. Moffett, *1500–1900*, 115.

52. Witek, "Schall von Bell," 734.

53. Moffett, *1500–1900*, 115. Competing with Muslims and traditional Chinese

emperor because, in those days, "nothing of importance was embarked on in public or private life without first consulting the aspect of the stars."[54] The German Jesuit Schall was appointed as head of the powerful Bureau of the Calendar and later became director of the Institute of Mathematics.[55] During the early Qing era, Schall developed personal relationships with the regent, Dorgon, and the Emperor Shunzhi, reflecting the golden age of Christians in China. Imperial support reached a high point in 1650 when Shunzhi allowed the Jesuits to retain their Beijing mission compound and renovate the church that Ricci founded in 1605 which had since fallen into disrepair.[56] The emperor also provided the Jesuits with an annual subsidy from the imperial treasury. In one notable incident, Adam Schall was asked to pray for a sick daughter of the emperor's mother, a staunch Buddhist. When the daughter recovered, the emperor's mother increased her support for Christians as her faith in Buddhism waned. With strong support from government officials, some estimate that the total number of Christians in China grew to about 150,000 by the year 1650 and around 255,000 by the year 1664.[57] However, as the number of believers grew, so did opposition from those who resisted foreign influence in China.[58]

Ferdinand Verbiest, a Flemish Jesuit missionary, succeeded Schall as the head of the Bureau of the Calendar.[59] Under the third Qing emperor,

---

astronomers, the Jesuits ultimately won control of the Bureau of the Calendar through their application of Western scientific knowledge and instruments to precisely predict important eclipses in 1611 and 1644. Moffett, *1500-1900*, 117.

54. Attwater and Duhr, *Adam Schall*, 17.

55. Moffett, *1500-1900*, 117–18. It is difficult to underestimate the importance of the calendar to the Chinese government. "The Calendar . . . was both popular and scholarly; astrological and astronomical. While it gave information on the phases of the moon, eclipses and so on, it provided also a plan or system by which fundamental agricultural life and the work of the community was regulated. . . . The whole represented for the Chinese a kind of chain linking the Celestial Empire on earth with that of the heavens themselves." Attwater and Duhr, *Adam Schall*, 16–17.

56. Witek, "Schall von Bell," 734. This Catholic church building is still standing today, although it has been rebuilt multiple times since being found by Matteo Ricci in 1605. One of four historic Catholic churches in Beijing, it is known as the Nantang (南堂, literally "South Cathedral") because of its location in the southern part of the city.

57. Moffett, *Beginnings to 1500*, 118–19. Attwater and Duhr offer a more modest estimate of 150,000 Catholics around the year 1644. Attwater and Duhr, *Adam Schall*, 734.

58. Chinese opposition, along with the growing influence of the Dominican and Franciscan missionary movement, would lead to Schall being ousted in his later years. Moffett, *1500-1900*, 119.

59. Moffett, *1500-1900*, 124–25; China Group, "Verbiest, Ferdinand."

Kangxi (ruled 1662–1723), Verbiest ascended to even higher ranks of the government than Schall or Xu did under previous rulers. As one of China's greatest emperors, Kangxi granted a high degree of religious freedom to his subjects. Impressed by Verbiest and the Jesuits, Kangxi issued a decree of toleration in 1671, granting the church the right to own land. In 1692, Kangxi issued an edict granting Christianity legal status in China.[60] The emperor's edict legitimized Christianity in China and helped to support the expansion of further missionary work in the coming years.

However, the Jesuits' privileged position did not last long. In a surprising turn of events, Kangxi was drawn into the Rites Controversy that divided Jesuits from their Dominican and Franciscan missionary counterparts. The key issue in this debate was the degree to which missionaries should accommodate Chinese cultural practices, including ancestor worship. Kangxi sided with the Jesuits' more accommodating position but was frustrated by the pope's rejection of these practices. The Rites Controversy was a key factor that contributed to the eventual decline of Jesuit missions in China.[61] Tensions with Rome escalated until 1720 when Emperor Kangxi, exasperated by Pope Clement XI's rejection of Chinese rites, rescinded his support for Catholic missionaries and restricted their ability to preach in China.[62] Even though Kangxi eventually turned against Christians, this still does not diminish the vital roles played by late Ming and early Qing emperors who were strong supporters of the church.

Government Officials as Proponents of the Gospel During the Republican Era (1912–1949): The Rise and Fall of the Nationalists

Despite many ups and downs, Christianity grew in China during several notable periods of government support during parts of the Tang, Yuan, Ming, and Qing Dynasties.[63] Another such period emerged in the mid-

---

60. "We decide therefore that all temples dedicated to the Lord of heaven, in whatever place they may be found, ought to be preserved, and that it may be permitted that all who wish to worship this God . . . according to ancient custom by the Christians. Therefore let no one henceforth offer them any opposition." Neill, *History of Christian Missions*, 189–90.

61. Moffett, *1500–1900*, 125–26.

62. These restrictions continued and were formalized in 1724 by an edict from Kangxi's successor, Yongzheng. Moffett, *1500–1900*, 130–33; Leung, "China," 141.

63. For the sake of this study, which focuses on government officials, I will not cover

twentieth century, during the era of the Republic of China (1912–1949). After the fall of the Qing Empire, China entered a period of political transition and frequent turmoil marked by internal strife and foreign conflicts. During this Republican era, the Nationalist Party (Kuomintang) rose to power and included several prominent Christian officials. While the role of Christianity in Nationalist politics is a complex topic, its influence on both the government and the church during this period is significant and worth exploring.[64]

In 1912, Sun Yat-sen, a Chinese Christian with Methodist ties, helped inaugurate the new Republic of China as its provisional president. In a move that alienated some in the Christian community, Sun left his first wife and married Soong Ching-ling, who came from a prominent and wealthy Christian family in Shanghai.[65] She was the second of three daughters born to Charlie Soong, a Vanderbilt-educated Chinese Methodist pastor who later became a businessman and an eminent leader of the Young Men's Christian Association (YMCA).[66] Although Sun's tenure

---

the important contributions of Robert Morrison, the first Protestant missionary to China (who arrived in 1807), or Hudson Taylor, the founder of the China Inland Mission (who arrived in 1865). Both men were instrumental in shaping modern Chinese Christianity by reaching the Chinese at the grassroots level rather than through engagement in the Qing imperial court. For more on the lives of Morrison and Taylor, see Broomhall, *Robert Morrison*; Taylor and Taylor, *Hudson Taylor's Spiritual Secret*.

64. The Nationalist Party's corruption or internal strife are well-documented elsewhere. While acknowledging these blemishes, I aim to offer a more balanced account by highlighting areas where the Nationalist government supported Christians. Moreover, China's Christian scene was far from homogenous. Both Catholics and Protestants claimed a significant number of Chinese adherents. In addition, the Protestant landscape was significantly shaped by the Fundamentalist-Modernist controversy that divided much of the American missionary force into competing theological camps. Broadly speaking, the theologically conservative Protestants were more focused on individual conversion while those who leaned liberal in their theology were more interested in social reform. Both the liberal and conservative wings of Christians would benefit from Nationalist leadership, though in different ways. Bays, *History of Christianity in China*, 121–28.

65. Without excusing Sun's behavior, we should note that it was not uncommon for Chinese men of this era to take secondary wives or concubines. Women, on the other hand, were expected to remain faithful to their husbands. This dynamic reflects the low state of women's rights in China at the time. Kennedy, "Activism Among Women," 8.

66. After serving as a Methodist pastor, Charlie Soong became a businessman while remaining in lay leadership in the local Christian community in Shanghai. The Soong family maintained a complex web of religious, political, and business ties. Bays, "Soong Family," 28–29; Crozier, *Man Who Lost China*, 114.

as Kuomintang president did not last long, he eventually passed the torch to his close associate, General Chiang Kai-shek, who later married the third Soong daughter, Mei-ling.[67]

Chiang Kai-shek is a notoriously enigmatic figure.[68] Chiang was a Confucianist and a revolutionary military leader who was married multiple times. During 1926–1927, Chiang fell in love with Soong Mei-ling. To gain the blessing of his future mother-in-law, Chiang promised to investigate the claims of Christianity and to study the Bible.[69] In 1927, Chiang married Soong Mei-ling and upheld his promise by maintaining daily habits of prayer and Bible reading even though he had not yet become a believer.[70] In his new wife, Mei-ling, Chiang had found a trusted confidant, spiritual mentor, and influential political advisor for the challenging years ahead.[71]

After a few years of considering Christianity, which included reading the New Testament twice, Chiang Kai-shek was still not ready to publicly embrace the faith. It would take a dramatic military victory to strengthen his convictions. In some ways, the Central Plain War of 1930 became for Chiang what the Battle of Milvian Bridge was for Constantine and the Thundering Legion was for Marcus Aurelius. During this battle, Chiang became separated from his troops and surrounded by enemy forces. Disoriented in combat, Chiang said a prayer in which he vowed to become a

---

67. Throughout his life, Chiang Kai-shek would carry on the ethos of Sun Yat-sen. These striking words are recorded in Chiang's will which he wrote in 1975: "I have always regarded myself as a disciple of Dr. Sun Yat-sen and also of Jesus Christ." Crozier, *Man Who Lost China*, 15.

68. On the perplexing combination of Chiang's Confucian and Christian beliefs, biographer Brian Crozier writes, "Such paradoxes are not rare in men who make their mark upon the history of their times" (Crozier, *Man Who Lost China*, 4). Powell points out that "neither enemy nor friend found it easy to understand Chiang's religion" (Powell, "Chiang Kai-shek," 3). As Crozier points out, the enigma of Chiang extended to multiple areas of his life. Though outwardly calm, he was also sometimes known for having a hot temper. Though outwardly tough, he kept a private diary in which he "was humbly self-critical" (Crozier, *Man Who Lost China*, 15).

69. Since her father, Charlie Soong, had died, Chiang Kai-shek was left to negotiate the terms of the marriage with her mother, Ni Guizeng. Incidentally, Ni Guizeng was a descendant of a prominent Christian family whose lineage traced back to Xu Guangxi, the Chinese Jesuit who served in the Ming imperial court after being discipled by Matteo Ricci. Bays, "Soong Family," 27.

70. Wang, "Chiang Kai-shek's Faith," 197. For a helpful analysis of Chiang Kai-shek's daily devotional practices as reflected in his personal diaries, see Bae, "Chiang Kai-shek and Christianity."

71. Bays, "Soong Family," 29.

Christian if God would deliver him from his enemy. Soon, a snowstorm arose that allowed him to reunite with his own troops and win the battle. A few weeks later, he was baptized in the home of his mother-in-law.[72] Although some questioned the sincerity of Chiang's conversion, his lifelong personal diaries attest to the earnestness of his faith.[73] Significantly, he continued his lifelong habits of prayer and Bible reading long after the death of his mother-in-law in 1931.[74]

After his conversion, Chiang was known to give public testimonies of his faith during Easter, Christmas, and other special occasions.[75] In his personal diary, he often reflected upon the Christian virtue of self-sacrifice and its potential to transform Chinese society.[76] As the leader of China's new republic, Chiang aspired to revolutionize the nation through Christian principles.[77] Chiang's ambition is reflected in these words which he wrote to the Christians of China during Christmas of 1945: "Our entire nation needs faith in revolution, honorable morality and a Christian spirit of sacrifice."[78] In Chiang's view, Christianity could come alongside Confucianism to help resolve China's social troubles, as reflected in a diary excerpt from 1937 in which he writes, "For the Chinese people Confucianism is the authentic source of morality and ethics, and the ancestry of political philosophy, while religion, or Jesus Christ's spirit of service and sacrifice ought to be the spiritual doctrine."[79] Despite Chiang's ambitions for China, his efforts were stifled by many factors, including the Japanese

---

72. Chiang's faith reached another significant milestone in December 1936. After being kidnapped in Xian, Chiang sensed God's hand at work through his wife, who came to negotiate his release. Bae, "Chiang Kai-shek and Christianity," 4–5; Wang, "Chiang Kai-shek's Faith," 197–98; Powell, "Chiang Kai-shek," 50.

73. Powell, "Chiang Kai-shek," 2, 51–52.

74. Wang, "Chiang Kai-shek's Faith," 197.

75. Wang, "Chiang Kai-shek's Faith," 198; Powell, "Chiang Kai-shek," 101. For example, Chiang's radio address during Easter 1938 was translated and published in the United States (Chiang, "Why I Believe in Jesus").

76. Bae, "Chiang Kai-shek and Christianity," 7.

77. In the first half of his Easter 1938 radio address, titled "Why I Believe in Jesus," Chiang argues that Jesus was a revolutionary who came to enact a national, social, and religious revolution (Chiang, "Why I Believe in Jesus," 723). The latter half of the speech focuses upon Jesus' "spirit of universal love" and the social impact that Christian faith can have upon China (Chiang, "Why I Believe in Jesus," 724).

78. Bae, "Chiang Kai-shek and Christianity," 7.

79. Chiang Kai-shek Diaries, Apr. 18, 1937, quoted in Bae, "Chiang Kai-shek and Christianity," 7.

invasion of China, strife within the Nationalist Party, and conflicts with the Chinese Communist Party.[80] Moreover, Chiang's authoritarian leadership style and collusion with the corrupt practices of the Nationalist Party alienated him from many.[81]

Nevertheless, under Chiang Kai-shek, believers in China benefitted from an overall environment of religious tolerance.[82] In parts of China, both Christian missions and Chinese indigenous churches flourished during the relatively tranquil mid-1930s.[83] Chinese Christians also influenced society through important initiatives related to women's rights, medical work, and educational reform.[84] Believers of this time period opposed social ills such as opium use and the practice of foot binding for girls, while also establishing Christian institutions such as hospitals, schools, and universities.[85] While the Nationalist government previously opposed religious education in schools, Chiang Kai-shek and Soong Mei-ling were instrumental in relaxing these regulations so that Christian schools were allowed to instruct students in the faith.[86] Some of Chiang's other attempts at integrating Christianity into

---

80. Chiang's focus on eliminating Communism from China even in the face of Japanese invasion left one of his biographers with the impression that Chiang "was prepared to pit Chinese against Chinese rather than to stand up to the invading foreigners" (Crozier, *Man Who Lost China*, 393). In one instance, the Nationalist government imprisoned a Christian preacher for hiding Communist guerrillas (Jing and Koesel, "Church and State," 127).

81. Powell, "Chiang Kai-shek," 54–78. Although a Christian, Chiang clearly had much room to grow in his faith. For instance, in 1948, when Chiang was about to be expelled from China by the Communists, he was known to drink heavily to help him sleep. Powell, "Chiang Kai-shek," 106.

82. Ma and Li, *Surviving the State*, 3.

83. Tiedemann, *1800–Present*, 659.

84. Powell, "Chiang Kai-shek," 60–61, 72–73. Up until this time, women were subjected to foot binding and arranged marriages in which they had little say in their choice of a husband. While husbands could have concubines, wives were expected to remain faithful to their husbands. In addition to Soong Mei-ling, other Chinese elite women of this era who embraced Christianity and social reform included Zeng Jifen (1852–1942) and her daughter Zeng Baosun (1893–1978). Kennedy, "Activism Among Women," 7–8, 11–14.

85. Ma and Li, *Surviving the State*, 3–4; Hodgkin, "Events in China During 1927," 18–19.

86. Under the influence of Western missionaries, Protestant schools sprang up all over China starting in the late 1800s (Bays, "Soong Family," 24). However, up until Chiang's reforms, the official Nationalist policy nevertheless restricted religious teaching in these schools (Capristo, "Mission Schools," 41–42).

Chinese culture were less successful.[87] Despite Chiang's eventual defeat by the Chinese Communist Party, the legacy of social reform, Christian institutions, and indigenous churches that flourished during Nationalist rule have left a lasting impact upon many Chinese lives.

In 1949, Mao Zedong secured the Chinese Communist Party's control over China, and Chiang Kai-shek relocated his Nationalist government to the nearby island of Taiwan.[88] Though the conversion of Chiang Kai-shek brought excitement to many Christians, his enigmatic career and defeat by the Communists meant that, despite his ambitions, he never became China's Constantine. Moreover, while the authenticity of Chiang's Christian faith has been legitimately questioned by some, it should be noted that Chiang was a new convert (like Naaman in 2 Kgs 5) who needed to undergo spiritual growth just like any other believer would.[89] However, due to his political position, Chiang also faced significant pressures that,

---

87. One such example was his attempt to integrate Confucian and Christian beliefs in the New Life Movement. Popularly known as the "Blue Shirts," adherents of Chiang's New Life Movement were subjected to an extreme authoritarian style of leadership that sought to bring about social change through a blend of Confucian and Christian teachings. Some believers supported the movement while other opposed it, and the movement ultimately did not prove very effective in reforming Chinese society (Bays, *History of Christianity in China*, 127–28; Crozier, *Man Who Lost China*, 11–12; Powell, "Chiang Kai-shek," 78–86). The New Life Movement declined in the late 1930s, and ironically, its ideals would be carried on by the YMCA, which was "a mildly incongruous choice since it meant that a Christian organisation was being asked to spread Confucian doctrines." Crozier, *Man Who Lost China*, 166.

88. After relocating to Taiwan, Soong Mei-ling experienced what she described as a genuine conversion. Despite having the outward appearance of a Christian, Mei-ling became troubled by the haunting realization that she lacked a personal relationship with God. One day, while reading the familiar biblical account of the crucifixion, Mei-ling experienced an "old-fashioned conversion" where she "suddenly realized for the first time that Christ's suffering was for her." From then on, she vowed to be "not only intellectually convinced but personally attached" to God (Tyson Li, *Madame Chiang Kai-shek*, 343). The latter years of Mei-ling's life would be marked by a humbler dependence upon God than the tumultuous earlier years in China. Following Chiang Kai-shek's death in 1975, Soong Mei-ling moved from Taiwan to the United States in 1976. She lived quietly in the New York City area with relatives until her death in 2003. Chu, "Soong Meiling and Her Times," 5.

89. Drawing upon the writings in Chiang Kai-shek's personal diary, Wang argues that Chiang relied heavily on his Christian faith to navigate diplomatic tensions with the United States during the Stillwell Incident of 1944. However, Wang "does not claim that Chiang was so ardently Christian throughout his life" or that "Christian ethics and principles were the only values governing [Chiang's] decisions during the Stillwell Incident or in other matters." Wang, "Chiang Kai-shek's Faith," 207.

when coupled with the lonely nature of his Christian life, sometimes led him towards questionable decisions.[90] Nevertheless, Chiang stands as one example of a government official who, in his own unique ways, served as a proponent of God's purposes during China's Republican era.

Government Officials as Proponents of the Gospel in China During the Communist Era (1949–Present): Growth Amid Regulation

In 1949, Mao Zedong declared the beginning of the People's Republic of China. The Chinese Communist Party, along with its atheistic ideology, had displaced the Nationalist Party and its Christian leader, Chiang Kai-shek. For some people, this transition signaled the rise of a new "evil empire" that was opposed to Christianity.[91] Surprisingly, even under Communist rule, some government officials continued to serve as proponents of the gospel in China. To see how this happened, we must briefly discuss the history of religious regulations in Communist China.

All religions, including Christianity, faced significant new restrictions under Communist rule. During the 1950s, the Chinese government established the Religious Affairs Bureau (RAB) to oversee China's five officially recognized religions (Buddhism, Taoism, Islam, Catholicism, and Protestantism).[92] While citizens were allowed to practice their faith, they

---

90. In the category of questionable choices, Wang cites Chiang's pledge to instruct his entire army to be baptized if China was victorious in battle at Hengyang. Wang, "Chiang Kai-shek's Faith," 207.

91. Not all Christians were against the Chinese Communist Party. By the late 1940s, some believers, including intellectuals such as Y. T. Wu (Wu Yaozong), had become "openly sympathetic to the communist movement and its victory." Wu was a national secretary for the YMCA and a leading voice for theologically liberal Protestants. Bays, *History of Christianity in China*, 160.

92. The Chinese government's oversight of religion reflects the complexity of its organizational structure. At the national level, the RAB was later incorporated into the State Administration of Religious Affairs (SARA). In 2018, SARA was formally dissolved, and its functions—including that of the RAB—were placed under the United Front Work Department (Jing and Koesel, "Church and State," 121–22). It is also worth noting that registration and enforcement are handled by separate government bureaus. As Palmer explains, "The RAB is responsible for managing the legal religious communities, while the Public Security Bureau (PSB) prosecutes religious activities deemed illegal. Since the RAB and PSB at a given level jurisdiction do not necessarily communicate with each other or have good relations, policy implementation is not always coherent." Palmer, "China's Religious Danwei," 25.

could only belong to local religious groups (e.g., temples, churches) that were officially sanctioned by the government. For Protestants, this meant worshiping within a local church that was registered under the state-recognized Three-Self Patriotic Movement (TSPM), which was established in 1954.[93] Initially, many Christians agreed to join the TSPM while others chose to worship in unregistered "house" churches.[94]

By the late 1950s, the government tightened its control over religion and eventually sought to suppress it entirely during the Cultural Revolution of 1966–1976.[95] During the Cultural Revolution, institutional Christianity (regardless of registration status) was banned from China. The TSPM was effectively closed, and any Christian gatherings had to be done in secret. Christians faced stiff persecution during this time and the years that followed.

In 1979, churches began to reopen under Deng Xiaoping's open-door policy.[96] With its sights set on economic development, the government's

---

93. Schak, "Protestantism in China," 72; Leung, "China," 145. The "three selves" of the TSPM refer to self-support, self-government, and self-propagation—ideas which the Chinese government borrowed from Western Protestant missionaries. While the TSPM was the government's system for regulating Protestants, a different approach (called the Catholic Patriotic Association) was needed for Catholics because the issue of self-government was at odds with oversight from the Vatican. Bays, *History of Christianity in China*, 159–60.

94. In these early years, the TSPM's leadership was largely directed by theologically liberal Protestants who were generally more accepting of government requirements than their conservative counterparts. Two notable evangelical representatives in TSPM leadership were Jia Yuming and Chen Chonggui (Marcus Cheng). Chen Chonggui, who served as president of Chunking (Chongqing) Theological Seminary, was ousted from his TSPM leadership role in 1957 after expressing objections towards the government's religious policy. Bays, *History of Christianity in China*, 166–68.

Though the registered and unregistered churches are sometimes viewed in stark contrast to one another, their relationship is often a bit more complex. Today, many churchgoers would sense little difference between the teaching they receive in a registered church compared to an unregistered one (Ma and Li, *Surviving the State*, 167). Thus, it is not uncommon for Christian leaders and parishioners to move back and forth between the TSPM and unregistered churches. In some locales, there is a strong partnership between registered and unregistered churches, and some local church leaders have been known to simultaneously hold pastorates at both registered and unregistered churches. Jin Mingri (Ezra Jin) is one prominent example of a former TSPM pastor who later became the lead pastor of an large, urban, unregistered church in Beijing (Ma and Li, *Surviving the State*, 169–72).

95. Schak, "Protestantism in China," 72; Leung, "China," 145; Bays, *History of Christianity in China*, 159.

96. Bays, *History of Christianity in China*, 185–90; Leung, "China," 145. After Mao

stance towards religion also began to shift. Recognizing the rapid growth of religion in China, the government outlined new religious policies in 1982. Significantly, these policies reaffirmed religious freedom and provided guidelines for religious practice.[97] Nevertheless, the official regulations left some details undefined.[98] These ambiguities have contributed to what sociologist Fengyang Yang describes as a triple religious market in China consisting of red (legal), black (illegal), and gray (neither legal nor illegal) religious activities.[99] Since many Christian activities fall into gray areas, the task of negotiation has become an increasingly important part of maintaining harmonious relationships between government officials and Christians.

Political scientists point out that under Mao Zedong, the government and church often related to one another in a paradigm of domination and resistance. After Mao, however, the paradigm shifted more towards a relationship of domination and *negotiation*.[100] Ambiguities in the official religious policy, coupled with understaffing in the government's Religious Affairs Bureau, meant that, in practice, religious freedom often depended on how local administrators chose to implement the official policies.[101] As is often the case in authoritarian regimes, mid- or lower-level officials aim to strike a balance between the demands of their superiors and the desires of their citizens. Officials may seek to maintain a public transcript that upholds government authority while also accommodating their constituents' needs and requests.[102] While this public transcript is set by the higher authorities, lower-level officials and their constituents sometimes have room to negotiate specific details on a case-by-case basis. The relationship between local

---

Zedong's death, Deng Xiaoping arose as China's next political leader.

97. Two important pieces of this policy were Article 36 of China's constitution and another document commonly known as "Document 19" (formally titled "The Basic Viewpoint and Policy on the Religious Question During Our Country's Socialist Period"). Bays, *History of Christianity in China*, 190.

98. For example, while Article 36 of the Chinese constitution affirms freedom of religious belief for its citizens and protects "normal [*zhengchang de*] religious activities," it stops short of defining what constitutes "normal" activities for religious adherents. Const. of the People's Republic of China [*Xianfa*] art. XXXVI (see People's Republic of China, "Constitution"); Vala, *Politics of Protestant Churches*, 36.

99. Yang, "Red, Black, and Gray Markets," 97.

100. Vala, *Politics of Protestant Churches*, 45.

101. Moreover, Chinese Christians who chose to resist government sanctions could do so while asserting that they were acting in obedience to Document 19 and the Chinese constitution, which granted some religious freedoms.

102. Vala, *Politics of Protestant Churches*, 11.

believers and their officials may sometimes reflect the types of negotiations that we saw in our earlier analysis of Daniel and the Babylonian officials in Dan 1–2 (see chapter 2). Like Ashpenaz and Arioch, Chinese officials can play key roles in crafting creative solutions for God's people.

In a large government system that oversees the lives of over one billion citizens, including millions of Christians, the implementation of official policies has hardly been uniform. Observers of China have pointed out that while religious regulations may be more strictly enforced in one area, the rules may be relatively relaxed in other regions.[103] This is because behind the enforcement of rules are countless individual officials—humans with free will, caught in webs of social relationships with both their superiors and their constituents.[104] Although officials in charge of religious regulation are typically not Christians, they are ordinary Chinese people who often have Christian friends or relatives.[105] At least on paper, most government officials are atheists, as is required for membership in the Chinese Communist Party. However, many officials, including some at the higher ranks, privately hold religious beliefs.[106] Moreover, as Vala points out, "due to vaguely defined terms and generalized implementation guidelines, the rules actually leave local authorities considerable discretion in implementation."[107] In addition to these ambiguities, government officials who oversee religious affairs are often severely outnumbered by Christians.[108] Therefore, without pressure from higher-level authorities, religious groups can often cultivate relationships of trust with local officials.[109]

The Zhejiang province in southeastern China is one area where Christians and the Communist government have historically had favorable relationships. Due to an overall friendly political climate in Zhejiang, the province has become home to thousands of churches, including many in the city of Wenzhou which has been called "China's Jerusalem."[110] Wenzhou is

---

103. Liu and White mention the southeast coastal region as one area where local officials have historically been more flexible in religious management. Liu and White, "Old Pastor and Local Bureaucrats," 584.

104. Vala, *Politics of Protestant Churches*, 13–14; Liu and White, "Old Pastor and Local Bureaucrats," 569.

105. Liu and White, "Old Pastor and Local Bureaucrats," 569.

106. Qian, "Everyday Religiosity," 91.

107. Vala, *Politics of Protestant Churches*, 37.

108. Vala, *Politics of Protestant Churches*, 42.

109. Vala, *Politics of Protestant Churches*, 13.

110. Aikman, *Jesus in Beijing*, 187; Yang, "Church Crosses in Zhejiang," 15–16.

a hotbed for Chinese entrepreneurs, many of whom are Christians.[111] These business-minded believers leverage their economic success to promote the cause of Christianity before their local officials. Some believers have served in public office, enabling Wenzhou Christians to negotiate exceptions, including permission to construct enormous church buildings whose architecture resembles multistory European cathedrals. Other Wenzhou Christian officials, including a high-ranking leader in the local chamber of commerce, have used their position to spread the gospel in the city.[112]

The trust relationships between Christians and government officials have been tested at times. Between the years 2013 and 2016, Zhejiang's provincial leader initiated a campaign to remove crosses from all churches across the province.[113] Although Christians in Zhejiang sustained significant losses, local officials played an important role to mitigate damages. As Yang points out, some of Zhejiang's local prefectures experienced relatively fewer cross removals despite having a higher number of churches.[114] Yang suggests multiple reasons for the uneven enforcement of orders across Zhejiang's prefectures. In general, local officials preferred to negotiate with church leaders rather than carrying out demolition orders. Many local officials delayed implementing orders to tear down crosses. Finally, many officials were unwilling to remove crosses because of pressures from Christian family members and friends.[115] The cross removal campaign,

---

111. In a 2008 study on Christianity in Wenzhou, Cao estimates that there are over twelve hundred churches serving seven hundred thousand to one million Protestants who comprise at least 12 percent of the city's population. Cao, "Boss Christians," 63–64.

112. Cao, "Boss Christians," 68.

113. This campaign, according to sociologist Fenggang Yang, was the government's most widespread effort to suppress Christianity since the Cultural Revolution. Over fifteen hundred crosses were removed, and a few churches, including the well-known Sanjiang Church in Wenzhou, were demolished entirely. Though the stated goal was to remove all crosses from Zhejiang's churches by the end of 2014, the campaign ended quietly in 2016 after meeting about one-third of the total goal. Efforts to remove crosses were hampered by Christian resistance in the form of courageous individuals standing up to guard their crosses and challenging the legal basis for the cross removal campaign. Yang, "Church Crosses in Zhejiang," 7, 11, 14.

114. Yang analyzed the number of churches and the number of cross removals per prefecture in Zhejiang. The miscorrelation between the number of churches and the number of cross removals reflects the different approaches taken by local officials across Zhejiang's various prefectural regions. Yang, "Church Crosses in Zhejiang," 18–19.

115. Yang points out that many officials did not implement the plan to demolish crosses until after being incentivized or repeatedly pressured by provincial authorities. Negotiation was attempted even in the case of the prominent Sanjiang Church, which

though initially targeting all of Zhejiang's roughly five thousand churches, ended quietly after reaching about one-third of the original goal. The provincial leader who initiated the campaign was eventually assigned to another role in Beijing.[116]

In Xiamen, a major coastal city in the Fujian province of southeast China, close relationships with local government officials resulted in less oversight for one pastor and his congregation. In their fascinating case study on this situation, Liu and White uncover "a level of engagement and social networking that often occurs between local officials and church leaders but is often absent in more macro analysis of church/state relations in contemporary China."[117] Liu and White's study focused upon Pastor Wen, the leader of Grace Church, a local TSPM congregation that registered with the government after 1979. Despite suffering as a Christian during the Cultural Revolution, Pastor Wen later developed close bonds with his local officials.[118] By informing local officials of his activities, Wen fostered a relationship of trust that he leveraged to negotiate for increased flexibility with the state.[119] In various instances, local RAB officials made exceptions to the rules, advocated for the church, or provided coaching on how to work within (or around) existing regulations. Working together, the officials and pastor crafted creative solutions by leveraging topics of mutual interest, such as the safety and orderliness of church gatherings. Although the officials were not always supportive, Wen found that his local RAB cadres "tend to avoid confrontation with the churches as long as church activities do not harm their political future. Therefore, in the absence of written reports, officials are happy to pretend not to know about particular affairs."[120] Wen's approach demonstrates that registration with the government can lay the foundation for fruitful negotiation between a church and

---

was later demolished. Yang, "Church Crosses in Zhejiang," 18.

116. Yang, "Church Crosses in Zhejiang," 13–14.

117. Liu and White, "Old Pastor and Local Bureaucrats," 565.

118. Born in 1930, Pastor Wen was labeled by the government as a "rightist" in 1957 and was persecuted for his faith during the Cultural Revolution. After enduring twenty-two years of suffering, the government removed Wen's "rightist" label in 1979. Wen later held administrative roles within the TSPM's registered church system in Xiamen. Liu and White, "Old Pastor and Local Bureaucrats," 515–74.

119. Liu and White, "Old Pastor and Local Bureaucrats," 574–79.

120. Liu and White, "Old Pastor and Local Bureaucrats," 575.

its local officials.¹²¹ These negotiations can, at times, result in less official oversight. Such negotiations often hinge upon lower-level officials who, at least in some regions, "tend to act as members of society rather than agents of state authority or firm policy implementers."¹²² In Xiamen, officials who were exposed to Christianity were friendlier towards believers because they recognized the benefits that Christians brought to the community.

The experiences of Grace Church in Xiamen reflect numerous instances in modern China where local officials granted increased flexibility toward their Christian constituents. Although not necessarily believers, many government cadres have friends or family members who are Christians.¹²³ Some reports mention Christian believers serving in various positions within the Chinese government, including as consulate officers, judges, and provincial leaders.¹²⁴ In one unusual example, a graduate from a state-sanctioned TSPM seminary found employment as a government official in the Religious Affairs Bureau. After twenty years of providing government oversight to churches, this official transitioned to pastoral ministry in the TSPM.¹²⁵

It is not just the registered TSPM churches that have opportunities to negotiate with their local officials. Hannah Nation recounts a story involving a local unregistered church's efforts to beautify the apartment building where the church rented property. Soon, their neighbors and local officials noticed the good work this church was doing.

> Not only did the church's immediate neighbors notice these actions, but likewise did the neighborhood security officers and policemen, and eventually the pastor was called to meet with these low-level magistrates. These local authorities chose not to interfere, and the church grew to more than five hundred congregants spread across multiple daughter churches. Until 2018, this large church was publicly engaged and maintained a friendly relationship with the local authorities. Since 2018, its relationship with authorities has changed.¹²⁶

---

121. Liu and White, "Old Pastor and Local Bureaucrats," 568.

122. Liu and White, "Old Pastor and Local Bureaucrats," 581.

123. Aikman, *Jesus in Beijing*, 10; Liu and White, "Old Pastor and Local Bureaucrats," 578.

124. Aikman, *Jesus in Beijing*, 8–9.

125. Vala, "Pathways to the Pulpit," 106–7.

126. Wang, *Faithful Disobedience*, 3.

Indeed, the political and religious climate in China has changed since 2018 when Xi Jinping's administration unveiled a broad-based agenda aimed at increasing the level of Sinicization (i.e., indigenization) for China's major religions.[127] In general, the new agenda has resulted in increased scrutiny of religious activities for both registered and unregistered churches.[128] Christians hold a variety of perspectives on Sinicization, with some viewing the government's agenda in a positive, neutral, or negative light.[129] Some suggest that Sinicization actually empowers Christians as they contextualize their theologies in ways that uphold the gospel while publicly expressing their deference to the official agenda. While Sinicization has brought increased pressure (and even imprisonment) for some believers, it can also lead to more opportunities for negotiation between local believers and their government officials.[130] Indeed, as the story of Christianity under China's Communist regime continues to unfold, we ought to expect some government officials to play vital roles in supporting the gospel.

---

127. Wayne Ten Harmsel offers the following helpful definition: "Sinicization is the natural process by which non-Chinese societies, or in this case, religions, come under the influence of Chinese culture. Missionaries typically refer to this as contextualization, and everyone sees it as inevitable, predictable, and a good thing. . . . In China, however, Sinicization has become a broiling controversy because, ironically, the molding of Christianity into Chinese culture seems to be emerging, not in its normal progression, from a grassroots, gradual change, but rather from a top-down, government-launched initiative. Rather than Christianity gradually influencing and seeping into the hearts and minds of the people, the Chinese government has determined that it should take the initiative and assertively mold Christianity into its culture." Ten Harmsel, *Registered Church in China*, 60.

128. Jing and Koesel, "Church and State," 122–28.

129. Yang views the government's Sinicization initiative as an effort to increase control over Christians. He maintains a distinction between cultural Sinification (i.e., contextualization, indigenization) from the government's political Sinicization (i.e., Chinafication) of religion. Ten Harmsel's analysis reflects the registered church's relatively positive (or neutral) posture towards Sinicization, while Wang Yi's perspective represents a more resistive stance taken by one prominent house church, the Early Rain Church in Chengdu. Yang, "Sinicization or Chinafication?," 16–17; Ten Harmsel, *Registered Church in China*, 58–68; Wang, *Faithful Disobedience*, 110–12, 195.

The approach taken by Wang Yi and his Early Rain Church have been criticized by some as "a bit extreme" (Ten Harmsel, *Registered Church in China*, 76). Importantly, Wang does not encourage most churches to openly resist the government regulations in the way his church is doing. By bearing the torch for other smaller churches, he aims to assert the church's legal rights so that "other churches can focus their energy on other things instead of legal matters." Wang, *Faithful Disobedience*, 197.

130. Ten Harmsel, *Registered Church in China*, 64–67.

Conclusion

Today, China is known as one of the most restrictive environments for Christians in the world.[131] In this chapter, we saw how government officials have served as surprising proponents of the gospel throughout five distinct periods of Chinese history from the Tang dynasty to the Communist era. Spanning the lowest to highest ranks of the government, some of these officials became believers while others were non-Christian sympathizers. Throughout China's dynastic period, Christians were able to garner the support of various sympathetic emperors. During China's Republican era, some of its most influential officials were believers who promoted Christian causes. Finally, during the Communist era, countless local officials have worked behind the scenes to advocate for Christians under their jurisdiction.

Viewed from a biblical perspective, the positive role of government officials in Chinese history should not surprise us since both the Old and New Testaments demonstrate that sympathetic officials have existed within ostensibly hostile regimes throughout human history. When we read of lower-level Communist officials advocating for believers, we are reminded of the Babylonian officials Arioch and Ashpenaz, who mediated for Daniel by negotiating exceptions to Nebuchadnezzar's edict. Chinese officials who converted or became friends of Christians prompt us to recall the string of Roman centurions whom we met in the pages of Luke–Acts. While we celebrate the conversion of Chinese officials, we are reminded that, like Naaman the Syrian commander, such individuals desperately need discipleship support as they face untold religious and political pressures while trying to nurture their newfound faith. The presence of Christians (and their supporters) in the upper tiers of the Chinese government remind us why Luke would dare to address his two-volume work to a high-ranking Roman official like Theophilus.

The story of government officials in China also presents a helpful contrast to the more often-told account of the gospel's spread throughout the Roman Empire. Although China never produced a ruler like Constantine, its rich history shows that Christianity has nonetheless grown deep roots into Chinese soil. This process has taken place over many centuries and can be likened more to a "'long conversation' between church and state"

---

131. Jing and Koesel, "Church and State," 107.

than a quick fix that aims to Christianize an empire overnight.[132] Throughout Christianity's nearly fourteen-hundred-year history in China, we see that while believers may benefit from government support, the church was never meant to depend upon favorable state policies. The resilience of the church in China through the ages reminds us that God's kingdom continues to advance despite opposition—and that he can even use government officials as unexpected allies in spreading the gospel to all nations.

---

132. Liu and White, "Old Pastor and Local Bureaucrats," 582. This "long conversation" complements Alan Kreider's notion of "patient ferment," which he uses to describe the advance of Christianity in the Roman Empire. Kreider, *Patient Ferment*, 7–12.

8

Conclusion

> "But Comrade Nikiforov," I protested, "these people didn't fight back. This wasn't like the other police actions we were on. They're a different kind of people."
>
> —Sergei Kourdakov (1951–1973), a former KGB officer, describing his first raid on Soviet Christians[1]

On the night of September 3, 1971, a young Soviet sailor leaped out of a Russian navy ship off the coast of Canada. A fierce storm provided just enough cover so that his fellow shipmen did not notice his bold escape. Sergei Kourdakov, a former persecutor of Christians, swam three miles in frigid waters before reaching shore. Growing up in the Soviet Union, Kourdakov became a committed Communist from a young age. He gradually climbed the ranks and joined the KGB where he supervised a group of officers. One day, Kourdakov's superiors ordered him to raid a house where Christians were gathered for worship.

Kourdakov recounts his confusion during this encounter. From his previous operations, he had become used to taking violent criminals into custody. But this gathering of believers was like no other group he had encountered before. He knocked on the door and was greeted by a kind voice asking if he belonged to the police. Taken aback by the gentleness of these Christians, Kourdakov thought to himself, "*Boy, is this stupid! We were sent to break up the Believers' service, and here I am, conducting a conversation*

---

1. Kourdakov, *Persecutor*, 134.

in whispering tones so I won't disturb the meeting!"[2] As the conversation unfolded, Kourdakov was struck by the calm and reasonable way in which the believers asserted their constitutional right to practice their religious beliefs. Trapped between the Soviet constitution and the commands of his superiors, Kourdakov eventually took two of the believers back to the police office. The opening quote of this chapter comes from Kourdakov's report to his commander describing how this raid was unlike any he had been on before. Though the young officer obeyed orders, a seed had been planted. Eventually, he became convinced of the truth of the Christian message. This realization later led him to leave Communism, convert to Christianity, and escape to Canada where he became an outspoken voice for freedom.

Sergei Kourdakov is a modern example of how government officials serving within a hostile regime can sometimes become surprising supporters of Christianity. In his testimony, we hear echoes of the centurion at the cross who, though tasked with executing Jesus, became the first one to declare the righteousness of the crucified Christ. Sergei Kourdakov is just one of countless officials throughout history who have become sympathetic towards Christianity despite serving in a government that opposes God and his purposes.

In this book, I argued for the importance of paying attention to Theophilus as the first recipient of Luke–Acts. Based on the usage of κράτιστος in Luke–Acts, I suggested that Theophilus was most likely a Roman official, even if Luke used a pseudonym to protect his recipient's identity. As he wrote to this official, Luke drew special attention to centurions as proponents of the gospel.

The clearest way to advocate for the gospel would be to become a follower of Jesus. At several key points in Luke–Acts, we find Roman officials who convert, including the centurion at Capernaum (Luke 7:1–10), the centurion at the cross (Luke 23:47), Cornelius (Acts 10:1—11:18), and Sergius Paulus (Acts 13:6–12). These morally upright men demonstrate the fittingness for a Roman official to believe the gospel. In the early centuries of church history, Christianity continued to spread among the ranks of government officials. The fourth century provides two clear examples of such officials. In Milan, Ambrose was elected bishop while serving as governor in northern Italy.[3] With the rise of Constantine in the same century, the gospel reached all the way to the Roman emperor himself.

2. Kourdakov, *Persecutor*, 132; emphasis original.
3. Swift, *Early Fathers*, 97.

CONCLUSION

While the most obvious way to support the gospel was to convert, nonbelieving officials could also support Christians by treating them fairly and facilitating the spread of the gospel "to the end of the earth" (Acts 1:8). As we saw in Acts, centurions protect Paul from danger, assert his citizenship rights, and escort him towards Rome (Acts 21:27–36; 22:25–26; 23:17, 23; 24:23). Julius the centurion exemplifies how an official might encourage believers and nonbelievers to work together for the common good (27:1–44). Besides portraying centurions as proponents of the gospel, Luke also presents several other believers who either served in political leadership or were closely associated with those in such positions. Several examples from early church history and Chinese history demonstrate the important roles that sympathetic officials played in the advance of the gospel all over the world.

Since officials have become proponents of the gospel throughout history, believers today should seek to present a rational case for their faith to government authorities. Just as Luke wrote to help Theophilus gain certainty concerning the things he had been taught, so believers today can work to show the reasonableness of the biblical faith to political leaders. As we do so, we also ought to pray for those in authority (1 Tim 2:1–2), including those whom we might naturally see as our enemies (Luke 6:28).

The story of Christianity is a fascinating journey that touches upon peoples and nations all over the world. With the spread of the gospel across time and places, Christians have encountered political powers in various cultural contexts. Just as Roman centurions became surprising proponents of the gospel in Luke–Acts, so Christians throughout the ages have also found unexpected support from officials serving within seemingly hostile regimes. Some of these officials embraced the Christian message as their own. Others stopped short of embracing the faith while nevertheless supporting its spread. To be clear, state support was often the exception rather than the norm, as many sympathetic officials were preceded and succeeded by officials who were less friendly towards Christianity.

Finally, I would like to reflect on two areas of application for believers today. First, I believe the message of this book ought to encourage Christians to pray for officials of every human government, especially those that persecute Christians. As we seek the advance of the gospel in difficult places, the collective witness of Luke's narrative and centuries of church history demonstrates that no human official or regime is beyond God's reach. Just as Roman centurions embraced faith in Jesus, so it is also possible for modern-day officials to convert to Christianity. We ought to pray for many such conversions to happen across all ranks of every government system today. When government authorities embrace the faith, we should be sympathetic concerning the unique pressures faced by those who serve in public office. Such individuals need discipleship and encouragement just like the rest of us do. Additionally, in cases where conversion does not occur, we should still pray for God to work in the hearts of sympathetic officials who will treat believers favorably. Several examples of centurions in Paul's trial narrative and various authorities throughout Roman and Chinese history remind us that nonbelieving officials can become the "most excellent" proponents of the gospel.

Second, I hope this book speaks to believers who serve within various roles related to the government. Even today, countless Christians courageously choose to remain embedded in regimes that sometimes seem hostile towards the church. By placing themselves in such difficult situations, these believers work for the common good of society and for the benefit of everyday Christians who are not as directly involved in governmental affairs. Such courageous civil servants deserve our respect and ought to be included in our prayers. Although Christians in America are perhaps more accustomed to thinking of other governments as hostile towards the gospel, the tensions between church and state have also escalated in our own country in recent years. The political polarization of our society is reflected in the uneasiness with which different segments of the church tend to view the government, depending on which political party is currently in power. Christians of more conservative convictions often feel genuinely concerned over the erosion of traditional biblical values in American society. In contrast, progressively minded believers are often equally concerned by a widespread neglect of Christian love in the name of winning culture wars. These types of tensions can be amplified in the lives of those who feel called to serve society through avenues such as military service, public education, and governmental office. Although I certainly do not claim to be a political expert, I believe the message of this book can help believers on both sides of the divide. I hope that the issues raised in this book will help believers who sometimes feel like they are serving within an evil empire. Sometimes, the pressures of serving an evil empire will conflict so directly with loyalty to Christ that faithful believers will find no way to remain in their positions. Other times, believers will find ways to creatively navigate their allegiances to Caesar and God in beautiful ways. As we considered how various officials served evil empires throughout history, I hope that many more individuals are encouraged to continue serving the public, despite the pressures that often come along with trying to live out the Christian faith as a civil servant.

In some sense, these are the same types of tensions that are faced by every believer who lives in this fallen world. All of us can relate to the pressures that come along with being embedded in a society that is hostile towards our faith. The overarching message of Theophilus and the centurions is that God is the supreme ruler over every human government. Throughout every generation, he has placed his own people within the ranks of seemingly evil empires. Each of these faithful officials serves as a pointer to the true king whose dominion will never end (Isa 9:7, Dan 7:14). One day, our Lord Jesus will take his throne as the rightful ruler over his redeemed people "from every tribe and language and people and nation" (Rev 5:9). In that day, the evil empire and its leaders will be replaced by the most faithful ruler that the world has ever known.

Bibliography

Adams, Edward. "The Ancient Church at Megiddo: The Discovery and an Assessment of Its Significance." *Expository Times* 120.2 (2008) 62–69.

Aikman, David. *Jesus in Beijing: How Christianity Is Transforming China and Changing the Global Balance of Power*. Washington, DC: Regnery, 2003.

Alexander, Loveday. *Acts in Its Ancient Literary Context*. Library of New Testament Studies 298. London: T&T Clark, 2007.

———. "Ancient Book Production and the Gospels." In *The Gospels for All Christians*, edited by Richard Bauckham, 71–105. Grand Rapids: Eerdmans, 1998.

———. *The Preface to Luke's Gospel: Literary Convention and Social Context in Luke 1.1–4 and Acts 1.1*. Society for New Testament Studies Monograph Series 78. Cambridge: Cambridge University Press, 1993.

———. "What If Luke Had Never Met Theophilus?" *Biblical Interpretation* 8 (2000) 161–70.

Anderson, R. H. "Theophilus: A Proposal." *Evangelical Quarterly* 69.3 (1997) 195–215.

Angelo, Camille Leon, and Joshua Silver. "Debating the Domus Ecclesiae at Dura-Europos: The Christian Building in Context." *Journal of Roman Archaeology* 37 (2024) 264–303.

Aristides. *Apology*. Translated by D. M. Kay. In *ANF* 9:263–79.

Athenagoras. *Plea for Christians*. Translated by B. P. Pratten. In *ANF* 2:129–48.

Attwater, Rachel, and Joseph Duhr. *Adam Schall: A Jesuit at the Court of China, 1592–1666*. Milwaukee, WI: Bruce, 1963.

Augustine of Hippo. *The City of God, Books I–VII*. Translated by Demetrius B. Zema and Gerald Groveland Walsh. Fathers of the Church 8. Washington, DC: Catholic University of America Press, 2008.

———. *The City of God, Books VIII–XVI*. Translated by Gerald G. Walsh and Grace Monahan. Fathers of the Church 14. Washington, DC: Catholic University of America Press, 2008.

———. *The City of God, Books XVII–XXII*. Translated by Daniel J. Honan and Gerald Groveland Walsh. Fathers of the Church 24. Washington, DC: Catholic University of America Press, 2008.

———. *Expositions on the Book of Psalms*. Translated by A. Cleveland Coxe. In *NPNF*[1] 8:1–683.

———. *Letters, Volume IV, (165–203)*. Translated by Wilfrid Parsons. Fathers of the Church 30. Washington, DC: Catholic University of America Press, 1981.

———. *Letters of St. Augustine*. Translated by J. G. Cunningham. In *NPNF*[1] 1:209–593.

Aune, David E. "Luke 1.1–4: Historical or Scientific Prooimion?" In *Paul, Luke and the Graeco-Roman World: Essays in Honour of Alexander J. M. Wedderburn*, edited by Alf Christophersen et al., 138–48. Journal for the Study of the New Testament Supplement Series 217. London: T&T Clark, 2003.

Bae, Kyounghan. "Chiang Kai-shek and Christianity: Religious Life Reflected from His Diary." *Journal of Modern Chinese History* 3 (2009) 1–10.

Barag, Dan, and David Flusser. "The Ossuary of Yehoḥanah Granddaughter of the High Priest Theophilus." *Israel Exploration Journal* 36 (1986) 39–44.

Bar-Efrat, Shimon. *Narrative Art in the Bible*. London: T&T Clark, 2004.

Barnes, Timothy David. *Constantine and Eusebius*. Cambridge: Harvard University Press, 1981.

Barrett, C. K. *A Critical and Exegetical Commentary on the Acts of the Apostles*. 2 vols. International Critical Commentary. Edinburgh: T&T Clark, 1994.

Bateman, Steve. "Lord over Raging Nations: Ronald Reagan's 'Evil Empire' Speech Turns 42." Gospel Coalition, Mar. 8, 2025. https://www.thegospelcoalition.org/article/reagan-evil-empire/.

Bauckham, Richard. "For Whom Were Gospels Written?" In *The Gospels for All Christians: Rethinking the Gospel Audiences*, edited by Richard Bauckham, 9–48. Grand Rapids: Eerdmans, 1998.

———, ed. *The Gospels for All Christians: Rethinking the Gospel Audiences*. Grand Rapids: Eerdmans, 1998.

———. "Response to Philip Esler." *Scottish Journal of Theology* 51 (1998) 249–54.

Bays, Daniel H. *A New History of Christianity in China*. Oxford: Wiley-Blackwell, 2012.

———. "The Soong Family and the Chinese Protestant Christian Community." In *Madame Chiang Kai-shek and Her China*, edited by Samuel C. Chu, 22–32. Norwalk, CT: Eastbridge, 2005.

Beck, Robert R. *A Light to the Centurions: Reading Luke-Acts in the Empire*. Eugene, OR: Wipf & Stock, 2019.

Bengel, John Albert. *Gnomon of the New Testament*. Edited by Andrew R. Fausset. 7th ed. 2 vols. Edinburgh: T&T Clark, 1887.

Bock, Darrell L. *Acts*. Baker Exegetical Commentary on the New Testament. Grand Rapids: Baker Academic, 2007.

———. *Luke*. 2 vols. Baker Exegetical Commentary on the New Testament. Grand Rapids: Baker Academic, 1994–1996.

———. *A Theology of Luke and Acts: Biblical Theology of the New Testament*. Biblical Theology of the New Testament. Grand Rapids: Zondervan, 2012.

Bovon, François. *A Commentary on the Gospel of Luke 1:1—9:50*. Vol. 1 of *Luke*, edited by Helmut Koester, translated by Christine M. Thomas. Hermeneia. Minneapolis: Fortress, 2002.

———. *A Commentary on the Gospel of Luke 19:28—24:53*. Vol. 3 of *Luke*, edited by Helmut Koester, translated by James Crouch. Hermeneia. Minneapolis: Fortress, 2012.

BIBLIOGRAPHY

Brent, Allen. "Luke-Acts and the Imperial Cult in Asia Minor." *Journal of Theological Studies* 48 (1997) 411–38.

Brink, Laurena Ann. "Unmet Expectations: The Literary Portrayal of Soldiers in Luke-Acts." PhD diss., University of Chicago, 2009.

Brodie, Thomas L. "Towards Unraveling the Rhetorical Imitation of Sources in Acts: 2 Kgs 5 as One Component of Acts 8,9–40." *Biblica* 67 (1986) 41–67.

Broomhall, Marshall. *Robert Morrison: A Master-Builder*. New York: Doran, 1924.

Brown, Andrew J. "The Gospel Commentary of Theophylact, and a Neglected Manuscript in Oxford." *Novum Testamentum* 49 (2007) 185–96.

Brown, Jeannine K. *The Gospels as Stories: A Narrative Approach to Matthew, Mark, Luke, and John*. Grand Rapids: Baker Academic, 2020.

———. "Narrative Criticism." In *Dictionary of Jesus and the Gospels*, edited by Joel B. Green et al., 619–24. IVP Bible Dictionary Series. Downers Grove, IL: InterVarsity, 2013.

Bruce, F. F. *The Book of Acts*. New International Commentary on the New Testament. Grand Rapids: Eerdmans, 1988.

Brueggemann, Walter. "2 Kings 5: Two Evangelists and a Saved Subject." *Missiology* 35 (2007) 263–72.

Bruehler, Bart B. "Expecting the Unexpected in Luke 7:1–10." *Tyndale Bulletin* 73 (2022) 71–89.

Cadbury, H. J. "Commentary on the Preface of Luke." In *The Beginnings of Christianity: The Acts of the Apostles*, vol. 2, edited by F. J. Foakes-Jackson and Kirsopp Lake, 489–510. London: Macmillan, 1922.

Campbell, J. B. *The Romans and Their World*. New Haven: Yale University Press, 2011.

Cao, Nanlai. "Boss Christians: The Business of Religion in the 'Wenzhou Model' of Christian Revival." *China Journal* 59 (2008) 63–87.

Capristo, Vincenza Cinzia. "The Mission Schools in Chiang Kai-shek's Nationalist China: Debate Within the Chinese Political World on Educational and Schools Matters in the Nationalist Period." *Portugese Journal of Asian Studies* 28 (2022) 37–50.

Cassidy, Richard J. "Paul's Proclamation of Lord Jesus as a Chained Prisoner in Rome: Luke's Ending Is in His Beginning." In *Luke-Acts and Empire: Essays in Honor of Robert L. Brawley*, edited by David Rhoads et al., 142–53. Princeton Theological Monograph Series 151. Eugene, OR: Pickwick, 2011.

———. *Society and Politics in the Acts of the Apostles*. Maryknoll, NY: Orbis, 1987.

Celsus. *On the True Doctrine: A Discourse Against the Christians*. Translated by R. Joseph Hoffmann. New York: Oxford University Press, 1987.

Chan, Michael. "Joseph and Jehoiachin: On the Edge of Exodus." *Zeitschrift für die alttestamentliche Wissenschaft* 125 (2013) 566–77.

Chase, Mitch. "The Angel Gabriel." Substack, Biblical Theology (blog), Dec. 7, 2023. https://mitchchase.substack.com/p/the-angel-gabriel.

Chen, Kevin. *Daniel: A Pastoral and Contextual Commentary*. Asia Bible Commentary. Carlisle, UK: Langham, 2025.

———. *The Messianic Vision of the Pentateuch*. Downers Grove, IL: InterVarsity, 2019.

Chiang, Kai-shek. "Why I Believe in Jesus." *Christian Century* 55.23 (1938) 723–24.

China Group. "Verbiest, Ferdinand." In *A Dictionary of Asian Christianity*, edited by Scott W. Sundquist et al., 872–73. Grand Rapids: Eerdmans, 2001.

———. "Xu Guangqi." In *A Dictionary of Asian Christianity*, edited by Scott W. Sundquist et al., 913. Grand Rapids: Eerdmans, 2001.

Chu, Samuel C. "Soong Meiling and Her Times (1897–2003)." In *Madame Chiang Kai-shek and Her China*, edited by Samuel C. Chu, 3–6. Norwalk, CT: Eastbridge, 2005.

Cohn, Robert L. "Form and Perspective in 2 Kings V." *Vetus Testamentum* 33 (1983) 171–84.

Collins, John. *Daniel: A Commentary on the Book of Daniel*. Hermeneia. Minneapolis: Fortress, 1993.

Cotton, Hannah M. "Some Aspects of the Roman Administration of Judaea/Syria-Palaestina." In *Lokale Autonomie und Ordnungsmacht in den kaiserzeitlichen Provinzen vom 1. bis 3. Jahrhundert*, edited by Werner Eck, 75–92. Berlin: Oldenbourg Wissenschaftsverlag, 2009.

Creamer, Jennifer M., et al. "Who Is Theophilus? Discovering the Original Reader of Luke-Acts." *In die Skriflig* 48 (2014) 1–7.

Crenshaw, James L. *Old Testament Story and Faith: A Literary and Theological Introduction*. Peabody, MA: Hendrickson, 1992.

Crozier, Brian. *The Man Who Lost China: The First Full Biography of Chiang Kai-shek*. New York: Scribner's, 1976.

De Boer, Martinus C. "God-Fearers in Luke-Acts." In *Luke's Literary Achievement: Collected Essays*, edited by C. M. Tuckett, 50–71. Journal for the Study of the New Testament Supplement Series 116. Sheffield: Sheffield Academic, 1995.

Deeg, Max. "A Belligerent Priest—Yisi and His Political Context." In *From the Oxus River to the Chinese Shores: Studies on East Syriac Christianity in China and Central Asia*, edited by Dietmar W. Winkler and Li Tang, 107–21. Orientalia-Patristica-Oecumenica 5. Vienna: LIT Verlag, 2013.

Dillon, Richard J. "Previewing Luke's Project from His Prologue (Luke 1:1–4)." *Catholic Biblical Quarterly* 43 (1981) 205–27.

Dunn, James D. G. *The Acts of the Apostles*. Grand Rapids: Eerdmans, 2016.

Du Plessis, Isak J. "The Lukan Audience—Rediscovered? Some Reactions to Bauckham's Theory." *Neotestamentica* 34 (2000) 243–61.

———. "Once More: The Purpose of Luke's Prologue (Lk I 1–4)." *Novum Testamentum* 16 (1974) 259–71.

Dupont, Jacques. *The Salvation of the Gentiles: Essays on the Acts of the Apostles*. Translated by John R. Keating. New York: Paulist, 1979.

Easter, Matthew C. "'Certainly This Man Was Righteous': Highlighting a Messianic Reading of the Centurion's Confession in Luke 23:47." *Tyndale Bulletin* 63 (2012) 35–51.

Edwards, James R. *The Gospel According to Luke*. Pillar New Testament Commentary. Grand Rapids: Eerdmans, 2015.

Effa, Allan. "Prophet, Kings, Servants, and Lepers: A Missiological Reading of an Ancient Drama." *Missiology* 35 (2007) 305–13.

Ehrensperger, Kathy. "Meeting the Romans: The Encounter of Paul and Sergius Paulus According to Acts." In *Cyprus Within the Biblical World: Are Borders Barriers?*, edited by J. H. Charlesworth and J. G. R. Pruszinski, 103–14. Jewish and Christian Texts in Context and Related Studies 32. London: T&T Clark, 2021.

Emadi, Samuel. *From Prisoner to Prince: The Joseph Story in Biblical Theology*. New Studies in Biblical Theology. Downers Grove, IL: IVP Academic, 2022.

Esler, Philip F. "Community and Gospel in Early Christianity: A Response to Richard Bauckham's Gospels for All Christians." *Scottish Journal of Theology* 51 (1998) 235–48.

———. *Community and Gospel in Luke-Acts: The Social and Political Motivations of Lucan Theology*. Society for New Testament Studies Monograph Series 57. Cambridge: Cambridge University Press, 1987.

Eusebius of Caesarea. *Ecclesiastical History*. Translated by Arthur Cushman McGiffert. In *NPNF*[2] 1:73–403.

Evans, Craig A. "Daniel in the New Testament: Visions of God's Kingdom." In *The Book of Daniel, Volume 2: Composition and Reception*, edited by John J. Collins and Peter W. Flint, 490–527. Vetus Testamentum Supplements. Leiden: Brill, 2001.

———. "Luke's Use of the Elijah/Elisha Narratives and the Ethic of Election." *Journal of Biblical Literature* 106 (1987) 75–83.

Fitzmyer, Joseph A. *The Acts of the Apostles: A New Translation with Introduction and Commentary*. Anchor Bible 31. Garden City, NY: Doubleday, 1998.

———. *The Gospel According to Luke (I–IX): Introduction, Translation, and Notes*. Anchor Bible 28. Garden City, NY: Doubleday, 1981.

Flessen, Bonnie J. *An Exemplary Man: Cornelius and Characterization in Acts 10*. Eugene, OR: Pickwick, 2011.

Friedeman, Caleb. "The Use of Daniel in Luke 1–2." In *The Revelation of the Messiah: The Christological Mystery of Luke 1–2 and Its Unveiling in Luke-Acts*, 91–136. Society for New Testament Studies Monograph Series. Cambridge: Cambridge University Press, 2023.

Gagnon, Robert A. J. "Luke's Motives for Redaction in the Account of the Double Delegation in Luke 7:1–10." *Novum Testamentum* 36 (1994) 122–45.

Galen. *Method of Medicine*. Translated by Ian Johnston and G. H. R Horsley. 3 vols. LCL. Cambridge: Harvard University Press, 2011.

Gamble, Harry Y. *Books and Readers in the Early Church: A History of Early Christian Texts*. New Haven: Yale University Press, 1995.

Garland, David E. *Luke*. Zondervan Exegetical Commentary Series: New Testament 3. Grand Rapids: Zondervan, 2011.

Gaventa, Beverly Roberts. *The Acts of the Apostles*. Abingdon New Testament Commentaries. Nashville: Abingdon, 2003.

Gerstmyer, Robert Henry Madison. "The Gentiles in Luke-Acts: Characterization and Allusion in the Lukan Narrative." PhD diss., Duke University, 1995.

Goldingay, John. *Daniel*. Word Biblical Commentary 30. Dallas: Word, 1989.

González, Justo L. *The Story of Christianity*. 2nd ed. 2 vols. New York: HarperCollins, 2010.

Green, Bradley G. *Augustine of Hippo: His Life and Impact*. Early Church Fathers. Fearn, Ross-shire: Christian Focus, 2020.

Green, Joel B. *Conversion in Luke-Acts: Divine Action, Human Cognition, and the People of God*. Grand Rapids: Baker Academic, 2015.

———. *The Gospel of Luke*. New International Commentary on the New Testament. Grand Rapids: Eerdmans, 1997.

———. *The Theology of the Gospel of Luke*. New Testament Theology. Cambridge: Cambridge University Press, 1995.

Hamilton, James M. *With the Clouds of Heaven: The Book of Daniel in Biblical Theology*. New Studies in Biblical Theology. Downers Grove, IL: IVP Academic, 2014.

Harnack, Adolf von. *Militia Christi: The Christian Religion and the Military in the First Three Centuries*. Translated by David McInnes Gracie. Philadelphia: Fortress, 1981.

Hart, T. "The Gospel of Luke: Year of Faith, Year of Mercy." *Bible Today* 50 (2012) 337–43.

BIBLIOGRAPHY

Hays, Richard B. *Echoes of Scripture in the Gospels*. Waco, TX: Baylor University Press, 2018.

———. *The Moral Vision of the New Testament*. New York: Harper Collins, 1996.

Head, Peter M., et al. "Papyrological Perspectives on Luke's Predecessors (Luke 1:1)." In *The New Testament in Its First Century Setting: Essays on Context and Background in Honour of B. W. Winter on His 65th Birthday*, edited by P. J. Williams, 30–45. Grand Rapids: Eerdmans, 2004.

Helgeland, John. "Christians and the Roman Army AD 173–337." *Church History* 43 (1974) 149–63, 200.

———. "Roman Army Religion." In *Band 16/2. Teilband Religion (Heidentum: Römische Religion, Allgemeines [Forts.])*, edited by Wolfgang Haase, 1470–1505. Rise and Decline of the Roman World 2. Berlin: De Gruyter, 1978.

Hemer, Colin J. *The Book of Acts in the Setting of Hellenistic History*. Edited by Conrad H. Gempf. Wissenschaftliche Untersuchungen Zum Neuen Testament 49. Tübingen: Mohr Siebeck, 1989.

Henze, Matthias. "The Use of Scripture in the Book of Daniel." In *A Companion to Biblical Interpretation in Early Judaism*, edited by Matthias Henze, 279–307. Grand Rapids: Eerdmans, 2012.

Heumann, C. A. "Dissertatio de Theophilo, Cui Lucas Historiam Sacram Inscripsit." In *Bibliotheca Historico-Philologico-Theologica: Classis IV, Fasciculus 3*, 483–505. Bremen, 1721.

Hirsch, E. D., Jr. *Validity in Interpretation*. New Haven: Yale University Press, 1967.

Hobbs, T. R. *2 Kings*. Word Biblical Commentary. Waco, TX: Word, 1985.

Hodgkin, H. T. "Events in China During 1927 and Their Effect on the Christian Church." In *The China Christian Year Book 1928*, edited by Frank Rawlinson, 6–21. Shanghai: Christian Literature Society, 1928.

Holmes, Michael W., ed. *The Apostolic Fathers: Greek Texts and English Translations*. 3rd ed. Grand Rapids: Baker Academic, 2007.

House, Paul R. *1, 2 Kings*. New American Commentary. Nashville: B&H, 1995.

Howell, Justin R. "The Imperial Authority and Benefaction of Centurions and Acts 10.34–43: A Response to C. Kavin Rowe." *Journal for the Study of the New Testament* 31 (2008) 25–51.

Huttunen, Niko. "Brothers in Arms: Soldiers in Early Christianity." In *Early Christians Adapting to the Roman Empire: Mutual Recognition*, Supplements to Novum Testamentum 179, 138–228. Leiden: Brill, 2020.

Jervell, Jacob. *The Theology of the Acts of the Apostles*. New Testament Theology. Cambridge: Cambridge University Press, 1996.

Jing, Peitong, and Karrie J. Koesel. "Church and State in Contemporary China: Securing Christianity." *Politics and Religion* 17 (2024) 107–37.

Johnson, Luke Timothy. *The Acts of the Apostles*. Sacra Pagina 5. Collegeville, MN: Liturgical, 1992.

———. *The Gospel of Luke*. Sacra Pagina 3. Collegeville, MN: Liturgical, 1991.

Josephus. *Jewish Antiquities*. Translated by Henry St. J. Thackeray et al. 9 vols. LCL. Cambridge: Harvard University Press, 1930–1965.

———. *Against Apion: Translation and Commentary*. Translated by John M. G. Barclay. FJTC 10. Leiden: Brill, 2007.

———. *The Life. Against Apion*. Translated by Henry St. J. Thackeray et al. LCL. Cambridge: Harvard University Press, 1926.

Just, Arthur A., Jr., ed. *Luke*. Ancient Christian Commentary on Scripture: New Testament 3. Downers Grove, IL: InterVarsity, 2003.

———. "Luke's Canonical Criterion." *Concordia Theological Quarterly* 79 (2015) 245–60.

Justin Martyr. *First Apology*. In *ANF* 1:163–87.

———. *Second Apology*. In *ANF* 1:188–93.

Karris, Robert J. *Luke, Artist and Theologian: Luke's Passion Account as Literature*. Theological Inquiries. New York: Paulist, 1985.

———. "Luke 23:47 and the Lucan View of Jesus' Death." *Journal of Biblical Literature* 105 (1986) 65–74.

Keener, Craig S. *Acts: An Exegetical Commentary*. 4 vols. Grand Rapids: Baker Academic, 2012–2015.

———. "Acts 10: Were Troops Stationed in Caesarea During Agrippa's Rule?" *Journal of Greco-Roman Christianity and Judaism* 7 (2010) 164–76.

Keil, C. F., and F. Delitzsch. *Commentary on the Old Testament: I and II Kings*. Translated by James Martin. Grand Rapids: Eerdmans, 1982.

Kennedy, Thomas L. "Activism Among Women of China's Traditional Elite." In *Madame Chiang Kai-shek and Her China*, edited by Samuel C. Chu, 7–15. Norwalk, CT: Eastbridge, 2005.

Kilgallen, J. J. "Luke Wrote to Rome—A Suggestion." *Biblica* 88 (2007) 251–55.

Kim, Ho Sung. "Collusion and Subversion: Luke's Representation of the Roman Empire." PhD diss., Drew University, 2009.

Kourdakov, Sergei. *The Persecutor*. Old Tappan, NJ: Revell, 1973.

Kreider, Alan. *The Patient Ferment of the Early Church: The Improbable Rise of Christianity in the Roman Empire*. Grand Rapids: Baker Academic, 2016.

Kreitzer, Beth, ed. *Luke*. Reformation Commentary on Scripture: New Testament 3. Downers Grove, IL: InterVarsity, 2015.

Kuhn, Karl Allen. *The Kingdom According to Luke and Acts: A Social, Literary, and Theological Introduction*. Grand Rapids: Baker Academic, 2015.

———. *Luke: The Elite Evangelist*. Collegeville, MN: Liturgical, 2010.

Kyrychenko, Oleksandr. *The Roman Army and the Expansion of the Gospel: The Role of the Centurion in Luke-Acts*. Berlin: De Gruyter, 2014.

Lenglet, Ad. "La structure littéraire de Daniel 2–7." *Biblica* 53 (1972) 169–90.

Leung, Ka-Lun. "China." In *A Dictionary of Asian Christianity*, edited by Scott W. Sunquist et al., 139–46. Grand Rapids: Eerdmans, 2001.

Levine, Amy-Jill, and Ben Witherington III. *The Gospel of Luke*. New Cambridge Bible Commentary. Cambridge: Cambridge University Press, 2018.

Li, Tang. "Sorkaktani Beki: A Prominent Nestorian Woman at the Mongol Court." In *Jingjiao: The Church of the East in China and Central Asia*, edited by Roman Malek, 349–56. Collectanea Serica. London: Routledge, 2006.

Litfin, Bryan M. "Tertullian of Carthage: African Apologetics Enters the Fray." In *The History of Apologetics: A Biographical and Methodological Introduction*, edited by Benjamin K. Forrest et al., 85–101. Grand Rapids: Zondervan Academic, 2020.

Liu, Jifeng, and Chris White. "Old Pastor and Local Bureaucrats: Recasting Church-State Relations in Contemporary China." *Modern China* 45 (2019) 564–90.

Ma, Li, and Jin Li. *Surviving the State, Remaking the Church: A Sociological Portrait of Christians in Mainland China*. Studies in Chinese Christianity. Eugene, OR: Pickwick, 2018.

MacMullen, Ramsay. *Christianizing the Roman Empire: (A.D. 100–400)*. New Haven: Yale University Press, 1984.

———. *Constantine*. Crosscurrents in World History. New York: Dial, 1969.

Maddox, Robert. *The Purpose of Luke-Acts*. Edinburgh: T&T Clark, 1982.

Maier, Walter A., III. "Hadadrimmon." In *The Anchor Bible Dictionary*, vol. 3, edited by David Noel Freedman, 13. New York: Doubleday, 1992.

———. "The Healing of Naaman in Missiological Perspective." *Concordia Theological Quarterly* 61 (1997) 177–96.

Marguerat, Daniel. *The First Christian Historian: Writing the "Acts of the Apostles."* Society for New Testament Studies Monograph Series 121. Cambridge: Cambridge University Press, 2002.

Marshall, I. Howard. *Acts: An Introduction and Commentary*. Tyndale New Testament Commentaries 5. Downers Grove, IL: InterVarsity, 1980.

———. *The Gospel of Luke: A Commentary on the Greek Text*. New International Greek Testament Commentary. Grand Rapids: Eerdmans, 1978.

———. *Luke: Historian and Theologian*. Grand Rapids: Zondervan, 1971.

———. "Review of *The Preface to Luke's Gospel: Literary Convention and Social Context in Luke 1:1–4 and Acts 1:1* by Loveday Alexander." *Evangelical Quarterly* 66 (1994) 373–76.

Marx, Werner G. "A New Theophilus." *Evangelical Quarterly* 52 (1980) 17–26.

Mitchell, Margaret M. "Patristic Counter-Evidence to the Claim That 'The Gospels Were Written for All Christians.'" *New Testament Studies* 51 (2005) 36–79.

Moffett, Samuel Hugh. *Beginnings to 1500*. Vol. 1 of *A History of Christianity in Asia*. New York: Harper Collins, 1992.

———. *1500–1900*. Vol. 2 of *A History of Christianity in Asia*. New York: Orbis, 2005.

Morris, Leon. *Luke: An Introduction and Commentary*. Tyndale New Testament Commentaries 3. Downers Grove, IL: InterVarsity, 1988.

Moule, A. C. *Christians in China: Before the Year 1550*. London: SPCK, 1930.

———. "Extracts from Marco Polo's Description of the World." In Moule, *Christians in China*, 128–43.

Moxnes, Halvor. "The Social Context of Luke's Community." *Interpretation* 48 (1994) 379–89.

Musurillo, Herbert, ed. *The Acts of the Christian Martyrs*. Translated by Herbert Musurillo. Oxford: Oxford University Press, 1972.

Neagoe, Alexandru. *The Trial of the Gospel: An Apologetic Reading of Luke's Trial Narratives*. Cambridge: Cambridge University Press, 2002.

Neill, Stephen. *A History of Christian Missions*. The Pelican History of the Church 6. Baltimore: Penguin, 1964.

Nelson, Richard D. *First and Second Kings*. Interpretation. Atlanta: John Knox, 1987.

Newsom, Carol A. *Daniel: A Commentary*. Old Testament Library. Louisville: Westminster John Knox, 2014.

Nolland, John. *Luke 1—9:20*. Word Biblical Commentary 35A. Dallas: Word, 1989.

Nwaoru, Emmanuel O. "The Story of Naaman (2 Kings 5:1–19): Implications for Mission Today." *Svensk Missionstidskrift* 96 (2008) 27–41.

Open Doors UK and Ireland. "World Watch List." Accessed July 1, 2025. https://www.opendoorsuk.org/persecution/world-watch-list/.

Origen. *Against Celsus*. Translated by Frederick Crombie. In *ANF* 4:395–669.

———. *Homilies on Luke and Fragments on Luke*. Translated by Joseph T. Lienhard. Fathers of the Church 94. Washington, DC: Catholic University of America Press, 1996.

Padilla, Osvaldo. *Acts of the Apostles: Interpretation, History, and Theology*. Downers Grove, IL: InterVarsity, 2016.

Palmer, David A. "China's Religious Danwei: Institutionalising Religion in the People's Republic." *China Perspectives* 2009.4 (2009) 17–30.

Pennington, Jonathan T. *Reading the Gospels Wisely: A Narrative and Theological Introduction*. Grand Rapids: Baker Academic, 2012.

The People's Republic of China. "Constitution of the People's Republic of China." 1982. English.gov.cn, People's Republic of China, last updated Nov. 20, 2019. https://english.www.gov.cn/archive/lawsregulations/201911/20/content_WS5ed8856ec6d0b3f0e9499913.html.

Pinter, Dean. "The Gospel of Luke and the Roman Empire." In *Jesus Is Lord, Caesar Is Not: Evaluating Empire in New Testament Studies*, edited by Scot McKnight and Joseph B. Modica, 101–15. Downers Grove, IL: InterVarsity, 2013.

Polo, Marco. *The Travels of Marco Polo the Venetian, with an Introduction by John Masefield*. London: J. M. Dent, 1928.

Powell, John Douglas. "Chiang Kai-shek and Christianity." Master's thesis, Texas Tech University, 1980.

Puskas, Charles B. *The Conclusion of Luke-Acts: The Significance of Acts 28:16–31*. Eugene, OR: Pickwick, 2009.

Qian, Linliang. "Everyday Religiosity in the State Sphere: Folk Beliefs and Practices in a Chinese State-Run Orphanage." *China Information* 30 (2016) 81–98.

Rackham, Richard Belward. *The Acts of the Apostles*. Westminster Commentaries. London: Methuen, 1919.

Radice, Betty, trans. *The Letters of the Younger Pliny*. Baltimore: Penguin, 1969.

Rapske, Brian. *The Book of Acts and Paul in Roman Custody*. Grand Rapids: Eerdmans, 1994.

Read-Heimerdinger, Jenny, and Josep Rius-Camps, eds. *Luke's Demonstration to Theophilus: The Gospel and the Acts of the Apostles According to Codex Bezae*. Translated by Helen Dunn and Jenny Read-Heimerdinger. London: Bloomsbury T&T Clark, 2013.

Reagan, Ronald. "Remarks at the Annual Convention of the National Association of Evangelicals in Orlando, FL." Presented at the Annual Convention of the National Association of Evangelicals, Mar. 8, 1983. https://www.reaganlibrary.gov/archives/speech/remarks-annual-convention-national-association-evangelicals-orlando-fl.

Robbins, Vernon K. "Luke-Acts: A Mixed Population Seeks a Home in the Roman Empire." In *Images of Empire*, edited by Loveday Alexander, 202–21. Journal for the Study of the Old Testament Supplement Series. Sheffield: Sheffield Academic, 1991.

Rossabi, Morris. *Khubilai Khan: His Life and Times*. Berkeley: University of California Press, 1988.

Rowe, C. Kavin. *World Upside Down: Reading Acts in the Graeco-Roman Age*. Oxford: Oxford University Press, 2009.

Runesson, Rebecca. "Centurions in the Jesus Movement? Rethinking Luke 7:1–10 in Light of the Gaianus Inscription at Kefar 'Othnay." *Journal of Biblical Literature* 142 (2023) 129–49.

Sauma, Rabban. "Ancestor Practices in the Muslim World: A Problem of Contextualization from Central Asia." *Missiology* 30 (2002) 323–45.

Schak, David C. "Protestantism in China: A Dilemma for the Party-State." *Journal of Current Chinese Affairs* 40 (2011) 71–106.

Schnabel, Eckhard J. *Acts*. Zondervan Exegetical Commentary Series: New Testament 5. Grand Rapids: Zondervan, 2012.

Schreiner, Patrick. *The Mission of the Triune God: A Theology of Acts*. Wheaton, IL: Crossway, 2022.

Shean, John F. *Soldiering for God: Christianity and the Roman Army*. Leiden: Brill, 2010.

Shelton, John. "The Healing of Naaman (2 Kgs 5.1–19) as a Central Component for the Healing of the Centurion's Slave (Luke 7.1–10)." In *The Elijah-Elisha Narrative in the Composition of Luke*, edited by John S. Kloppenborg and Joseph Verheyden, 65–87. Library of New Testament Studies. London: Bloomsbury Academic, 2014.

———. "Naaman and the Centurion (2 Kings 5 and Luke 7)." Master's thesis, University of Limerick, 2013.

Sherwin-White, A. N. *Roman Society and Roman Law in the New Testament*. Sarum Lectures 1960–1961. Oxford: Clarendon, 1963.

Skinner, Matthew L. *Locating Paul: Places of Custody as Narrative Settings in Acts 21–28*. Academia Biblica 13. Atlanta: Society of Biblical Literature, 2003.

Smith, Abraham. "'Do You Understand What You Are Reading?': A Literary Critical Reading of the Ethiopian (Kushite) Episode (Acts 8:26–40)." *Journal of the Interdenominational Theological Center* 22 (1994) 48–74.

Speidel, Michael P. "The Roman Army in Judaea Under the Procurators: The Italian and Augustan Cohort in the Acts of the Apostles." *Ancient Society* 13/14 (1982–1983) 233–40.

Stein, Robert H. *Luke*. New American Commentary. Nashville: B&H, 1993.

Strauss, Mark L. *Four Portraits, One Jesus: A Survey of Jesus and the Gospels*. Grand Rapids: Zondervan, 2007.

———. *Four Portraits, One Jesus: A Survey of Jesus and the Gospels*. 2nd ed. Grand Rapids: Zondervan Academic, 2020.

Streeter, Burnett Hillman. *The Four Gospels: A Study of Origins*. London: Macmillan, 1924.

Strelan, R. "A Note on Asphaleia (Luke 1.4)." *Journal for the Study of the New Testament* 30 (2007) 163–71.

Sun, Jianqiang. "Re-Dating the Seven Early Chinese Christian Manuscripts: Christians in Dunhuang Before 1200." PhD diss., Leiden University, 2018.

Swift, Louis J. *The Early Fathers on War and Military Service*. Message of the Fathers of the Church 19. Wilmington, DE: Glazier, 1983.

Tajra, Harry W. *The Trial of St. Paul: A Juridical Exegesis of the Second Half of the Acts of the Apostles*. Wissenschaftliche Untersuchungen Zum Neuen Testament I 35. Tübingen: Mohr Siebeck, 1989.

Talbert, Charles H. *Reading Luke: A Literary and Theological Commentary*. Reading the New Testament. Macon, GA: Smyth & Helwys, 2002.

Tang, Li. "A Preliminary Study on the Jingjiao Inscription of Luoyang: Commentary, Text Analysis and English Translation." In *Hidden Treasures and Intercultural Encounters: Studies in East Syriac Christianity in China and Central Asia*, edited by Dietmar W. Winkler and Li Tang, 109–32. Orientalia-Patristica-Oecumenica 1. Vienna: LIT Verlag, 2009.

Tang, Xiaofeng, and Yingying Zhang. "Fangshan Cross Temple (房山十字寺) in China: Overview, Analysis and Hypotheses." In *Yearbook of Chinese Theology 2018*, edited by Paulos Z. Huang et al., 82–94. Leiden: Brill, 2019.

Tannehill, Robert C. *Luke*. Abingdon New Testament Commentaries. Nashville: Abingdon, 1996.

———. *The Narrative Unity of Luke-Acts: A Literary Interpretation*. 2 vols. Philadelphia: Fortress, 1986–1990.

Tanner, J. Paul. "The Literary Structure of the Book of Daniel." *Bibliotheca Sacra* 160 (2003) 269–82.

Taylor, Howard, and Geraldine Taylor. *Hudson Taylor's Spiritual Secret*. Edited by Gregg Lewis. Grand Rapids: Discovery, 1990.

Ten Harmsel, Wayne. *The Registered Church in China: Flourishing in a Challenging Environment*. Eugene, OR: Pickwick, 2021.

Tepper, Yotam, and Leah Di Segni. *A Christian Prayer Hall of the Third Century CE at Kefar 'Othnay (Legio): Excavations at the Megiddo Prison 2005*. Jerusalem: Israel Antiquities Authority, 2006.

Tertullian of Carthage. *Apology*. Translated by S. Thelwall. In *ANF* 3:17–60.

———. *On Idolatry*. Translated by S. Thelwall. In *ANF* 3:61–77.

———. *On the Crown*. Translated by S. Thelwall. In *ANF* 3:93–104.

———. *To Scapula*. Translated by S. Thelwall. In *ANF* 3:105–8.

Tertullian, and Minucius Felix. *Apologetical Works and Octavius*. Translated by Rudolph Arbesmann et al. Fathers of the Church 10. Washington, DC: Catholic University of America Press, 2008.

Thompson, Glen L. *Jingjiao: The Earliest Christian Church in China*. Grand Rapids: Eerdmans, 2024.

Thompson, Michael B. "The Holy Internet: Communication Between Churches in the First Christian Generation." In *The Gospels for All Christians: Rethinking the Gospel Audiences*, edited by Richard Bauckham, 49–70. Grand Rapids: Eerdmans, 1998.

Tiedemann, R. G., ed. *1800 to the Present*. Vol. 2 of *Handbook of Christianity in China*. Handbook of Oriental Studies 15. Leiden: Brill, 2010.

Troftgruben, Troy M. *A Conclusion Unhindered: A Study of the Ending of Acts Within Its Literary Environment*. Wissenschaftliche Untersuchungen Zum Neuen Testament II 280. Tübingen: Mohr Siebeck, 2010.

Tyson Li, Laura. *Madame Chiang Kai-shek: China's Eternal First Lady*. New York: Grove, 2006.

Ullendorf, Edward. "Candace (Acts 8:27) and the Queen of Sheba." *New Testament Studies* 2 (1955) 53–56.

Vala, Carsten T. "Pathways to the Pulpit: Leadership Training in 'Patriotic' and Unregistered Chinese Protestant Churches." In *Making Religion, Making the State: The Politics of Religion in Modern China*, edited by Yoshiko Ashiwa and David L. Wank, 96–125. Stanford, CA: Stanford University Press, 2009.

———. *The Politics of Protestant Churches and the Party-State in China: God Above Party?* Routledge Research on the Politics and Sociology of China. New York: Routledge, 2018.

Von Rad, Gerhard. "Naaman: A Critical Retelling." In *God at Work in Israel*, 47–57. Nashville: Abingdon, 1980.

BIBLIOGRAPHY

Von Soden, Hermann Freiherr. *Die Schriften des Neuen Testaments in ihrer ältesten erreichbaren Textgestalt hergestellt auf Grund ihrer Textgeschichte*. Göttingen: Vandenhoeck & Ruprecht, 1911.

Walaskay, Paul W. *"And So We Came to Rome": The Political Perspective of St. Luke*. Society for New Testament Studies Monograph Series 49. Cambridge: Cambridge University Press, 1983.

Walls, Andrew F. *The Cross-Cultural Process in Christian History: Studies in the Transmission and Appropriation of Faith*. Maryknoll, NY: Orbis, 2002.

Walton, Steve. "The State They Were In: Luke's View of the Roman Empire." In *Rome in the Bible and the Early Church*, edited by Peter Oakes, 1–41. Grand Rapids: Baker Academic, 2002.

Wang, Peter Chen-main. "Chiang Kai-shek's Faith in Christianity: The Trial of the Stilwell Incident." *Journal of Modern Chinese History* 8 (2014) 194–209.

Wang, Yi. *Faithful Disobedience: Writings on Church and State from a Chinese House Church Movement*. Edited by Hannah Nation and J. D. Tseng. Downers Grove, IL: InterVarsity, 2022.

Watson, Brian. "The Political Theology of Dietrich Bonhoeffer and the Ethical Problem of Tyrannicide." Master's thesis, Louisiana State University, 2015.

Wilken, Robert Louis. *The Christians as the Romans Saw Them*. 2nd ed. New Haven: Yale University Press, 2003.

Wilson, Stephen G. *The Gentiles and the Gentile Mission in Luke-Acts*. Society for New Testament Studies Monograph Series 23. Cambridge: Cambridge University Press, 1973.

Witek, John W. "Schall von Bell, Johann Adam." In *A Dictionary of Asian Christianity*, edited by Scott W. Sunquist et al., 734–35. Grand Rapids: Eerdmans, 2001.

Witherington, Ben, III. *The Acts of the Apostles: A Socio-Rhetorical Commentary*. Grand Rapids: Eerdmans, 1998.

Witherup, Ronald D. "Cornelius Over and Over and Over Again: 'Functional Redundancy' in the Acts of the Apostles." *Journal for the Study of the New Testament* 15.49 (1993) 45–66.

Wright, Benjamin G., III. *Letter of Aristeas*. Commentaries on Early Jewish Literature 8. Berlin: De Gruyter, 2015.

Yamazaki-Ransom, Kazuhiko. "God, People, and Empire: Anti-Imperial Theology of Luke-Acts in Light of Jewish Portrayals of Gentile Rulers." PhD diss., Trinity Evangelical Divinity School, 2006.

Yang, Fenggang. "The Failure of the Campaign to Demolish Church Crosses in Zhejiang Province, 2013–2016." *Review of Religion and Chinese Society* 5 (2018) 5–25.

———. "The Red, Black, and Gray Markets of Religion in China." *Sociological Quarterly* 47 (2006) 93–122.

———. "Sinicization or Chinafication? Cultural Assimilation vs. Political Domestication of Christianity in China and Beyond." In *The Sinicization of Chinese Religions: From Above and Below*, edited by Richard Madsen, 16–43. Religion in Chinese Societies 18. Leiden: Brill, 2021.

Yang, J. C. "Hsu Kuang-Chi." In *Eminent Chinese of the Ch'ing Period (1644–1912)*, vol. 1, edited by Arthur W. Hummel, 316–19. Washington, DC: US Government Printing Office, 1944.

Yates, Kenneth Wayne. "Centurions in Luke/Acts." PhD diss., Dallas Theological Seminary, 2014.

Yin, Xiaoping. "The Institution of Chongfu Si of the Yuan Dynasty." In *Winds of Jingjiao: Studies on East Syriac Christianity in China and Central Asia*, edited by Dietmar W. Winkler and Li Tang, 311–32. Orientalia-Patristica-Oecumenica 9. Vienna: LIT Verlag, 2016.

Zeichmann, Christopher B. "Military Forces in Judaea 6–130 CE: The Status Quaestionis and Relevance for New Testament Studies." *Currents in Biblical Research* 17 (2018) 86–120.

———. *The Roman Army and the New Testament*. Lanham, MD: Lexington, 2018.

General Index

Abednego, 12–17, 20n19
Abimelech, 11n2, 84n31
Adams, Edward, 96n3, 97n4
Agabus, 71
Agrippa. *See* Herod Agrippa I, Herod Agrippa II.
Aikman, David, 142n110, 145n123, 145n124
Aixue, 127–28
Alexander, Loveday, 30, 33n12, 34–36, 38n38, 39–40, 44n70, 47–50, 78n3, 94n73
Alexandria, 105
Alopen, 121–22, 124n22
Ambrose of Milan, 38, 150
Anderson, R. H., 40
Angelo, Camille Leon, 96n3
Antipas. *See* Herod Antipas.
Antipatris, 73
Antonia Fortress. *See* Roman military at Antonia Fortress.
Antoninus Pius, 100
Apollos, 43, 44
Archelaus. *See* Herod Archelaus.
Arikbuka, 128–29
Arioch, 14–15, 28, 142, 147
Aristides, 100
Artaxerxes, 11n2
Ashpenaz, 13–15, 28, 142, 147
Athenagoras, 100

Attwater, Rachel, 132n54, 132n55, 132n57
Augustine of Hippo, 9, 98, 112–16, 117
Aune, David E., 36
Aurelius, Marcus, 100, 102, 108, 135

Babylon, 12–19, 85n35, 113
Bae, Kyounghan, 135n70, 136n72, 136n76, 136n78, 136n79
Bar-Efrat, Shimon, 11n3
Bar-Jesus. *See* Elymas.
Barag, Dan, 40n59
Barclay, John M. G., 34n17
Barnabas, 90, 93
Barnes, Timothy David, 108n69, 109n75, 109n77
Barrett, C. K., 67n75, 90n61
Bateman, Steve, 1n2
Bauckham, Richard, 6n13, 31–32, 49, 82
Bays, Daniel H., 133n64, 134n66, 135n69, 135n71, 137n86, 138n87, 139n91, 140n93, 140n94, 140n95, 140n96, 141n97
Beck, Robert R., 38, 55n13, 55n15, 64n59
Belshazzar, 18n12
Bengel, John Albert, 40, 46n77
Bernice, 46, 88n53
Besas, 105
Bock, Darrell L., 39n50, 52, 63n52, 65n61, 66, 67n75, 87n42, 89n56, 93n68, 93n71

GENERAL INDEX

Bonhoeffer, Dietrich, 3n6
Boniface, 113–16
Bovon, François, 42n67, 45n72, 65n64
Brent, Allen, 39
Brink, Laurena, 7n19, 55n15, 56
Brodie, Thomas L., 68n81
Broomhall, Marshall, 133n63
Brown, Andrew J., 41n62
Brown, Jeannine K., 5n8, 5n11
Bruce, F. F., 86n39, 87n42
Brueggemann, Walter, 19n16, 21n22
Bruehler, Bart B., 55n16, 63n49, 63n50

Cadbury, H. J., 33n15, 34, 38n38, 38n41, 41–42, 44n70, 44n71
Caesar. *See* Roman Empire, emperor.
Caesarea Maritima, 5n12, 7–8, 45, 54, 59–61, 68, 71, 73–74, 94n73
Caligula, 74n106, 78
Campbell, J. B., 58n27, 58n28, 58n30, 59n31, 102n24
Candace, 86–88
Cao, Nanlai, 143n111, 143n112
Capernaum, 59, 96. *See also* centurion(s) at Capernaum.
Capristo, Vincenza Cinzia, 137n86
Cassidy, Richard J., 81, 94n73
Celsus, 99–100
centurion(s)
  basic responsibilities, 61
  as benefactors, 60, 63, 65, 68–69, 74, 78, 96–97
  at Calvary, 65–68, 92, 150
  at Capernaum, 56, 59, 62–65, 67–68, 92, 97, 100, 114, 150
  "chain of" in Luke–Acts, 6–7, 8, 55, 68, 150
  Cornelius, 5n12, 56, 67–70, 82, 87, 92, 97, 100, 114, 116, 150
  ethnicity, 57, 61, 63, 68, 71, 74
  Gaianus, 96–97
  in Paul's trial narrative, 70–73, 151
  Julius, 56n21, 74–75, 151
  languages spoken, 61
  Marinus, 104–5
  positive roles in Luke–Acts, 6–7, 10, 12, 28, 51, 55, 62–76, 116, 150–51
  promotion process, 61, 104
  scholarship on, 51, 55–57
  social status, 61
Chan, Michael, 84n31
Chase, Mitch, 18n15
Chatman, Seymour, 5n11
Chen Chonggui (Cheng, Marcus), 140n94
Chen, Kevin, 12n4, 84n31
Chiang, Kai-shek, 135–39
chiastic structure, 16n9 22–23
China
  Beijing, 118–19, 130, 132, 140n94
  Bible in, 121–22
  Buddhism in, 118, 121, 123, 125, 132, 139
  Christianity in, 4, 9, 118–48, 139
  Christians serving in government, 126–28, 130–33, 136–39, 143, 145
  Communist Party, 138, 139–46
  Confucianism in, 121, 123, 136, 138n87
  Constitution, 141n97, 141n98, 141n101
  Cultural Revolution, 140, 143n113, 144n18
  "Document 19," 141n97, 141n101
  Dunhuang, 121n8, 124n22
  Fangshan Cross Temple, 118–19
  Guangzhou, 129–30
  Islam in, 125, 131, 139
  Luoyang Stele monument, 124n22
  Ming dynasty, 118, 120, 129–31
  missionaries to, 125–26, 129–33
  Mongols in, 124–29
  Nanjing, 130, 131
  Nationalist Party (Kuomintang), 134–39
  Public Security Bureau, 139n92
  Qing dynasty, 120, 131–33
  registered churches. *See* Three Self Patriotic Movement (TSPM).
  Religious Affairs Bureau, 139, 141, 144–45
  Republican era, 120, 133–39
  Rites Controversy, 133
  Shanghai, 134

GENERAL INDEX

Sinicization, 146
State Administration of Religious Affairs (SARA), 139n92
Tang dynasty, 119, 120–24
Taoism in, 121, 123, 125, 139
Three Self Patriotic Movement (TSPM), 140, 144, 145, 146n129
United Front Work Department, 139n92
unregistered churches, 140, 145, 146n129
Wenzhou ("China's Jerusalem"), 142–44
women in, 125, 134, 137
Xiamen, 144–45
Xian Stele monument, 120
Young Men's Christian Association (YMCA) in, 134, 138n87, 139n91
Yuan dynasty, 120, 124–29
Zhejiang province, 142–44
Zhenjiang, 126–27
China Group, 130n48, 131n49, 131n50, 132n59
Chrysostom, John, 41n62
Chu, Samuel C., 138n88
Chuza, 92
Codex Bezae, 6n13
Cohn, Robert L., 19n17, 22
Collins, John, 17n11, 18n13
common good, 75–76, 112–13
communism, 1, 9, 149–50. *See also* China, Communist Party.
conscience, 11, 13, 23–24, 29
Constantine, 96n3, 104n39, 107–11, 128–29, 135, 138, 147, 150
Cornelius. *See* centurion(s), Cornelius.
Cotton, Hannah M., 60n34
Creamer, Jennifer M., 44n70, 45n72, 49n89
Crenshaw, James L., 24n28
Crozier, Brian, 134n66, 135n67, 135n68, 137n80, 138n87
culture, 4, 11, 13, 24, 28, 59, 83, 85–86, 95, 103–6, 120, 130, 133
Cyrus, 11n2, 122

Daniel, 8, 11–18, 28, 131, 142, 147

Darius, 16–17
David, 114
De Boer, Martinus C., 55, 69n86
Deeg, Max, 123n16, 123n17
Deng Xiaoping, 140
Di Segni, Leah, 96n1, 96n3
Diocletian, 103, 108
Dillon, Richard J., 44n70
Domitian, 39
Domitilla, 39
Donatists, 115n114
Du Plessis, Isak J., 6n13, 32, 42n68, 44n69, 44n70, 44n71
Duhr Joseph, 132n54, 132n55, 132n57
Dunn, James D. G., 39n50, 42, 47n78, 49n90
Dupont, Jacques, 68n76

Easter, Matthew C., 6n18, 55n14, 66n66, 66n67, 66n68, 67n74
Ebed-melech, 88
Edessa, 102n27
Edict of Milan, 96n3, 108
Edict of Toleration, 108
Edwards, James R., 53n5, 63n48, 64n57, 64n58
Effa, Allan, 19n16, 24
Egypt, 12, 38n41, 84–86, 88
Ehrensperger, Kathy, 89n57, 89n58, 90–91
Elisha, 11, 19–28
Elymas, 90
Emadi, Samuel, 84n31
Ephesus, 71, 94n73
Erasmus, Desiderius, 39n45
Esler, Philip F., 31n5, 55n9, 79n6, 81–82
Esther, 84n31
Ethiopia, 86–89
Ethiopian eunuch, 67n75, 86–89, 92, 93, 101
Eusebius of Caesarea, 49n88, 100n15, 102n25, 104–5, 108n66
Evans, Craig A., 63n49
exceptions to laws, 12–15

Felix, Antonius, 41, 45, 72–73, 80
Festus, Porcius, 41, 45–46, 73, 80

Fitzmyer, Joseph A., 39n45, 42n67, 45n74, 70
Flavius Josephus, 33–34, 40, 60n38, 61, 69n87, 88
Flessen, Bonnie J., 55n14, 56
Flusser, David, 40n59
France, R. T., 5n11
Friedeman, Caleb, 18n15

Gagnon, Robert A. J., 55n14
Gaianus, Gaianus Inscription. *See* centurion(s), Gaianus.
Gaius Caligula. *See* Caligula.
Galen, 35n22, 35n29, 46n77, 47
Galilee, 57–59, 60n35, 61, 63
Gallio, 90
Gamble, Harry Y., 32n9, 33n10, 33n11, 39–40
Garland, David E., 39n50, 48, 65n63, 66
Gaventa, Beverly Roberts, 68n76, 68n77, 69n85
Gehazi, 19n18, 25
gentile inclusion
 in Luke–Acts. *See* Luke–Acts, gentiles in.
 in Old Testament, 25–29
Germany, 3n6, 131
Gerstmyer, Robert Henry Madison, 55n13, 69n86, 69n88, 91n63
God
 as deliverer from danger, 18
 fearers of, 2, 38, 55, 69, 76
 as sovereign ruler, 12, 15, 18, 28, 153
 worship of, 11, 16–18, 21–25, 99, 101, 103, 104, 105, 111
Goldingay, John, 13n5, 13n6
González, Justo L., 96n3, 108n64, 108n65, 108n67, 109n76, 109n79, 110n81, 110n82, 110n84, 110n89, 111n91, 111n93, 111n95
government officials
 believers serving as, 1–2, 3–4, 11–17, 38, 84–86, 93, 107–11, 113–16, 126–28, 130–33, 136–39, 150, 152–53.
 conversion of, 11, 17–18, 21–29, 48–49, 62–65, 65–66, 67–70, 86–89, 89–91, 107–9, 135–36, 150

 discipleship of, 24, 27, 110–11, 130, 135–36, 138–39, 147, 152
 low-ranking, 7, 11–17, 77, 83, 95, 141–42, 144–45, 147
 high-ranking, 1–2, 6, 8, 11–26, 41–49, 51, 77–78, 83, 87, 89–91, 95, 100–101, 107–11, 112, 113, 117, 119, 121–24, 125–29, 130–33, 133–39, 141, 146
 as mediators, 13–16, 142–43, 143, 144, 148
 supporters of God's people, 11–16, 107–111, 120, 121–24, 125–28, 132–33, 136–39, 142, 144, 150–52
Green, Bradley G., 115n114
Green, Joel B., 35n24, 53n7, 55n9, 62n47, 64n60
Guo Ziyi, 122–23

Hadrian, 100
Hamilton, James M., 16n9, 85n35
Harnack, Adolf von, 100n14, 102n27, 102n29, 105
Hart, T., 38
Hays, Richard, 10, 29n36, 54n8
Head, Peter M., 38n41
Helgeland, John, 103–4, 105n48, 106n56, 108n64, 109n74
Hemer, Colin J., 37n36, 73n103
Henze, Matthias, 85n35
hermeneutics, 4–5
Herod
 Agrippa I, 60, 74n105, 80
 Agrippa II, 42, 46, 73, 79n5, 80
 Antipas, the Tetrarch, 58–59, 63, 65, 79–80, 92–93, 101
 Archelaus, 60
 The Great, 58–61
Heumann, C. A., 41, 80–81
Hippolytus, 107
Hiram, 11n2
Hirsch, E. D., Jr., 5n7
Hobbs, T. R., 19n18
Hodgkin, H. T., 137n85
Holmes, Michael W., 49n88
House, Paul R., 21n22, 21n23
Howell, Justin R., 55n14, 56, 57n22
Huttunen, Niko, 55, 61n45

GENERAL INDEX

idolatry, 11, 18, 22–25, 106–7, 110
Italy, 5n12, 56n21, 59, 69, 73–74, 129, 150. *See also* Roman military, Italian cohort; Rome.

Jairus, 83n26
Jehoiachin, 84n31
Jeremiah, 88
Jerusalem, 6, 8, 12, 45, 51, 53–54, 59, 61, 67, 70–73
Jervell, Jacob, 81
Jesus Christ
  birth and childhood, 53n4, 54
  death, 65–67, 93
  at Gethsemane, 106–7
  journey to Jerusalem, 53–54
  as king, 65, 153
  as Lord, 56, 66, 81, 95
  resurrection, 53n4, 67
  as "righteous," 65–66, 92
  as Savior, 52
  Second Coming, 112, 153
  as Son of Man, 12
  on trial, 65, 79, 106
Jewish War, 58
Jia Yuming, 140n94
Jin Mingri (Ezra Jin), 140n94
Jing, Peitong, 137n80, 139n92, 146n128, 147n131
Joanna, 92–93
John the Baptist, 61–62, 93, 102, 107, 114, 115
Johnson, Luke Timothy, 44n69, 63n52, 63n53, 65n64, 66n71, 66n72, 68n79, 68n82, 69n85, 70n91, 70n92, 71n93, 72n94, 73n101, 74n107, 75n110
Joseph, 13–14, 84–86
Josephus. *See* Flavius Josephus.
Judaea. *See* Judea.
Judea, 57–58, 60, 65, 67, 71
Julius. *See* centurion(s), Julius.
Just, Arthur A., Jr., 38n39, 39
just war theory, 113–16
Justin Martyr, 100, 101

Kangxi, 133
Karris, Robert J., 65n64
Keener, Craig S., 5n12, 32n8, 69n84, 72n95, 72n97, 73n100, 73n102, 73n103, 84n28, 84n29, 86n36, 86n37, 86n38, 86n40, 86n41, 87, 88n49, 88n50, 88n51, 88n52, 93n69, 93n70, 93n71, 93n72
Keil, C. F., 24
Kennedy, Thomas L., 134n65, 137n84
Khan, Genghis, 125
Khan, Kublai, 118, 125–29
Kilgallen, J. J., 31n2, 38
Kim, Ho Sung, 6n16
Koesel, Karrie J., 137n80, 139n92, 146n128, 147n131
Kourdakov, Sergei, 149–50
Kreider, Alan, 108n68, 108n69, 110n86, 111n90, 111n92, 115n114, 148n132
Kreitzer, Beth, 39n45
Kuhn, Karl Allen, 6n16
Kyrychenko, Oleksandr, 6n17, 55n15, 56, 65n62, 66n65

Lenglet, Ad., 16n9
Leung, Ka-Lun, 133n62, 140n93, 140n95, 140n96
Levine, Amy-Jill, 93n67
Li, Jin, 137n82, 137n85, 140n94
Li, Tang, 125
literary patronage 39–40
Litfin, Bryan M., 100n18
Liu, Jifeng, 142n103, 142n104, 142n105, 144–45, 148n132
Luke–Acts
  alleged historical inaccuracies, 7n19, 56, 63n50, 69n84
  allusions to Daniel, 18–19
  allusions to Naaman, 27–28
  audience, 31–33, 35–47, 49, 56–57, 82
  author, 6, 36
  conversion in, 62, 64, 66–70, 87–89, 90, 92, 116

Luke–Acts *(continued)*
  gentiles in, 51–52, 56, 62, 63n52, 67, 68n76, 82, 86–87, 94
  geographical spread of gospel, 53–54, 67, 70, 86, 94
  historical reliability, 5n12, 35, 37, 57, 63, 69n84, 73n102, 73n103, 74n105, 74n106, 82
  the Holy Spirit in, 67–71
  irony in, 56
  Jerusalem Council, 67n75, 70
  Jews in, 52, 63n52, 69n85, 70–71, 79, 82, 83n26, 87n42
  literary unity, 33n14, 35n24, 43–47, 52–54
  pairs of narratives in, 53n4, 68n76, 68n77, 68n79
  and the poor, 52, 53n4, 82
  praising God in, 66
  prefaces, 33–37, 42–47
  proclamation of gospel in, 67, 69, 71, 75–76, 83–84, 89, 92, 94
  purpose of, 37, 43
  reiteration in, 68, 70
  relationship to oral tradition, 35n29
  Roman Empire in, 3–8, 78–83, 89–92, 92–93, 94–95, 110
  salvation theme, 52–53, 62–63, 69, 75, 81–82, 89, 94
  similarities to extrabiblical literature, 33–36
  soldiers in, 52, 55, 82
  tax collectors, 52
  temple in, 54, 71, 84
  theology of, 52, 63n52, 66, 75
  women in, 52, 53n4, 92
Lysias, Claudius, 43, 45, 71–73

Ma, Li, 137n82, 137n85, 140n94
MacMullen, Ramsay, 108–11
Maddox, Robert, 53n6
Maier III, Walter A., 19n16, 20n19, 22n24, 23n26, 24n31, 26n34
Manaen, 93
Mao Zedong, 139, 141
Mar Sargis, 126–27
Marguerat, Daniel, 55, 68n80

Marinus. *See* centurion(s), Marinus.
Marshall, I. Howard, 33n13, 39n45, 39n50, 52, 55n9, 63n53, 63n54, 64n55, 64n56, 64n57, 66n68, 66n71, 66n72, 75n110, 90n61, 91n63
Marx, Werner G., 39n49, 40n55, 42, 79n5
Mason, Steve, 60n38
Megiddo, 96–97
Melchizedek, 84n31
Meroë, 87n44, 87n47, 88n52
Meshach, 12–17, 20n19
Milvian Bridge, Battle of the, 108, 128, 135
missiology, 19n16, 22n24, 24
Mitchell, Margaret M., 31n5, 32n6, 37n37, 41n62
Moffett, Samuel Hugh, 119, 121n8, 121n9, 122n11, 122n12, 124, 125, 126n27, 126n29, 127n32, 127n33, 127n34, 128n38, 128n39, 128n40, 128n41, 130n44, 130n45, 130n46, 130n47, 130n48, 131n49, 131n50, 131n51, 131n53, 131n55, 131n57, 131n58, 131n59, 133n61, 133n62
Mordecai, 84n31
Morris, Leon, 64n56, 92
Morrison, Robert, 133n63
Moses, 84–86
Moule, A. C., 126n27, 126n29, 126n30, 127n31, 127n35, 128n40
Moxnes, Halvor, 31n2, 38
Musurillo, Herbert, 104

Naian, 128–29
Namaan, 8, 10, 11, 19–28, 63, 64, 111, 119n7, 138, 147
narrative analysis, 4, 11n3, 16, 19, 27–28, 55, 68n76, 70, 75–76, 85n33
Nation, Hannah, 145
Neagoe, Alexandru, 45n73, 80n12
Nebuchadnezzar, 12–18, 119n6, 147
Nehemiah, 84n31
Neill, Stephen, 133n60
Nelson, Richard D., 27n35
Nestorianism, 121n8, 125n23
Newsom, Carol, 13, 14n8, 17n11, 18n13

GENERAL INDEX

Nolland, John, 40n56, 42n67
Nwaoru, Emmanuel O., 19n16, 25n33

Origen, 37, 99n7, 100n12, 100n13

pacifism, 106–7, 109 112, 115
Padilla, Osvaldo, 84n28, 84n29, 84n30
Palmer, David A., 139n92
Parsons, Wilfrid, 113n106
Paul
    conversion of, 68
    as evangelist, 70, 75, 89, 94–95
    nephew of, 73
    as prisoner, 71–75, 77, 94–95
    as Roman citizen, 6, 56n21, 72
    in Rome, 6n15, 54
    sea voyage, 74–75
    on trial, 8, 42–47, 70–73, 79–80, 83
Pennington, Jonathan T., 5n9, 5n10
Persia, 119n5, 121
persecution, 2, 4, 9, 13–14, 16–17, 67, 70–73, 98, 101, 103, 105, 108, 109, 112, 120, 123–24, 140, 143, 146, 149–50, 151
Peter, 44, 68, 70, 76, 83, 89, 106
Philip, 86–87
Philo of Alexandria, 40, 69n87, 86n38
Pinter, Dean, 78n1, 79n4, 80n11
Pliny the Younger, 80n12, 98–99
Polo, Marco, 118, 125–26
Pontius Pilate, 79
Potiphar, 85n34
Powell, John Douglas, 135n68, 136n72, 136n73, 136n75, 137n81, 137n84, 138n87
prayer, 1–2, 7, 66, 69, 151–52
Puskas, Charles B., 94n73

Qian, Linliang, 142n106
Quadratus, 49n88, 100
Queen of Sheba, 11, 88

Rackham, Richard Belward, 79n5
Rapske, Brian, 94n74
Read-Heimerdinger, Jenny, 6n13
Reagan, Ronald, 1–3
religious liberty, 2, 133, 137, 141, 152

Ricci, Matteo, 129n43, 130–32, 135n69
Rimmon, 23–24
Rius-Camps, Josep, 6n13
Robbins, Vernon K., 78n2, 81
Roman Empire
    aristocracy, 39
    book production in, 32–33, 39–40
    Caesar. *See* Roman Empire, emperor.
    Christianity in, 9, 80–82, 96, 98–117
    Christianization of, 108–11
    citizenship, 9, 59–60, 72
    emperor, 45, 54, 59, 72, 74n106, 77, 78, 80, 83, 94–95, 104, 107–11, 117, 130. *See also* Antoninus Pius; Aurelius, Marcus; Caligula; Constantine; Domitian; Hadrian; Tiberius; Trajan.
    emperor worship, 20n19, 103–5
    in Luke–Acts. *See* Luke–Acts, Roman Empire in.
    military. *See* Roman military.
    officials' familiarity with gospel, 46
    philosophical schools, 35
    portrayal in Luke–Acts, 6
    tax collectors, 7, 52, 62, 79, 82
Roman military
    at Antonia Fortress, 70–71, 73n102
    Augustan cohort, 56n21, 69n84, 74
    auxiliaries, 58, 59, 60, 61, 65, 68, 70–71, 73n103, 74n105, 103n32
    camp, 103, 106
    cavalry units (*alae*), 58
    centurions. *See* centurion(s).
    ceremonial events, 103, 104
    Christians and the, 98, 102–3, 104–5, 106–7, 113–16
    ethnicity, 57–59, 61, 65n62, 68, 71, 74n106
    extortion practices, 60, 64–65
    infantry units (*cohortes*), 58
    Italian cohort, 5n12, 56n21, 69
    Legio X Fretensis, 104
    Legio XII Fulminata, the "Thundering Legion," 102–3, 108, 135
    legionaries, 58, 102–3, 104
    liturgical calendar, 103

Roman military *(continued)*
   mixed infantry and cavalry units
     (*cohortes equitatae*), 58
   non-combat duties, 60
   organization, 57–60, 102n24
   praetorian guard, 59, 77
   religious practices, 103–6, 109
   royal forces, 58–59, 60, 61, 63, 65n62
   symbols and standards, 103, 104–6,
     108–9
Rome, 54, 75–76, 94–95, 133
Rossabi, Morris, 125n25
Roth, Jonathan, 60n38
Rowe, C. Kavin, 79n7, 80n10, 80n11, 81,
   95n75, 104n37
Ruggieri, Michele, 130n44
Runesson, Rebecca, 97n4, 97n5

Samaria, Samaritan(s), 54, 60, 65n62, 67,
   73n103, 74n105, 86
Sauma, Rabban, 19n16, 24n28
Schaff, Philip, 102n29
Schak, David C., 140n93, 140n95
Schall von Bell, Adam, 131–33
Schnabel, Eckhard J., 91n64
Schreiner, Patrick, 52n2
Sebaste. *See* Samaria, Samaritan(s).
Septuagint, 41n61, 87n45, 93n69
Sergius Paulus, 80, 89–91, 92, 100, 101,
   150
Shadrach, 12–17, 20n19
Shean, John F., 109n72, 110n86
Shelton, John, 63n49
Sherwin-White, A. N., 59n33
Sidon, 28, 62, 74
Silk Road, 120, 125
Silver, Joshua, 96n3
Simeon, 62–63
Simon the Magician, 86, 91n64
Skinner, Matthew L., 94n74
Smith, Abraham, 87n45, 87n48, 88n52,
   89n55
Soong, Charlie, 134n66
Soong, Mei-ling, 135–37, 138n88
Sorkaktani Beki, 125
Soviet Union, 1–2, 149–50

Speidel, Michael P., 69n84
Star Wars, 1, 3
Stein, Robert H., 39n45, 42n67, 52n2,
   53n4
Stephen, 66, 76, 83–86
Strauss, Mark, 5n9, 31n5
Streeter, Burnett Hillman, 39
Strelan, Rick, 44n70
Sun, Jianqiang, 124n22
Sun, Yat-sen, 134, 135n67
Swift, Louis J., 100n16, 103n32, 104n39,
   107n60, 107n62, 107n63, 112n96,
   112n97, 113n106, 115n111,
   115n113, 150n3
Syria, 11, 19–28, 59, 65n62, 71, 121
Syriac, 118

Taiwan, 138
Taizong, 121–22
Tajra, Harry W., 45n73, 79n8, 80n9
Talbert, Charles H., 64n56
Tang dynasty, 9
Tang, Li, 124n22
Tang, Xiaofeng, 118n2, 119n3, 119n4
Tannehill, Robert C., 6n13, 33n14,
   47n79, 48n83, 52, 63n51, 66n70,
   67n75, 70n89, 72n95, 72n96,
   73n99, 74n104, 74n108, 75,
   76n112, 83
Tanner, J. Paul, 16n9
Taylor, Geraldine, 133n63
Taylor, Howard, 133n63
Taylor, Hudson, 133n63
Ten Harmsel, Wayne, 146n127, 146n129,
   146n130
Tepper, Yotam, 96n1, 96n3
Tertullian of Carthage, 9, 48n87, 96, 98,
   100–101, 102, 104n39, 105–7,
   112
Theophilus
   appearances in papyri, 38n41
   etymology of name, 37–38, 40
   as historical person, 39, 42
   as Jewish reader, 40, 42, 46, 48
   as literary patron, 33, 39–40, 46
   as "most excellent," 6, 41

as prototypical reader, 37–38, 41, 46
as pseudonym, 38, 47–49, 79n5, 150
as Roman official, 6, 31, 41–51, 57, 77, 79n5, 80–81, 91, 111, 117, 147
Theophylact of Ohrid, 41
Thompson, Glen L., 122n10, 122n13, 122n15, 123, 127n35, 128n36, 128n37
Thompson, Michael B., 31
Tiberius, 74n106, 78
Tiedemann, R. G., 137n83
Titus Flavius Clemens, 39
totalitarianism, 1
Trajan, 98–99
Troftgruben, Troy M., 94n73
Tyre, 11n2, 62
Tyson Li, Laura, 138n88

Ullendorf, Edward, 88n54
United States, 1–2, 152

Vala, Carsten T., 141n98, 141n100, 141n102, 142, 145n125
Valignano, Alessandro, 130n44
Verbiest, Ferdinand, 132–33
Von Rad, Gerhard, 20n20, 20n21
Von Soden, Hermann Freiherr, 41n62

Walaskay, Paul W., 80–81
Walls, Andrew F., 129n43
Walton, Steve, 6n16, 55n9, 78n1, 78n2, 79n7, 80n11, 81, 83n24

Wang, Peter Chen-main, 135n70, 136n72, 136n74, 136n75, 138n89, 139n90
Wang Yi, 145n126, 146n129
Watson, Brian, 3n6
White, Chris, 142n103, 142n104, 142n105, 144–45, 148n132
Wilken, Robert Louis, 35n29, 80n12, 99n6, 99n7, 99n9
Wilson, Stephen G., 68n78
Witek, John W., 131n52, 132n56
Witherington III, Ben, 57n23, 69n84, 73n103, 81, 93n67
Witherup, Ronald D., 68n79
Wright III, Benjamin G., 40n54
Wu, Y. T. (Wu Yaozong), 139n91

Xavier, Francis, 129n43
Xi Jinping, 146
Xu, Guangxi, 130–31, 133, 135n69

Yamazaki-Ransom, Kazuhiko, 6n16
Yang, Fenggang, 141, 142n110, 143–44, 146n129
Yang, J. C., 130n48
Yates, Kenneth Wayne, 6n17, 55n15
Yin, Xiaoping, 122n14, 128n36
Yisi, 122–23

Zeichmann, Christopher B., 56–61, 63, 65n11, 65n62, 69n83, 71n93, 73n102, 74n106
Zhang, Yingying, 118n2, 119n3, 119n4

Ancient Document Index

Old Testament

Genesis

12:3	85n33
18:4	23n27
39:6	12
41:12	12
41:33	13
41:38	17n10
41:39	13
41:42	85n32
41:45	13, 85n32
42:7–17	85n33
42:25–28	85n33
42:30	85n33
42:35	85n33
43:16–34	85n33
44:4–15	85n33
47:7	85n33
47:10	85n33
48:9	85n32
50:26	85n32

Exodus

4:18	24

Numbers

12	19n17
21:15	23n27

Deuteronomy

23:1	87

Judges

6:12	20
11:1	20
16:26	23n27

Ruth

2:1	20

1 Samuel

9:1	20
15:15	41n61
20:42	24

2 Samuel

1:6	23n27

ANCIENT DOCUMENT INDEX

1 Kings

10:1–13	88
10:1–2	87n45
10:9	88
11:28	20
12:8	93n71
12:10	93n71
12:14	93n71

2 Kings

4:1–7	20
4:8–37	20
4:38–44	20
4:38–41	19n17
4:42–44	19n17
5–7	23n27
5	26, 68n81, 138
5:1–27	8, 11, 19–28, 64
5:1	20, 26, 27
5:2	21
5:3	21, 27
5:5	21
5:7	21
5:8	21
5:10	21, 64n57
5:11–14	26
5:11	21
5:12	21
5:14–19	26
5:14	21
5:15–19	22–24
5:15	21–22
5:16	22, 25
5:17	22
5:18	22–24, 25, 26, 111
5:19	24
5:19b–27	25
5:20–27	25
5:20	25
5:26	25
5:27	25–26
6:1–7	19n17
7	26
7:1–20	25–26
7:2	22–23, 26
7:3–10	26
7:17–20	26
7:17	22–23, 26
15:14–23	93n69
24	19n17

2 Chronicles

9:1–12	88
9:8	88
13:18	23n27
14:10	23n27
16:7	23n27
36:22–23	122

Ezra

1:1–4	122

Job

8:15	23n27
24:23	23n27

Psalms

16:6	41n61
23:5	41n61
34:5	118
68:31	87n45

Proverbs

3:5	23n27

Isaiah

9:7	153
10:20	23n27
30:12	23n27
31:1	23n27
45:14	87n45
50:10	23n27
56:3–7	88n51

Jeremiah

29:7	113
38:4–6	88
38:7–13	88

Ezekiel

29:7	23n27

Daniel

1–6	8, 11–18
1–2	12–16, 142
1	15, 17n11
1:2	15
1:3	13
1:4	12, 13, 86
1:5	13
1:6–7	13
1:7	13
1:8	13
1:9	13, 15
1:10	13
1:11	13
1:15	14
1:17–20	14
1:17	12, 15
1:21	14
2–7	16
2	15, 16n9
2:1–3	14
2:4	14
2:5	14
2:8	14
2:10	14
2:12–13	14
2:12	14–15
2:13	14
2:14	14
2:15	14–15
2:17–23	16
2:24	14
2:25	14
2:27–28	16
2:47	15
2:48	15
2:49	15
3	13, 16–17
3:8–12	16
3:12	17
3:27	17
3:28	17
3:30	17
4	16n9, 17n11
4:5	17
4:8	13, 17, 18n12
4:9	13
4:19	13
4:34–35	18
4:34	17
4:37	17–18
5	16n9, 18n12
5:11	18n12
5:14	18n12
5:18–21	18n12
6	13, 16–17
6:3	16
6:4–13	16
6:8	17
6:12	16
6:13	17
6:24	17
6:25–26	18
6:26–27	17, 18
6:28	17
7	16n9
7:13	18
7:13–14	12, 17, 18
7:14	153
8:27	14
10:1	13
11:43	87n45

Amos

6:2	41n61

Micah

3:11	23n27

# ANCIENT DOCUMENT INDEX

Apocrypha

2 Maccabees

3:2	41n61
4:12	41n61

3 Maccabees

1:2	41n61

New Testament

Matthew

1:1–17	33
5:39	115n114
12:42	88
20:8	92n66
22:17–21	78n1
26:52	106

Mark

1:1–3	33
12:14–17	78n1

Luke

1–4	78n3
1:1–4	33–36, 42–47
1:1–2	37
1:2	42, 46
1:3–4	30, 35, 37, 46
1:3	6, 30, 33–34, 37, 39n45, 41–43, 44n69, 46, 48, 111
1:4	37, 43, 44–45, 47
1:5—4:30	44n70
1:5–25	53n4, 54
1:5–7	53n4
1:9	6n15
1:20	53n4
1:26–56	52, 53n4
1:26–38	53n4
1:27	53n4
1:44	53n4
1:52	52
1:57–80	53n4
1:77	75n110
2:1–21	53n4
2:1	78
2:8–20	52
2:20	66n68
2:22	6n15
2:25–35	53n4
2:32	54, 62–63
2:36–38	52, 53n4
2:41–51	54
2:49	54
3	62
3:1	78, 93
3:3	62
3:12–14	82
3:12–13	52
3:12	79
3:14	52, 60, 61–62, 64, 65, 69, 79, 102, 107, 114, 115
3:19–20	64, 79
3:19	93
4:3	65
4:9	65
4:14—9:50	6n15
4:15–37	62
4:15	66n68
4:16–30	27
4:18	52, 53
4:24–27	27–28
4:25–27	68n76
4:27	10, 64
4:31–37	53n4
4:33–37	62
4:37–40	62
4:38–41	52
4:38–39	53n4
4:41	62
4:44	62
5:1–11	62
5:12–15	62
5:17–26	62
5:25	66n68
5:26	66n68
5:27–32	52, 62

ANCIENT DOCUMENT INDEX

5:27–28	79	13:30	53
5:30	79	13:31	64, 79, 93
6:6–11	62	14:10	38n40
6:17–19	52	14:11	52
6:17	62	14:12	38n40
6:20–26	53	15:1–2	52
6:20	52	15:1	79
6:28	1, 7, 66, 151	15:4–7	53n4
7	57n23, 62	15:6	38n40
7:1–10	6, 8, 28, 51, 53n4, 55–56, 62–65, 68, 75, 79, 83n26, 92, 114, 150	15:8–10	53n4
		15:9	38n40
		15:29	38n40
		16:9	38n40
7:4–5	60, 63	17:15	66n68
7:5	68–69, 97	18:2–7	53n4
7:6	38n40, 63	18:9–14	52, 53n4, 79
7:7–8	64	18:11	79
7:9	51, 63n49, 64	18:13	66
7:11–17	52, 53n4	18:14	52
7:16	66n68	18:25–26	43–44
7:22	52	18:35–43	53n4
7:34	38n40	18:43	66n68
7:36–49	53n4	19:1–10	52, 53n4, 79
7:50	75n110	19:7	79
8:1–3	52	20:19–26	54
8:3	53, 92–93, 101	20:22–25	78n1
8:12	75n110	20:25	77, 83, 101, 104, 117
8:26–39	53n4		
8:40–56	53n4	20:45–47	53n4
8:41–42	83n26	21:1–4	53n4
8:48	75n110	21:12–13	83
8:50	75n110	21:16	38n40
9:7–9	79, 93	22:47—23:49	54
9:9	64	23:1–25	79
9:48	53	23:2	78n1
9:51—24:53	6n15	23:4	79
9:51—19:27	54	23:7–12	93
9:51	53–54, 70	23:11	64, 65, 79
11:3	88	23:12	38n40
11:5	38n40	23:14	79
11:6	38n40	23:15	79
11:8	38n40	23:18–23	70
11:31	88, 88n54, 89	23:22	79
12:4	38n40	23:24–25	79
13:1	79	23:34	7, 66
13:13	66n68	23:37	65
13:29	88, 89	23:41	65n64

Luke (continued)

23:47–48	66
23:47	6, 8, 55, 60, 65–67, 68, 71, 72, 76, 79, 92, 150
23:48	66
23:49	66, 93
23:50	53, 65n64
23:55	93
24:1–12	53n4
24:10	93
24:13–35	53n4
24:47	68n76
24:53	54

John

1:1–18	33
19:12–15	78n1
20:29	64

Acts

1:1	6n13, 30, 33, 34, 46n77
1:4	54
1:8	6n15, 51, 53, 54, 67, 70, 75, 86, 88, 89, 94, 151
2:1–11	67
2:8–11	68n76
2:11	69n86
2:14	68n76
2:17	68n76, 69
2:21	68n76
2:36	43, 44
2:38–39	68n76
2:47	69n85
3:9	69n85
3:14	66
4:1–22	83
4:9	75n110
4:17–42	83
4:21	66n68
4:36–37	53
5:23	43, 44
6:5	69n86, 86
6:8	69n85
6:13–14	85
6:13	84
7:1–60	83, 84–86
7:2–6	84
7:9–16	84
7:9	84
7:10	84, 85
7:11–14	85
7:13	85
7:15	84
7:17–43	84
7:21	86
7:22	84, 86
7:27	84, 86
7:29	84
7:30–31	84
7:33–34	84
7:35–36	86
7:35	84, 86
7:36	84
7:39–40	84
7:41–43	84
7:44–45	84
7:48–50	84
7:51	84
7:52	66, 84
7:53	84
8	91n64
8:1–25	67
8:4–8	86
8:7	91n64
8:9–25	86
8:14–17	67
8:26–40	86–89, 92, 101
8:27–28	67, 87
8:27	86, 88, 88n54
8:31	87
8:34	87
8:35	87
8:37	87
8:39	88
9:1–19	68n79
9:31	67
10:1—11:18	8, 55–56, 67–70, 76, 80, 114, 150

ANCIENT DOCUMENT INDEX

10	28, 51, 56, 57n23, 69	13:50	69
		14:1	70
10:1–48	6, 68, 92	14:2	70
10:1–8	68n77	14:5	70
10:1–2	5n12	14:19	70
10:1	56n21, 69	14:27	70
10:2	69, 97	15:7–11	67n75, 68n76, 69
10:9–16	68n77	16:12	77
10:14	56n20	16:14–15	70
10:17–23a	68n77	16:14	69
10:23b–29	68n77	16:23	43, 44
10:24	38n40, 69	16:24	43, 44
10:28	68	16:30–34	70
10:30–33	68n77	16:37–39	72
10:34–43	68n77, 69	17:4	69
10:34	56	17:5	70
10:43	69	17:7	78
10:44–48	56n20, 68n77	17:12	70
10:45	67	17:17	69
10:47–48	69, 87	17:34	70
11:1–18	68n77	18:2	78
11:1	67	18:7	69
11:3	69	18:12	89n58, 90
11:4–18	68	18:25–26	44
11:14	69	18:25	43, 44
11:17–18	56n20	18:26	43, 44
11:18	66n68, 67, 69	19:24–27	99
11:28	78	19:31	38n40
12:1–23	80, 93	19:38	89n58
12:1–19	69	20:22	71
12:3	93n70	21:7–14	73
13	69, 89, 91n64, 93	21:11	71
13:1	92–93, 101	21:13	70–71
13:4–12	89–91, 101	21:20	66n68
13:6–12	92, 150	21:21	44n71
13:6	90, 91n64	21:24	44n71
13:7	80, 89n58, 90, 91	21:26—26:32	42–47
13:8	89n58, 90	21:27—23:35	8, 70–73, 80
13:12	70, 89n58, 90	21:27–36	71, 151
13:16	69	21:27	71
13:26	69	21:30–31	71
13:38	68n76	21:31	70n92
13:43	69n86	21:32	6, 71–72
13:45	70	21:33	71
13:46–49	70	21:34	43, 45
13:46	68n76	21:39	56n21, 72
13:48	66n68	22:1–21	71

Acts (continued)

22:1	45
22:3	43
22:6–21	68n79
22:14	66
22:22–24	71
22:25–26	72, 151
22:25	72
22:26	72
22:27–30	72
22:28	71, 72n98
22:30	43, 45, 73
23:1—26:32	83
23:10	71, 73
23:11	76
23:12–35	72, 74
23:12–15	73
23:15	43, 45
23:17	71, 72–73, 151
23:20	43, 45
23:23–35	71
23:23–30	72n95
23:23	72–73, 151
23:26	6, 41, 43, 46, 71
23:31–32	73
23:31	73n103
24:3	6, 41, 43, 46
24:8	45
24:10–21	95
24:21	95
24:22	43, 45, 80
24:23	8, 70, 72–74, 76, 80, 151
24:24–27	45
24:25	80
24:26	80
24:27	73
25:8–12	54, 94
25:8	78
25:9–11	54
25:9	73
25:10	78
25:11–12	72–73
25:11	45, 78
25:12	78, 130
25:13	88n53
25:21	78
25:25	78
25:26–27	80
25:26	43, 45
26:1–32	73
26:2–29	95
26:5	43
26:12–18	68n79
26:16	42n68, 46
26:25–27	46n75
26:25	6, 41, 43, 46
26:26	45n73, 46
26:27	46
26:28	42
26:31–32	80
26:32	54, 78, 94
27:1–44	8, 70, 74–75, 80, 151
27:1–28	76
27:1	56n21, 69n84, 74, 78
27:2	74
27:3	38n40, 74
27:6	74
27:10	74
27:11	75
27:20	75
27:24	78
27:25	75
27:30	75
27:31–32	75
27:31	75
27:34	75
27:42	74
27:43	75
28	78n3
28:16–31	6n15, 54, 94–95
28:16	94
28:19	78, 94
28:24	94
28:28	68n76, 94
28:31	94

Romans

13:1–7	107

1 Corinthians

7:7	114

Galatians

4:2	92n66

Philippians

1:12–14	77
4:22	77, 95

Colossians

4:14	36

1 Timothy

2:1–2	151

2 Timothy

2:9	77
4:11	36

Titus

3:4	74

Philemon

24	36

1 Peter

1:1	113
1:8	64
2:17	11, 104n38

Revelation

4:10	106
5:9	153

Greco-Roman Writings

Galen, Method of Medicine

1–4	35n22
1.1	47
2.1	47
3.1	47

Josephus, Against Apion

1.1	33–34, 36n30
2.1	34
2.296	34n19

Josephus, Jewish Antiquities

17.198–99	61n46
18.123–24	40n57
19.297	40n57

Pliny the Younger, Epistles

10.96	99
10.97	99n10

Early Christian Writings

Aristides, Apology

Introduction	49n88, 100n15

Athenagoras, Plea for Christians

Introduction	100n15

Augustine, Against Faustus

22.74	115

Augustine, City of God

3.14	113, 115
15.4	113
15.5	113
15.14	114
19.17	113n99
19.26	113

ANCIENT DOCUMENT INDEX

Augustine, *Expositions on the Psalms*

62.4	112n98

Augustine, *Letters*

93.1–2	115n114
93.9	115n114
138.13	115n114
138.14	115n114
189	112, 113–16
189.4	114
189.5	114
189.6	114, 115, 116
189.7	116
220.7	113n106
229.2	115n111

Eusebius, *Ecclesiastical History*

4.3.1–3	100n15
4.3.1–2	49n88
5.5	102n25
6.41.16	105n45
6.41.22	105n46
7.15.1–5	104n40
7.15.1	104–5
7.15.2	105
8.17.6–10	108n66

Justin Martyr, *First Apology*

1	49n88, 100n17
7	101n20
12	101
14	101
17	101

Justin Martyr, *Second Apology*

1	49n88, 100n17

Hippolytus, *Apostolic Tradition*

16.11	107

Origen, *Homilies on Luke*

1.6	37

Origen, *Against Celsus*

1.27	99–100
8.68	100n13

Tertullian, *Apology*

1	96, 100n18
1.1	49n88
5	102
42	102

Tertullian, *On Idolatry*

17	104n39, 106n54
19	106

Tertullian, *On the Crown*

7	106
9	106
10	106
11	101n39, 104n39, 106–7, 112n96
14	106n53

Tertullian, *To Scapula*

1	49n88
2	102–3
4–5	48n87
4	102
5	101

Epistle to Diognetus

1.1	49n88

Letter of Aristeas

49	40n54

www.ingramcontent.com/pod-product-compliance
Lightning Source LLC
Chambersburg PA
CBHW072129160426
43197CB00012B/2039